The School-to-Prison Pipeline

The School-to-Prison Pipeline

Structuring Legal Reform

Catherine Y. Kim, Daniel J. Losen,
and Damon T. Hewitt

NEW YORK UNIVERSITY PRESS
New York and London

NEW YORK UNIVERSITY PRESS
New York and London
www.nyupress.org

References to Internet websites (URLs) were accurate at the time of writing.
Neither the author nor New York University Press is responsible for URLs
that may have expired or changed since the manuscript was prepared.

Library of Congress Cataloging-in-Publication Data
Kim, Catherine Y.
 The school-to-prison pipeline : structuring legal reform /
Catherine Y. Kim, Daniel J. Losen, and Damon T. Hewitt.
p. cm.
Includes bibliographical references and index.
ISBN 978-0-8147-4843-5 (cl : alk. paper) —
ISBN 978-0-8147-4844-2 (e-book)
1. School discipline—Law and legislation—United States.
2. Juvenile delinquents—Legal status, laws, etc.—United States.
3. Right to education—United States. 4. Law reform—United States.
5. Educational change—United States.
I. Losen, Daniel J. II. Hewitt, Damon. III. Title.
KF4159.K56   2010
344.73'079—dc22   2010018811

New York University Press books are printed on acid-free paper,
and their binding materials are chosen for strength and durability.
We strive to use environmentally responsible suppliers and materials
to the greatest extent possible in publishing our books.

Manufactured in the United States of America

10 9 8 7 6 5 4 3 2 1

Contents

Acknowledgments

The authors wish to thank the many friends and colleagues who provided invaluable contributions and assistance, generating new ideas, drafting sections, reviewing drafts, editing, and researching: Deborah Gershenowitz, Stuart Biegel, Angela Ciolfi, James Ryan, Olga Akselrod, Holly Thomas, Cynthia Rice, Barbara Duffield, Lee Gelernt, Kathleen Boundy, Elisa Hyman, Ron Lospennato, Jeff Spitzer Resnick, Ruth Zweifler, Aaron Caplan, Sarah Dunne, Nancy Talner, Rose Spidell, Dean Hill Rivkin, Emily Chiang, Alexis Agathocleus, Graham Boyd, Jim Freeman, Daniel Farbman, Lisa Thurau-Gray, Craig Goodmark, Laval Miller Wilson, Robin Dahlberg, Marsha Levick, Katayoon Majd, Nancy Rosenbloom, Christopher Tan, Dennis Parker, Chris Hansen, Chloe Cockburn, Salima Tongo, Nicole Dixon, David Blanding, Melissa Francisco, Angelia Dickens, Norman Chachkin, Chinh Le, Lia Epperson, Anurima Bhargava, Kimberly Liu, Joe Duff, Leah Aden, Anita Khandelwal, Nisha Agrawal, Johanna Wald, Jennifer Honig, Gary Orfield, Katie Schaaf, Jared Sanchez, Bernardine Dohrn, Joe Tulman, Victor Goode, Barbara Kaban, Vincent Warren, Mark Soler, Kim Brooks-Tandy, Camille Holmes, Leslie Gross-Davis, Josh Dohan, Jenny Chou, Monique Dixon, Ilze Hirsh, Allen J. Rom, Joe Scantlebury, Jesse Hahnel, John Affeldt, Russell J. Skiba, Judith Storandt, Martha Stone, Amy McManus, Deborah Archer, Janet Stotland, Len Reiser, Jessica Price, Justin Ashenfelter, Junyeon Park, Tona Boyd, Rebecca Horowitz, Jennifer Liu, Julie Zwibelman, Courtney Chai, Anthony Delgado, Judie Pisnonant, Julie Hernandez, Randolph Frazier, Stacey Moore, the law firm Skadden, Arps, Slate, Meagher & Flom, especially Ronald Tabak and associates Brenna DeVaney, Aleah Borgard, Rose Jenkins, Amy Lambert, Sigrid Neilson, Joe Satorius, Albert Song, and Blair Thetford, and the many other folks who contributed to this project.

Introduction

The School-to-Prison Pipeline presents the intersection of a K–12 educational system and a juvenile justice system, which too often fail to serve our nation's at-risk youth. In many cases, these failures are attributable not to the children themselves but rather to deficiencies in the institutions charged with caring for them. For the past several years, policymakers, educators, academics, advocates, the media, and the public at large have paid increasing attention to these deficiencies—at the national, state, and local levels—which disserve our youth by reducing the likelihood that they will remain in school and ultimately graduate and instead increasing the likelihood that they will become involved with the courts and ultimately be detained or incarcerated.

At its core, the pipeline results from the failure of public institutions to meet the educational and social development needs of a large segment of the children they are charged with serving. Toward the front end of the pipeline, the denial of adequate educational services sets up many students for failure. Overcrowded classrooms, racially and socioeconomically isolated environments, a lack of effective teachers and school leaders, and insufficient funding for "extras" such as counselors, special education services, and even textbooks lock too many students into second-rate educational environments.[1] These deficiencies increase students' disengagement and the likelihood of their dropping out and later becoming involved with the courts.[2] Even worse, some schools may actually encourage dropouts in response to unintended pressures from test-driven accountability regimes, which create incentives to push out low-performing students to boost overall test scores.[3]

Unfortunately, the youth who suffer disproportionately from these practices are likely to be precisely those who need the most support, including low-income students, students of color, English language learners, homeless youth, youth in foster care, and students with disabilities. And, of course, many students fall into more than one of these categories.

Although data on the impact of the pipeline on some of these at-risk categories are not generally available, extensive data on its impact on students of color and children with disabilities are available and consistently demonstrate alarming disparities. From 1973 to 2006, the percentage of African American students enrolled in public schools who were suspended at least once in a given year rose from 6 percent to 15 percent.[4] And although suspension rates have nearly doubled for all students, racial disparities in suspension rates have grown considerably worse over the past thirty years. For example, thirty years ago, Black students were approximately twice as likely to be suspended as their white counterparts; today, they are more than three times as likely to be suspended.[5] When the data are broken down by race *and* gender, the disparities are even greater. In 2002–2003, the risk of suspension for African American males was nearly 18 percent, as compared to just over 7 percent for white males.[6] In most large districts across the nation, middle-school suspension rates for minority students are consistently over 20 percent, and in many cities it is not uncommon for over half the African American males to have been suspended at least once in a given year.[7] Latino and Native American students are also faring worse.[8]

As in the case with school suspensions, children of color are disproportionately impacted by School-to-Prison Pipeline policies that lead to court involvement. In 2003, African American youths made up 16 percent of the nation's overall juvenile population but accounted for 45 percent of juvenile arrests.[9] And these disparities cannot be attributed to an increase in the frequency of bad conduct among minority children—studies show that African American students are more likely than their white peers to be suspended, expelled, or arrested for the *same kind* of conduct at school.[10]

Children who have special learning or emotional needs are also particularly vulnerable to being pushed out of mainstream schools and into the juvenile justice system. While only approximately 9 percent of children in public schools have been identified as having disabilities that impact their ability to learn,[11] a survey of correctional facilities found that nationally approximately 33 percent of youth in juvenile corrections had been previously identified as eligible for special education under the Individuals with Disabilities Education Act.[12]

Lacking resources, facing incentives to push out low-performing students, and responding to public misperceptions about school safety, many schools have embraced draconian school discipline policies, including zero-tolerance rules that automatically impose severe punishments regardless of circumstances. Although the necessity of discipline in schools goes without saying, schools in recent years have begun exercising their disciplinary authority to suspend and expel students more frequently and in far more questionable circumstances. In 2004, there were over 3.2 million school suspensions and over 106,000 expulsions; in some states, the number of suspensions exceeded 10 percent of the number of students enrolled.[13] Schools that rely on zero-tolerance and other punitive measures to maintain discipline, rather than incorporating developmentally appropriate and proven effective responses, are contributing to the problem.

Exclusion from the classroom for even a few days disrupts a child's education and may escalate misbehavior by removing the child from a structured environment, which gives the child increased time and opportunity to get into trouble. Studies show that a child who has been suspended is more likely to be retained in his or her grade, to drop out, to commit a crime, and to be incarcerated as an adult.[14]

As the number of students excluded from our nation's public schools grows, policymakers, educators, and communities must decide what to do with these children. In some jurisdictions, these students have no right to education at all or are deemed to have waived that right.[15] Where alternative schooling is provided, but the education or environment is substandard, alternative school may make matters worse since struggling students need more support, not less. On the one hand, alternative schools and programs may function as valuable interventions to serve the heightened needs of at-risk students. On the other hand, where they are poorly operated, such schools may actually enhance the risk of student disengagement and dropout.[16]

Another development exacerbating the pipeline is the overreliance on police measures to maintain discipline—in a growing number of schools, teachers and principals have gone from *in loco parentis* to *in loco politia*.[17] Schools use law enforcement tactics including random sweeps, searches of students, drug tests, and interrogations,[18] and they increasingly rely on sworn police officers to patrol their hallways.[19] As a result, a growing number of youth are being arrested and processed through courts for misconduct at school.[20]

Despite the fact that our juvenile justice system is premised on the concept of rehabilitation of youth, the School-to-Prison Pipeline frequently flows in only one direction. Toward the back end of the pipeline, once children become involved with the courts, they may find it increasingly difficult to reenter the mainstream education system. They may be denied procedural due process protections while being processed through court,[21] they may be inappropriately detained,[22] they may be denied educational opportunities while detained or incarcerated,[23] and, finally, they are likely to face barriers to their reentry into traditional schools.[24] The vast majority of these students never graduate from high school.[25]

Policies that lead to overdetention and overincarceration of children are counterproductive to the goal of preventing problematic behavior. A report by the National Center on Education, Disability and Juvenile Justice analyzes empirical studies to conclude that "incarceration is a spectacularly unsuccessful treatment."[26] Similarly, the Federal Advisory Committee on Juvenile Justice concludes, "research by criminologists over the past several years has shown that punitive consequences do not, in fact, reduce criminal behavior and in some cases actually increase it."[27]

In each of these ways, opportunities for youth caught in the School-to-Prison Pipeline are curtailed, imposing significant multigenerational costs. The costs to families and communities are tremendous, and since some of the greatest economic benefits of earning a diploma are realized in the next generation, the most significant loss is in the future.[28] This loss to society is immeasurable. Not only do communities lose the potential talents that these students offer, but they also commit themselves to expending vast resources—far greater than the resources it would take to fund public education adequately—to address the problems that these students are likely to pose when they become adults.

The School-to-Prison Pipeline thus refers to the confluence of education policies in underresourced public schools and a predominantly punitive juvenile justice system that fails to provide education and mental health services for our most at-risk students and drastically increases the likelihood that these children will end up with a criminal record rather than a high school diploma. Given the devastating impact on not only the children themselves but also the communities in which they live, challenging and limiting the impact of the pipeline presents one of the most urgent challenges in civil rights today.

For these reasons, the Racial Justice Program of the American Civil Liberties Union Foundation, the NAACP Legal Defense and Educational Fund, Inc., and the Civil Rights Project at UCLA developed this book to identify the most damaging trends associated with the pipeline and to analyze theories and strategies that have been employed to challenge them through structural reform litigation. The School-to-Prison Pipeline involves a great deal of subtleties and complexities, and litigators and scholars have devoted lifetimes to them; this book is not intended as an exhaustive list of ideas for structural reform litigation in this area. Rather, it seeks to provide a starting place for discussing these issues by exploring an array of legal claims and theories that may prove useful in shutting down one or another piece of the pipeline. These claims range from well-established approaches replete with multiple precedents and analyses to newer theories and strategies that are just beginning to be explored. Some employ federal law, while others rely on more protective state laws. Where possible, the authors have identified strategic strengths and weaknesses, from a legal perspective as well as from a policy perspective, involved with different legal claims.

Chapter 1 explores legal theories to challenge the pipeline where it begins—in underresourced public schools. It seeks to connect evidence of a relationship between low or inadequate resources and outcomes associated with the School-to-Prison Pipeline in an attempt to generate remedies that address these underlying deficiencies. The chapter explores the contours of a child's right to education under the U.S. Constitution and federal statutes, as well as under state law.

Chapter 2 discusses the impact of aspects of the School-to-Prison Pipeline on particular populations, identifying the grave disparities in areas such as suspensions, expulsions, and law enforcement referrals for certain identifiable subgroups of youth. The chapter begins with an analysis of strategies to protect the rights of children of color under both federal and state laws. The second section explores the rights of English language learner (ELL) students and undocumented students. The third section discusses protections for homeless youth and children in foster care.

Chapter 3 concentrates on the particular rights of students with special needs. First, the chapter examines the extraordinarily high and disproportionate rates of school failure and disciplinary removal of students with disabilities and how the failure properly to ensure the legal rights and procedural protections afforded to students with disabilities contributes to their disproportionate representation in the pipeline to prison. Second, the chapter describes the legal protections available to students with disabilities, focusing in particular on the federal Individuals with Disabilities Education Act and Section 504 of the Rehabilitation Act. Third, the chapter sets forth case studies of structural reform litigation that have succeeded in obtaining comprehensive remedies to the School-to-Prison-Pipeline.

Chapter 4 explores systemic problems associated with inappropriate school discipline, including overly draconian student codes of conduct. First, it describes the rise of zero-tolerance disciplinary policies across the country, and second, it turns its attention to possible procedural due process claims to challenge student removals. The third section discusses substantive challenges to the punishment itself, not just the procedures by which the punishment was imposed. The fourth section discusses the potential for a specific subset of due process challenges: that school discipline rules may be void for vagueness. The fifth section discusses challenges to school discipline rules on the grounds that those rules constitute unlawful restrictions on First Amendment–protected expressive conduct. Finally, the sixth section discusses the emerging trend of automatic suspensions for students who are arrested for off-campus conduct.

Chapter 5 addresses the growing phenomenon of disciplinary alternative educational schools and programs, exploring the right to alternative education for suspended and expelled youth and the right to an adequate education once in these schools and programs. The first section introduces the concept of alternative schools and programs, describing the different types that exist and the students who attend them. The second section addresses the problem in jurisdictions where children do not have access to alternative education while they are suspended or expelled; it explores legal strategies to secure the right to continued education for these disciplined students. The third section describes the right to challenge a district's attempt to transfer a child involuntarily to an alternative placement. The fourth section explores the quality of education and related services in these alternative programs and assesses strategies to ensure that alternative schools and programs meet minimum requirements. Finally, the fifth section discusses barriers to returning to mainstream schools upon completion of a term at an alternative school or program.

Chapter 6 discusses issues resulting from the increased policing of school hallways. It describes case law analyzing students' criminal procedural rights when they are subject to searches, seizures, questioning, and interrogation by school officials, as well as by school resource officers and other law enforcement. The first section of the chapter explores the scope of students' rights where school officials (e.g., principals and teachers) implement policelike searches, seizures, and questioning. The second section proposes approaches for holding law enforcement accountable for their conduct in public schools. The third section discusses affirmative challenges to school-specific statutes and ordinances frequently used to criminalize school misconduct.

Chapter 7 focuses on the back end of the pipeline, exploring challenges to the ways in which the judicial system draws children in and keeps them in the School-to-Prison Pipeline. For advocates new to the area, the first section provides an introductory overview of the salient features of the juvenile justice system. The second section discusses the potential for systemic challenges to the initial referral or arrest of children. In the third section, the chapter explores the rights of incarcerated children, focusing in particular on the right to education. Finally, the fourth section explores the rights of court-involved youth to reenter the mainstream educational system.

Although the problems associated with the School-to-Prison Pipeline are daunting, they are not intractable. The first step toward dismantling the pipeline is to take a critical look at existing policies and practices. In many instances, state and local educational agencies fail to keep the data necessary for such a critical look. In the vast majority of cases where the records do exist, data demonstrate that policies or practices seen in the School-to-Prison Pipeline are counterproductive and lack a pedagogical underpinning. In fact, many of these policies not only label children as criminals but also encourage children to lose hope, making it more likely that they will wind up behind bars.

In the long run, it will be necessary to address head-on the grave crisis and racial disparities in public education. Although programs can be created to address some of the individual needs of students, it will take a true community reinvestment in our schools to give students the educational opportunities that will allow them to realize their potential. Instead of excluding so many children from educational opportunity, school systems must provide services in a manner consistent with the notion that every child can succeed. The goal of creating safe, sustainable school communities depends on it.

1

The Right to Education

The School-to-Prison Pipeline, as a concept, implies that schools are not meeting educational and social development needs of a large segment of children. Despite the tremendous importance of public education, the system is plagued by inadequate resources, especially in districts marked by concentrated poverty and racial isolation.[1] Students in underresourced schools and districts, with too little access to experienced and highly qualified educators, with curriculum resources that do not prepare them for college, with inadequate exposure to the arts, and in facilities that are unsafe and poorly equipped and have too few early intervention programs for struggling students are at high risk of academic failure.[2]

In some instances, these underresourced schools and districts may employ practices that are genuine attempts to address real problems but that ultimately prove counterproductive. The lack of resources combines with mounting pressures imposed by test-driven accountability and creates perverse incentives for school officials actively to push the neediest children out of their schools. These push-outs range from nondisciplinary measures, such as disenrolling truant youth from high school or counselors encouraging struggling students to enroll in GED programs, to harsher forms of exclusion, including frequent suspensions, expulsions, and school-based arrests.

As a society, we rely too much on juvenile court referrals and incarceration to respond to problematic behavior, even though research demonstrates that investing resources in education can improve behavior and prevent delinquency, saving money in the long term. For example, a team of economists from Columbia, Princeton, and Queens College predicts that increasing high school graduation rates would decrease violent crime by 20 percent and drug and property crimes by more than 10 percent.[3] These economists calculate that each additional high school graduate yields an average of greater than $26,500 in lifetime cost savings to the public from averted costs associated with crime.[4] Similarly, Nobel-laureate economist James Heckman, most famous for his research demonstrating the long-term benefits of high-quality preschool, has more recently acknowledged the importance of high quality K–12 education, especially where it can optimize the benefits of preschool.[5] These analyses support the idea that interventions for students of all ages will pay dividends. When the full scope of benefits is considered, and factors such as increases in productivity, tax revenues, and family stability and reductions in the need for public support such as welfare are included, the benefits grow exponentially while the costs remain the same.[6] As economists increasingly demonstrate the cost savings of investing in education, and as struggling state governments confront the growing costs of incarceration, there may be important opportunities for advocates to push for investments in education-based remedies and to push against the frequent use of exclusion from education as a response to misbehavior. Because inadequate educational resources are one of the root causes of the School-to-Prison Pipeline, it is imperative to explore litigation remedies that go beyond the immediate harmful policies or practices. When possible, advocates should consider litigation that might drive resources, not only toward improving the quality of education generally, but toward specific programs designed to reduce the use of suspensions, expulsions, and school-based arrests and toward improving rates of graduation for students, including those who have been incarcerated or educated in alternative schools. This chapter primarily explores ways in which litigators might identify and incorporate evidence of a relationship between low or inadequate resources and outcomes associated with the School-to-Prison Pipeline in an attempt to generate remedies that address these underlying deficiencies. In addition, this chapter, as well as chapter 4, looks at the use of rights-based litigation to provide more immediate relief from policies and practices that push children out of school.

The threshold question is, do all children have a right to education? If so, what is the extent of that right and what are the related implications for litigation? This chapter separates this basic inquiry into two distinct questions under federal and state law depending on the type of remedy sought. The first section explores litigation to stimulate broad and deep systemic school reform. There, the question becomes, to what extent do students have protection against the kind of education resource deficiencies that are believed to contribute to high dropout rates, delinquent behavior, and incarceration? The second section of this chapter explores how rights-based litigation might provide relief for the large numbers of students denied access to, or discouraged from attending, school. In answering each question the chapter provides a brief review of education rights under the U.S. Constitution and federal statutes, followed by a review of the contours of the "right to education" under state law.[7]

In each section, strategies for impact litigation are discussed in terms of their potential to contribute to a remedy to the School-to-Prison Pipeline. As a practical matter, even comprehensive and systemic litigation is unlikely, *alone,* to provide a permanent solution. Whatever potential gains may be achieved through court orders or required legislative responses, successful implementation over the long term is critically important. Public education is a highly complex institution with many obstacles to implementing reforms of the system. Therefore, this chapter concludes by suggesting that litigators pursuing education-rights-based impact litigation coordinate their efforts with grassroots and legislative advocates to reap long-term benefits.

A. REMEDIES TO RESOURCE DEFICIENCY AND THE RIGHT TO EDUCATION

1. RESOURCE REMEDIES AND THE RIGHT TO EDUCATION UNDER FEDERAL LAW

For many years, advocates viewed language from *Brown v. Board of Education,*[8] which underscored the importance of education to other civil rights including voting, freedom of expression, and citizenship, as suggesting that the U.S. Constitution protects the right to an education.[9] Although the Court did not expressly declare education as a fundamental right, its description of segregation as denying an "important" interest in education left room for interpretation.[10] The Supreme Court held that if a state provided education, it must provide it in a manner to ensure equal educational opportunity.[11] Although the extent to which the legal system could require and enforce the right to equal educational opportunity remained in dispute, many civil rights advocates believed that *Brown* and other precedents had created an opportunity to reform school funding mechanisms that resulted in an inequitable distribution of resources along the lines of race and class.[12]

But in 1973, the Supreme Court decided *San Antonio Independent School District v. Rodriguez.*[13] In that case, a group of low-income residents from the Edgewood district of metropolitan San Antonio challenged the state's unequal public schools funding system on behalf of students in poor districts throughout Texas.[14] They claimed the funding system violated the Equal Protection Clause, and they won in the lower court.[15] Reversing that ruling, the Supreme Court clarified that there was no federally guaranteed right to an education under the U.S. Constitution.[16]

Therefore, the short answer to the threshold question is that there is no "fundamental right" to education under the federal Constitution. Nor was poverty regarded as a "suspect category." Without either, the school finance system was subjected to "rational basis" review and survived this relatively low level of judicial scrutiny. Had either a fundamental right or suspect category been found, "strict scrutiny" would have been applied and, as the *Rodriguez* Court suggested, the Texas school funding system of 1973 would not have been able to satisfy the standard of meeting a "compelling interest."[17]

The long answer, however, is far more complicated. While the Supreme Court reversed the lower court, the decision in *Rodriguez* introduced a new adequacy rationale into the legal discourse by suggesting that the Constitution might be violated if education expenditures fell short of "some identifiable quantum of education," which the Court conceded was a necessary "prerequisite to the meaningful exercise" of the constitutionally protected right to free speech and right to vote.[18] This adequacy rationale may be a powerful concept, but at the federal level, it has not been powerful enough to encourage or support resource litigation in the absence of a fundamental right to education. However, advocates interested in securing the necessary resources for all students have pursued the adequacy rationale in state court pursuant to "education clauses" in state constitutions.

Before examining the contours of state law, it is important to note that the adequacy rationale made its mark in federal statutes.[19] Most notable is that pursuant to the Elementary and Secondary Education Act of 1965 (ESEA), recipients must meet numerous federal "adequacy" requirements.[20] Those requirements, however, are applicable only to entities that actually receive federal funds under Title I.[21] Entities that reject Title I funding are not required to comply with Title I requirements, even if they receive other types of federal funding.[22]

Some advocates have argued that, in addition to imposing certain federal requirements on states and districts, the ESEA[23] (which is the largest source of federal grant money to public schools) provides enforceable rights to students and their families. For example, pursuant to No Child Left Behind Act's (NCLB's) amendments to the ESEA, students who attend a school deemed to be "in need of improvement" on the basis of student performance on standardized tests for two or more consecutive years must be provided with an opportunity (including transportation) to transfer to a nonfailing school.[24] Yet federal courts have thus far ruled that students and families do not have standing to enforce this right because NCLB lacks an explicit "private right of action."[25]

Despite the obstacles to litigation to enforce NCLB, litigators should familiarize themselves with the various requirements the statute imposes on states, including those relating to investigation of complaints, collection and reporting of data, school and district accountability for improving performance, and the provisions of the Safe and Drug-Free Schools and Communities Act. Even without an express private right of action, there may be ways to challenge the inadequate provision of education in public schools in violation of NCLB through administrative complaints[26] or through state courts. And, as discussed in the next section, the NCLB provisions, including those requiring the collection and reporting of data, may prove important to school resource litigation pursuant to state law.

2. RESOURCE LITIGATION UNDER STATE LAW

In the absence of a federal right to education for the general K–12 population, litigators have turned to state law to secure such a right. Right-to-education challenges seeking broad-based systemic reforms explore the quality of education that states are obligated to provide. The question becomes whether a given state, pursuant to state law, must provide more than the minimal rights suggested by *Rodriguez*.

The answers differ from one state to the next. Every state has language pertaining to a right to education or compulsory education under the state constitution or statute or both.[27] Many state courts have held that the state constitution or other state law creates a fundamental right to a free public education.[28] In others, state law has been interpreted as affording no fundamental right and no greater protection than federal law. In theory, at least, jurisdictions that recognize a fundamental right to education under a state constitution would apply strict scrutiny and require a compelling state interest to justify a denial of education, whereas jurisdictions that do not recognize a fundamental right to education under the state constitution would apply only rational basis review.[29] Yet, in other states, courts have found that state law, unlike federal law, creates an obligation to provide public education without explicitly equating this obligation with that of protecting a fundamental right to education. In some of these states, such as New Jersey[30] and Texas,[31] courts have required a new system of financing or a redistribution of resources conforming to what might be regarded as a substantial (but not fundamental) right to education pursuant to the language found in the education clauses of their respective state constitutions.[32]

Even where state law would appear to provide a more substantial right to education than federal law does,[33] litigators have had varying degrees of success litigating pursuant to these education clauses found in the state constitutions.[34] Despite the victories, many confounding obstacles can undermine the potential for litigation to drive resource remedies. Therefore, advocates need to examine closely the contours of the right to education in each state individually.[35]

Equally important are the practical issues litigators must consider before delving into complex litigation aimed at systemic reform. Litigators in the field describe the need for careful strategic planning with multiple players, difficult decisions about the quantity and quality of the evidence that must be presented, and full reviews of the political landscape, not to mention their own capacity to maintain their efforts to ensure the successful implementation of any hard-won remedies.[36] This chapter is not intended as a comprehensive review of all these issues. Nor does it provide a summary of the relevant law in each of the fifty states. Instead, it provides an overview of the kinds of issues and obstacles that confront impact litigation under state right-to-education law.[37]

a. Obstacles to Using Resource Litigation to Drive Remedies

One major concern is that state courts are often reluctant to force legislatures to remedy a failure to provide an adequate education, even when they have acknowledged a violation of a state constitutional right to education. In settlements as well as cases in which state liability is fully litigated, all or part of the remedy may be left in the hands of the state's legislature. The degree to which a right to education can generate comprehensive reforms with regard to the distribution of educational resources may be the product of the discourse between the courts and the legislature.

For example, in Massachusetts, in the 1993 case *McDuffy v. Secretary of Executive Office of Education,* the state's supreme court held that the state had violated its constitutional obligation to educate its children when evidence demonstrated that students in less affluent school districts were offered significantly fewer educational opportunities and lower educational quality than their counterparts in wealthier districts.[38] The court also directed that a single justice "retain jurisdiction to determine whether, within a reasonable time, appropriate legislative action has been taken."[39] The legislature responded immediately with a substantial redistribution of state education funds and a state action plan for further equalization of educational opportunity. But more recently, in 2005, in the related *Hancock* litigation, the state's supreme court reviewed a report from Judge Botsford, the lower court judge in charge of monitoring the state's remedy in *McDuffy.* Judge Botsford concluded that the state legislature's actions had proven insufficient to meet the constitutional obligations.[40] Although Massachusetts's highest court in *Hancock* agreed with Judge Botsford's factual findings, the majority opinion overruled her conclusions of law, explaining the apparent inconsistency as follows:

> I accept those findings, and share the judge's concern. . . . The public education system we review today, however, is not the public education system reviewed in McDuffy. Its shortcomings, while significant in the focus districts, do not constitute the egregious, Statewide abandonment of the constitutional duty identified in that case. . . . No one, including the defendants, disputes that serious inadequacies in public education remain. . . . By establishing objective competency goals and the means to measure progress toward those goals, . . . and by directing significant new resources to schools with the most dire needs, I cannot conclude that the Commonwealth currently is not meeting its constitutional charge.[41]

In other words, in *Hancock* the court affirmed that the state had a constitutional obligation to provide an adequate education but balked at requiring the state legislature to provide a remedy for the undisputed inadequacy observed in several districts. After *Hancock,* advocates question the extent to which the collective rights that appeared firm under *McDuffy* remain enforceable.[42] The *Hancock* case illustrates how judicial determinations shaping the contours of the right to education in a given state may evolve into a highly contextual analysis that qualifies that right based on the effort of the legislature to provide a remedy.

Resource remedies have proven elusive in other states, too. In Ohio, the state's highest court found that the state's system of school finance violated the Ohio constitution but has not sought to force the state legislature to remedy the violation.[43] Similarly, in 1993, in *Alabama Coalition for Equity v. Hunt,* a plaintiff coalition sued the governor and other state officials contending that the state's public school system was constitutionally inequitable and inadequate and thus violated the state's education and due process clauses.[44] The trial court found defendants liable and adopted a remedy plan. The Alabama Supreme Court, however, in 1997 vacated the remedy order.[45] While holding that the trial court was authorized to rule on the constitutionality of the state's school system and was empowered to order a specific remedy, it held that the trial court needed to wait a reasonable time for the legislature to formulate an educational system before it could implement its own plan.[46] Then, in 2002, the court reopened the case on its own initiative and dismissed.[47] Notably, the court left the liability order intact but held that the imposition of "any specific remedy that the judiciary could impose would, in order to be effective, necessarily involve a usurpation of that power entrusted exclusively to the Legislature."[48] These precedents and others[49] compromise the ability of advocates to rely exclusively on litigation to secure and enforce a right to education under state law, particularly where comprehensive remedies to insufficient resources would require an act by the state legislature.

On the other hand, in the recent case *Lobato v. State of Colorado,* challengers to the state's system of financing public education appealed the state's trial court decision that the issue raised was a political question and therefore not justiciable under the state's constitution.[50] The state's court of appeals affirmed, but the Colorado Supreme Court reversed. In reversing, the state supreme court held that whether the public school financing system violated the constitutional mandate for a "thorough and uniform" system of public schools was a justiciable issue.[51] However, the Colorado Supreme Court also held that the constitutionality of the state's finance system would be evaluated by "rational basis review."[52]

These examples suggest that the contours of the right to education under state law are not particularly stable within any given state. However, the legal landscape can also change dramatically for the better. In 1995, the Florida Supreme Court declined to declare a school funding scheme constitutionally inadequate because there were "no judicially manageable standards available to determine adequacy" and because such a judicial determination would violate the doctrine of separation of powers.[53] After losing that case, Florida education advocates succeeded in amending the language of the constitution's education clause to provide a delineated and higher standard of adequacy, opening the door for future adequacy suits.[54] Since this change, one Florida court, in *Crowley v. Pinellas County School Board,* permitted systemic actions against individual districts to go forward.[55]

b. The Potential for Right-to-Education Resource Cases in State Courts to Remedy the School-to-Prison Pipeline

Despite the complexity of education-resource litigation, and the often changing legal landscape, it is important to note that there has been a great deal of successful impact litigation in state courts around the right to education.[56] Since *Rodriguez,* lawsuits challenging the method of funding public schools or the adequacy of school resources have been brought in approximately forty-five states.[57]

While there is a robust debate regarding the efficacy of lawsuits that focus on the equitable distribution of finances versus those that focus on adequacy or on comparability of resources, litigation of either kind has rarely pursued remedies for ending the pipeline to prison in a conscious manner.[58] Rather than describe the debate, this chapter focuses on how lawsuits brought on right-to-education grounds—either in the equity or adequacy areas—might drive remedies that purposefully address the School-to-Prison Pipeline by reallocating resources and establishing effective monitoring programs.

There is an active bar of impact-litigation attorneys with expertise in comprehensive lawsuits involving systemic reform asserting the denial of the right to education, and new cases are filed every year. Considering that School-to-Prison Pipeline remedies are likely to produce large cost savings over time,[59] it may be especially useful for impact litigators, especially those already engaged in school resource litigation, to add elements to their legal claims that are more likely to generate remedies that will curb the pipeline.

There are two important right-to-education considerations for litigating against the pipeline:

- Where school resource cases are being contemplated, currently litigated, or settled, impact litigators could encourage greater attention to School-to-Prison Pipeline factors as evidence of a legal violation as well as important considerations for the remedy phase;[60] and
- Pursuant to some state constitutions, there may be viable causes of action seeking pipeline-specific remedies against a specific district or on behalf of subgroups that may be at a higher risk for incarceration.

(1) Leveraging Existing Statewide Adequacy Suits to Challenge the School-to-Prison Pipeline

Where school resource cases are being contemplated, currently litigated, or settled, the core recommendation is that advocates consider framing legal arguments or settlements so that broad and comprehensive cases include vehicles for pipeline-specific remedies. To illustrate this point, three types of remedies are described that might serve this purpose.

(a) Seek Resources That Matter Most

The first type of remedy, often found in right-to-education litigation, seeks to provide a wide range of resources relevant to ending the School-to-Prison Pipeline, including but not limited to high-quality preschool; highly effective teachers; support for students with disabilities and mental health issues, including access to guidance counselors, school psychologists, and well-trained special educators; effective instruction for English language learners;

reasonable class sizes; safe and healthy facilities; school libraries; and up-to-date college-bound curriculum and curriculum resources.

Often cases that have sought this type of remedy have relied on low graduation rates, low rates of qualified teachers, and inadequate special education resources to help establish a violation. The recently settled *Williams* case in California focused largely on evidence of overcrowding and poor facilities, but it also included evidence of limited access to effective instruction such as high teacher-pupil ratios, the lack of specialists available to serve English language learners and students with disabilities, and disparities in access to experienced and certified teachers.[61] Similarly, in *Campaign for Fiscal Equity v. State*, the New York Supreme Court found the quality of New York City's public school teachers to be inadequate, as measured by certification levels and the quality of their undergraduate education,[62] and discussed particular remedies relating to the number of qualified teachers, principals, and other personnel.[63] Of these resources, improvement to the quality of teachers and administrators may have the largest impact on the pipeline, as research demonstrates that a principal's attitude and beliefs about discipline have a large effect on suspension rates when demographics are controlled.[64]

(b) Request More Pipeline-Specific Remedies

The second type of remedy, largely absent from current litigation, would include resources that specifically target the students at greatest risk of failing school and becoming court-involved. These resources are often omitted from the remedies pursued or granted in right-to-education cases, even though the poor educational outcomes of these at-risk students are used as evidence of inadequacy. In contrast to the alignment of evidence and remedies regarding teacher quality, data demonstrating high rates of suspension have been presented in only a few adequacy cases, and few court decisions mention the issue.[65] Likewise, despite strong evidence suggesting a link, juvenile incarceration rates have rarely been raised in the context of educational adequacy cases. Most courts do examine graduation rates as probative evidence of an inadequate education,[66] but they rarely provide remedies specifically targeting an improvement in graduation rates.[67]

The frequent use of graduation rates in right-to-education cases illustrates the potential for expanding the type of remedies sought in these cases. Remedies in right-to-education cases often entail a "costing out" analysis to determine how resource needs can be met. Ideally, even in cases where resource needs are reduced to dollars and cents, advocates could include the estimated costs of providing effective dropout intervention programs or positive behavioral interventions and supports programs designed to lower rates of disciplinary exclusion, which, as discussed at the outset, economists suggest are cost-effective. Similarly, remedies could also call for more programmatic support for students who are overaged or have been court-involved, to ensure that these youth are fully considered in any remedy designed to boost school resources.

(c) Add Greater Safeguards to Ensure Full Implementation

A third consideration would be to incorporate more comprehensive monitoring and evaluation provisions as part of the remedy phase, specifically, data elements that are relevant to assessing the scope of the School-to-Prison Pipeline in a given jurisdiction. For example, given that graduation rates are often used as evidence of inadequacy, remedies designed to make the distribution of funds or resources more equitable, including those that direct more funds for dropout intervention programs, should be monitored to see whether real improvements to graduation rates result. Longitudinal data on rates of discipline, grade retention, school referrals to law enforcement, and school-based arrests should also be collected and reported as part of the monitoring of the remedy.

(2) Strategies and Other Considerations for Discrete Adequacy Cases

Given the complexity and enormity of statewide educational adequacy cases, litigators should give careful consideration to questions of organizational capacity. Even success in discrete cases requires a large commitment of resources for years beyond the actual litigation. That said, in some states, advocates might explore the viability of more discrete adequacy claims brought to generate pipeline-specific remedies.

A preliminary review of state cases suggests that in some states, viable pipeline-specific claims might even be brought on behalf of a particular subgroup (e.g., racial minorities) or against a single school district. These possibilities are briefly outlined below. The ideas presented here should not be construed as recommendations or endorsements. Rather, they are presented to broaden the scope of challenges litigators might consider. If an approach proves legally viable, nonlegal factors, such as the impact on coalition building, should be considered carefully prior to deciding on any particular course of action.

(a) Adequacy Lawsuits on Behalf of an Identifiable Subgroup

The first method to narrow a potentially unwieldy statewide adequacy claim would be to file on behalf of a limited subgroup, such as racial minorities, students with disabilities,[68] or, more generally, students "at risk" of failure.[69] Given the disproportionate rate at which these subgroups fall prey to the pipeline, a suit narrowed in this manner may help ensure that the remedies are targeted to protect the groups most in need.

One example suggesting that filing a discrete adequacy lawsuit on behalf of a particular subgroup of students holds potential is the aforementioned case of *Hunt v. Alabama*.[70] There a plaintiff class representing students with disabilities joined the larger lawsuit against the state, arguing that the state had provided inadequate funding for special education programs.[71] Plaintiffs claimed that Alabama's system was inequitable and inadequate, in violation of the state's education clause and due process.[72] The subclass of students with disabilities asserted two additional claims: that children with disabilities were entitled to an "appropriate education and special services" under Alabama statute and that the mechanism for distributing special education funds was arbitrary and violated the due process clause of the Alabama constitution.

The trial court found that significant disparities in funding existed between different districts, which resulted in students receiving different resources depending on where they attended school.[73] With respect to special education, the court found these funding disparities to extend to the opportunities provided to students with disabilities, asserting that "it is clear that the quality of a child's special education program—facilities, instruction, special or related services such as speech, physical and vocational therapy—depends entirely upon the system in which the child attends school."[74] In addition, the court determined that with regard to the specific subclass, the state system of public schools had failed to provide appropriate instruction and special services to children with disabilities, based on seven components.[75] Finally, the court ordered the state to establish a system of public schools that met the constitutional standards of equity and adequacy for all schoolchildren, including those with disabilities.[76] Unfortunately, as noted earlier, in 2002, the Alabama Supreme Court reopened the case on its own initiative and dismissed it.[77] On a more positive note, a motion to dismiss a lawsuit brought by advocates in Colorado who joined several historically disadvantaged subgroups in *Lobato* was denied.[78] The plaintiffs alleged that the finance system "particularly fails to provide a constitutionally adequate education to students with disabilities and to students from lower socio-economic backgrounds, ethnic and racial minorities, and non-English speaking families."[79]

As with any litigation, advocates should carefully anticipate foreseeable pitfalls and the risks of unintended consequences. Particularly with respect to resource suits on behalf of particular identifiable subgroups, advocates should carefully consider developing coalitions and allies and guard against accusations that remedies on behalf of a particular group would simply result in a redistribution of an inadequate pie.

(b) Adequacy Suits Seeking Specific Programs

Another possibility for filing a discrete and possibly more manageable resource case would be to file a lawsuit to implement specific *programs* targeted at a specific subgroup. One such example is a lawsuit filed in Michigan, on behalf of students with disabilities, to secure specific programming for this subgroup.

In *Durant v. State,* the Michigan Supreme Court consolidated three separate lawsuits challenging the state system of funding certain educational programs including special education.[80] The court held that Michigan had violated the state constitution by underfunding special education and special education transportation.[81] The state constitution prohibited defendants from reducing the state's share of special education funding because they were required by law to maintain proportional funding levels for programs mandated by the state.[82] The court awarded the plaintiffs both declaratory relief and a damages judgment for school districts for the amount of underfunding for three school years, totaling more than $200 million.[83] Unfortunately, however, when plaintiffs returned to court seeking additional funds on adequacy grounds on several occasions, the court refused to require further payments and eventually found the state's system of funding to pass constitutional muster.[84]

Given the partial success of the Michigan case, in some states it might be possible to pursue a right-to-education case on behalf of particular subgroups to secure specific programmatic remedies, such as dropout intervention programs, greater counseling and mental health support on behalf of students with emotional issues, or funding for other programmatic interventions that are scarce but have proven effective, especially in states with minimal investments of this nature.

(c) Litigation against a Particular School District

Leveraging adequacy suits to challenge the School-to-Prison Pipeline could involve naming public school districts as well as states as defendants. Such an approach, responding to both the limited capacity of advocates and the preference of state courts to avoid confrontations with legislatures, might even go as far as filing a suit against a school district but not the state. This approach has not been widely explored. It may be that the opportunity to bring a right-to-education case against a district would only be viable in a handful of states with strong right-to-education law and would depend on the district being regarded as sharing the constitutional obligation with the state.

(i) State and District Liability

Several cases have allowed a state to assert a cross- or third-party claim against a district, suggesting that student-plaintiffs may also allege district liability. The case of *Bradford v. Maryland State Board of Education* commenced in 1994 when the parents of students filed a class action lawsuit in state court against the state on behalf of "present and future students in the Baltimore City Public Schools who are at risk of educational failure."[85] In October 1995, the state filed a third-party claim against the city, in which it averred that the city had "totally failed to manage adequately the Baltimore City Public School system" and that "any inadequacies in the education received by the children of Baltimore City are a direct result of that failure and can only be remedied by a total restructuring of the management of BCPS."[86] The state asked that the city be held liable for the plaintiffs' claims should they prevail and that the city school system be restructured. On November 26, 1996, the parties in both cases entered into a consent decree that created a partnership between the city and the state and provided for five remedies: a significant restructuring of the governance of the city's public school system, the provision of certain additional funding by the state for fiscal years 1998–2002, the development of a plan to increase student achievement, interim and final review and evaluation of progress, and the continuance of jurisdiction by the court.[87]

(ii) Districts Alone

It is conceivable that lawsuits targeting a single district, alone, being smaller in scope, might also be more manageable for advocates with organizational resource limitations. Litigants exploring this possibility should first determine the viability of such claims in their respective jurisdictions and then determine whether the harms to be addressed, as well as the remedies needed, are sufficiently *intra*district in nature to warrant this approach.

The conventional wisdom in educational resource cases calls for challenging the state because the resource deficiencies most commonly associated with the School-to-Prison Pipeline are state driven. In many cases that would be accurate, but as Jonathan Kozol points out, profound intradistrict inequities in the distribution of important resources may also be at play.[88] Civil rights advocates have long been concerned about intradistrict resource inequities that flow along the lines of race and class. In a 2000 report to Congress, the U.S. Department of Education described its efforts to develop a guidance on the enforcement of Title VI in response "to the increase in lawsuits and OCR [Office for Civil Rights] complaints alleging inequities in the quality and quantity of educational opportunities based on race, ethnicity and economic status," stating that such a guidance would consider four major components: staff, programs, instructional support, and facilities.[89] While litigators should consider filing federal administrative complaints pursuant to Title VI regulations, similar theories might be viable pursuant to state law in state court.

For example, in 1986, in a lawsuit brought pursuant to California's Equal Protection Clause, which recognizes disparate impact causes of action, four residents of Los Angeles County filed a suit as taxpayers against the Los Angeles County Unified School District, the district superintendent, and the Board of Education of the City of Los Angeles that successfully challenged intradistrict funding inequities.[90] The suit alleged that the district violated equal protection by disproportionately allocating educational resources among its schools. Eventually, the parties settled, and the ensuing consent decree required equalization of funding on a per-pupil basis, provisions for more equitable distribution of experienced teachers, and a cap on the size of new and existing schools.[91]

A few other examples of resource cases brought against districts pursuant to state law suggest that this largely unexplored strategy may be viable in at least some jurisdictions outside of California. In the aforementioned Florida case *Crowley v. Pinellas County School Board,* the court found that plaintiffs had standing to sue a district under the state constitution for failure to provide an adequate education, but only for bringing systemic challenges.[92] In *Schroeder v. Palm Beach County School Board,*[93] however, the ACLU Racial Justice Program filed a class action complaint against the Palm Beach County School Board and the Palm Beach County School Superintendent alleging that the district failed to provide an adequate education as required under the state constitution, which guarantees a "uniform, efficient, safe, secure, and high quality education," evidenced by the dismal graduation rates in that county. The lawsuit alleged that one in three Palm Beach County students do not graduate in four years and that the graduation rates for children of color were even worse. However, the Florida circuit court in Palm Beach County granted defendants' motion to dismiss, concluding that the relevant constitutional provision provided an individual private right of action to sue the state but not an individual school district.[94] Plaintiffs refiled their lawsuit containing the same allegations, but this time, they sued the state and not the district. The lawsuit remains pending.

As these few cases suggest, the viability and benefits of suing individual districts *alone* are not well established. However, cases permitting a state defendant to assert a cross- or third-party claim against a district lend support for the proposition that at least in some states a district is responsible, and thus liable, for the provision of an adequate education, strengthening the argument that districts may be named as defendants alone.[95] Furthermore, the concept of district responsibility for adequate education is well established as a matter of federal policy, such as under NCLB, albeit with regard to outcomes and not resources.

(3) The Potential Influence of the No Child Left Behind Act in Right-to-Education Cases

Whether the central target is a school, a district, or a state, the No Child Left Behind Act (NCLB)[96] may present both obstacles and opportunities for impact litigators seeking to improve the adequacy of education resources as a remedy to the School-to-Prison Pipeline. In the aforementioned Massachusetts case *Hancock v. Commissioner of Education,* the state defended against that inadequacy claim, in part, by citing its adoption of "an accountability system that identifies struggling schools and districts and targets assistance to them," consistent with the parameters of NCLB.[97] The *Hancock* ruling itself was filled with references to the way in which the state had instituted a system to ensure adequacy and had showed signs of progress.[98] Just having an operational system was apparently sufficient.

On the other hand, the existence of clear standards for what children should learn, and NCLB-driven accountability requirements built off these standards that frame persistently underperforming schools as inadequate, may provide opportunities for litigants seeking to improve and enforce the educational rights of children. Litigants, especially in states where the educational rights of children are well established and justiciable might argue that NCLB accountability measures provide concrete and objective standards for measuring an "adequate" education. In such states, finding that a district or school fails to meet these measures provides evidentiary support for a claim of inadequate education under state constitutional law.

For example, in the aforementioned *Lobato v. State of Colorado,* the plaintiffs had argued that the state violated the education clause by failing to provide sufficient funds to enable the school districts to satisfy both the content standards and performance objectives in the education reform legislation. As evidence, plaintiffs cite data indicating that students of color, English language learner ("ELL") students, students with disabilities, and economically disadvantaged students failed to meet certain proficiency targets set by the Consolidated State Plan, a plan adopted by the state in order to comply with the requirements of the No Child Left Behind Act of 2001, 20 U.S.C. §§ 6301–6578 (2006).[99]

In this way, NCLB may provide especially strong support for discrete claims brought on behalf of particular subgroups. A core concept of NCLB is that the overall performance of a school or a district can be determined based on the outcomes for just one subgroup; persistently poor performance results for racial or ethnic minorities, students with disabilities, English language learners, or socioeconomically disadvantaged students can trigger accountability measures such as the state's takeover of the school district. Moreover, NCLB includes low graduation rates as an indicator of what is adequate. Properly implemented, graduation-rate accountability can serve as a counterbalance to perverse incentives of test-driven accountability systems that allow schools to push low achievers out in order to push test scores up.

Whether education reform remedies are driven by litigation or policy, impact litigation can have unintended consequences. Arguably, adequacy cases that focus on a limited number of outcomes, such as test-score improvements, without tracking rates of suspension, graduation, and incarceration, may actually exacerbate push-out pressures. In other words, litigation that focuses too heavily on low test scores to establish inadequacy and monitors test scores as the primary indicator to evaluate the implementation of the remedy could inadvertently add a new form of high-stakes testing accountability replete with incentives for schools to improve scores at the expense of more substantive indicators of a high-quality education.[100]

Although adding School-to-Prison Pipeline indicators such as grade retention, rates of suspension, and graduation to such litigation might mitigate these issues, many researchers and advocates have expressed concerns that NCLB's standards-based reforms with accountability focused on school and district performance (often lacking resources) creates incentives to drive low-achieving students, and students exhibiting challenging behavior, out of school. Advocates that use the failure to meet NCLB standards as evidence should be cognizant of these risks and consider adding safeguards and additional evaluation factors to remedies beyond current state or federal accountability schemes.

The need to safeguard the possible unintended "push-out" effects of systemic resource litigation that uses NCLB accountability standards brings us to the second overarching question of this chapter: to what extent can legal challenges grounded in the right to education push back on education policies and practices that push students out or deny children access to schools?

B. RIGHT-TO-EDUCATION REMEDIES TO POLICIES AND PRACTICES THAT DENY ACCESS OR PUSH CHILDREN OUT OF SCHOOL

As mentioned in the introduction to this chapter, there are compelling reasons for advocates to push back on educational policies and practices that have the effect of pushing students out of school. Besides federal policy, there are policies and practices initiated at the state, district, and school levels that may even more directly contribute to pushing students out.

Similar to concerns expressed about NCLB accountability, state policies, such as the use of high school exit exams, intended to improve school performance, may also create perverse incentives for school systems to push low-performing students out so that they are not part of the overall test-taking pool. States have historically used testing to evaluate schools as well as students. In a recent study, one scholar found that for similar offenses, schools meted out longer suspensions on students who performed poorly on Florida's standardized tests than they did on higher-performing students.[101] Additionally, this "punishment gap" grew substantially during the period when standardized tests were administered, providing evidence that schools use "selective discipline" to "reshape the testing pool" by keeping low-performing students out of school during testing days.[102]

As Joe Tulman has suggested in discussing the education rights of students with disabilities, raising awareness of students' educational rights is an important response. If lawyers can make it much harder for schools to push kids out by frequently representing those who are suspended or expelled, and can repeatedly challenge a district's failure to meet its educational obligations, such resistance may encourage districts to reconsider policies that push students out in favor of longer-term remedies involving early interventions and a commitment of resources.[103] Litigation in response to disciplinary removals is covered in depth in chapters 3 and 4. This section introduces rights-based litigation pursuant to both due process and equal protection claims and describes systemic challenges to school exclusion and nondisciplinary "push-out" practices not covered in the other chapters.

1. PROTECTION AGAINST DENIAL OF ACCESS TO EDUCATION IN FEDERAL AND STATE LAW

a. Access Denial and the Equal Protection Clause of the U.S. Constitution
The Constitution protects students from being denied access to educational opportunities on the basis of their membership in certain classes. For example, in *Plyler v. Doe,* the Supreme Court struck down a Texas statute that effectively denied undocumented children access to the public schools.[104] Children with disabilities are similarly protected from exclusion from schools on the basis of their disability under the federal Equal Protection Clause. In two cases, *Pennsylvania Association for Retarded Children (PARC) v. Commonwealth*[105] and *Mills v. Board of Education,*[106] federal district courts held that the routine exclusion of students with disabilities from public schools for fear that they would not behave properly violated the Equal Protection Clause.[107] For many years the common practice was to treat students with disabilities as second-class citizens or to deny access altogether.[108] The rulings in *Mills* and *PARC* became codified in the Education for All Handicapped Act, now known as the Individuals with Disabilities Education Act (IDEA).[109]

In another exclusion case, *Lau v. Nichols,* plaintiff students who were limited in English proficiency (LEP; also referred to as English language learners or ELL students) argued that the denial of additional supports and instruction effectively excluded them from educational opportunity although they were permitted to attend school physically.[110] The Supreme Court, interpreting Title VI regulations, concluded that these children were in fact constructively excluded from school in violation of antidiscrimination law.[111] Within weeks, Congress codified the *Lau* ruling by passing the Equal Educational Opportunity Act (EEOA).[112] The EEOA is regarded as "rights enforcing" in that the rights guaranteed are not predicated on a specific grant to the state of federal funds under the statute. The EEOA sets forth an affirmative duty requiring states to take "appropriate" action to provide English language learners with an equal educational opportunity.[113] Other federal antidiscrimination laws, including Title VI of the Civil Rights Act of 1964 and Section 504 of the Rehabilitation Act of 1973, are similarly rights enforcing and may help ensure access to public education.

b. Access Denial and the Equal Protection Clause in State Constitutions
Where the evidence suggests that a protected class of students is subjected to disciplinary removal more than other groups, or routinely
receives fewer educational resources, this different treatment implicates a
possible equal protection violation. As discussed in chapter 2, with a few
exceptions, most states require that either a fundamental right is at stake
or there is evidence of *intentional* discrimination against a "suspect" class
to review an equal protection claim under the "strict scrutiny" standard.
In other words, in many cases the state's equal protection clause affords
no greater utility than the federal equal protection clause. However, the
contours of state law often do not mirror federal law so precisely, and
therefore equal protection arguments pursuant to the language in state
constitutions are worth pursuing in many states, even when the state's
education clause does not provide in explicit terms a "fundamental right."
As the litigators in the successful *Montoy v. Kansas* litigation describe
their experience, "Schools for Fair Funding asserted an equal protection claim, a due process claim, and a claim under the Kansas Constitution's education Article VI. The Kansas Supreme Court dismissed the
equal protection and due process claims leaving only the Article VI claim
. . . [and] applied an equal protection–type analysis and Schools for Fair
Funding prevailed."[114]

2. PROTECTIONS AGAINST REMOVAL FROM SCHOOL FOUND IN
FEDERAL LAW

a. Fundamental Rights and Due Process Protections for
Pushed-Out Students at the Federal Level

Unfortunately, access is often insufficient to ensure that, once enrolled, students are not forced to leave school. Once a state decides to provide a public
education for all children, students and their families develop a constitutionally protected interest against arbitrary denials of public education. In *Goss
v. Lopez*, as described in detail in chapter 4, the Supreme Court held that
children maintain a property and liberty interest in attending public school
such that the state may not deny schooling without affording procedural due
process.[115] Similarly, substantive due process arguments may be used to challenge arbitrary denials of a public education.[116] Students attending a public
school also maintain their constitutional right to free speech, and the state
may not take away their right to education for violating a school's limit on
free speech that is unconstitutional.

b. Fundamental Rights and Due Process Protections for Pushed-Out Students at the State Level

Advocates concerned about due process violations should carefully analyze right-to-education precedents in their state courts for specific reference to "fundamental rights."[117] As mentioned in section A of this chapter, courts do not uniformly interpret provisions that obligate a state to provide education as implicitly guaranteeing education as a "fundamental" right. In states that describe the right to education as "fundamental," courts theoretically do apply strict scrutiny and the concomitant "compelling interest" standard when a suspension or expulsion is challenged.[118] But in other states, courts may conclude that students who misbehave waive their "fundamental" right, and thus, strict scrutiny need not be applied.[119]

Further, some states courts have drawn a distinction between the state's obligation to provide education to all students as part of a public system of education and its interpretation of an individual's rights when he or she sues a public school, district, or state alleging that his or her individualized right to education has been denied.[120] For example, in Massachusetts, in *Doe v. Superintendent of Schools,* the state supreme court acknowledged precedent imposing on states an "obligation to educate its children" and thus requiring a redistribution of educational resources to comply with the state constitutional right to education, but nonetheless the court "decline[d] to hold . . . that a student's right to education is a 'fundamental right' which would trigger strict scrutiny analysis whenever school officials determine, in the interest of safety, that student's misconduct warrants expulsion."[121] Other states appear to interpret their state constitutions in a similar fashion.[122]

The complexity of the legal landscape at the state level is further complicated by the wide variety of state statutory protections, which sometimes strengthen the right to education and corollary due process rights. From one state to the next there may be differences in enrollment requirements and safeguards, differences in the age range covered by the right to education, and differences in due process to challenge discipline and access to alternative education, to name a few.

Advocates seeking to challenge an exclusionary practice should consider claims sounding in both state and federal law and may find it advantageous to combine federal and state causes of action. The following case study involves a mixed state and federal lawsuit brought in federal court, where the state statutory provisions were critically important to the claims.

a. Challenging Nondisciplinary Exclusions from School: Case Study of *Ruiz v. Pedota*

Not all students who are pushed out of classrooms are removed for disciplinary reasons. In some cases, students may be disenrolled for academic reasons, and in others, they may be removed from school rolls for truancy. In addition to raising due process arguments to challenge disciplinary removals, lawyers can combine state education requirements with state and federal due process arguments to challenge the push-out of children for nondisciplinary reasons.

A lawsuit brought by Advocates for Children of New York (AFC) provides one model to challenge these types of practices. A report issued in 2002 documented that more than fifty thousand high school students were being "discharged" from the New York City school system each year without receiving a diploma—a number significantly higher than the officially reported dropout rates.[123] In January 2003, AFC filed suit in *Ruiz v. Pedota* in federal district court against Franklin J. Lane High School, on behalf of all students who had been excluded, expelled, or discharged from the school for reasons of age, lack of sufficient credits, failure to pass Regents exams, poor grades, and/or truancy.[124] Many of these children had been informed by school officials that their only educational option was to attend a GED program.[125] Plaintiffs brought claims under both federal and state law, including the Due Process Clause of the Fourteenth Amendment, section 1983, and New York State education law.[126]

New York State law provides that any person under twenty-one years of age is entitled to attend a public school and mandates full-time instruction until the age of seventeen.[127] State law also provides various protections limiting the circumstances under which an involuntary school transfer can occur.[128] Further, New York's law guarantees certain services for students who are struggling academically or who have attendance or behavioral problems; these services include guidance for educational progress, individual counseling, tutoring, and modified curricula.[129]

In response to the suit, the Department of Education immediately allowed the named plaintiff to reenroll and sent notice to more than five thousand recently discharged students, informing them of their right to return to school until the age of twenty-one.[130] In addition, when the suit was settled, the discharged students received priority enrollment in night or summer school,[131] and the Department of Education revised its policies to require a planning interview to be conducted before any student is discharged to a program that does not award high school diplomas. Further, the department both posted public advertisements and mailed personal notice to public school students informing them of their right to attend high school and to refuse to be transferred to a GED program.[132] Although the state Department of Education never admitted liability, and the federal court never reached a ruling, *Ruiz v. Pedota* demonstrates how legal theories pursuant to state law may be particularly useful for impact litigators seeking to challenge similar push-out practices in their own jurisdictions. Examination of due process arguments in response to *disciplinary* exclusions, as opposed to the nondisciplinary exclusions discussed here, are described in chapter 4.

b. Referencing International Human Rights Law in
    Pipeline Right-to-Education Cases

Advocates should also explore international human rights law in the course of lawsuits and administrative complaints to enforce the right to an education for children. In 2008, a report issued by the ACLU, the ACLU of Connecticut, and the Allard K. Lowenstein International Human Rights Clinic at Yale Law School entitled *Dignity Denied: The Effect of "Zero Tolerance" Policies on Students' Human Rights* analyzes the myriad of ways that human rights standards as set forth in international treaties may be implicated by zero-tolerance policies or the denial of access to education.[133]

The following three treaties are just a sample of human rights laws that may be relevant to right-to-education arguments set forth in this chapter: (1) the Convention on the Rights of the Child (CRC)[134] guarantees several basic human rights for children, including the rights to education, free expression, and freedom from discrimination; (2) the International Convention on the Elimination of All Forms of Racial Discrimination (CERD),[135] as ratified, sets forth the human right to be free from discrimination, including specifically in the context of education, and prohibits any "distinction, exclusion, restriction or preference" that has the "purpose or effect" of racial discrimination; and (3) the International Covenant on Economic, Social and Cultural Rights (ICESCR)[136] requires states to make compulsory primary education available to all children.

Referencing these and other provisions highlights the concerns about educational neglect and abusive school policies that pave the path from school to prison. Over time, these treaties and international declarations may gain strength and precedential authority in our courts or may help convince state and federal legislatures to enact laws that would effectuate them. A similar noteworthy development is that the American Bar Association recently and unanimously passed three resolutions based on the organization's call for a right to high-quality education. The second resolution (118B) in particular encourages the development of laws and greater law enforcement to prevent the exclusionary and push-out practices. It reads as follows:

RECOMMENDATION

RESOLVED, That the American Bar Association urges federal and state legislatures to pass laws and national, state, and local education, child welfare, and juvenile justice agencies to implement and enforce policies that:

1. Help advance the right to remain in school, promote a safe and supportive school environment for all children, and enable them to complete school;
2. Limit exclusion from and disruption of students' regular educational programs as a response to disciplinary problems;
3. Provide full procedural protections, including the opportunity to have representation by counsel in proceedings to exclude students from their regular education program, appropriate provisions of due process in other school disciplinary processes, and implementing disciplinary procedures in a fair, non-discriminatory and culturally responsive manner;
4. Reduce criminalization of truancy, disability-related behavior, and other school-related conduct; and
5. Establish programs and procedures to assist parents, caregivers, guardians, students, and their legal representatives in understanding and exercising student rights to remain in school; and

FURTHER RESOLVED, That the American Bar Association urges federal and state legislatures to legally define, and assure standardized on-going monitoring, reporting, and accountability for, measuring graduation rates, school dropout rates, school truancy, and disciplinary violations resulting in student suspensions and expulsions, with data disaggregated by race, disability and other disparately affected populations, and ensure that no group of students is disparately subjected to school discipline or exclusion."[137]

C. CONCLUSION

Whether advocates pursue comprehensive resource litigation to strike at underlying contributing factors, pursue more discrete and immediate chal- lenges to prevent student push-outs and ensure students have and maintain access to educational opportunities, or seek greater legal protections for children by pressing for the creation and implementation of new laws, it is important that remedies consider monitoring and oversight to ensure effec- tive implementation over time.

Advocates should also consider these right-to-education cases as an orga- nizing vehicle for grassroots advocacy aimed at reforming the system in any way they can. In fact, often advocacy groups have organized around the issues highlighted by more general right-to-education cases, pursuing rem- edies through the political process simultaneously during the legal process and using the same evidence to raise the issues in the public policy arena.[138] As Jeannie Oakes, John Rogers, Gary Blasi, and Martin Lipton conclude in *Grassroots Organizing, Social Movements, and the Right to High-Quality Edu- cation,* "Establishing education as a fundamental right requires social move- ment activism."[139] They add that "legal victories are often implemented with little fidelity or not implemented at all unless they are broadly supported by public norms."[140] The authors recommend that lawyers, organizers, phi- lanthropies, and others form strategic relationships.[141] Although limits on resources and capacity will necessarily constrict the ability of any one orga- nization to pursue school-to-prison litigation that aims at the root causes of the phenomenon, it may also be true that efforts to stop push-out practices will require a greater degree of organization and collaboration between liti- gators and other advocates if the benefits of successful litigation are to be long lasting. Despite these complexities, advocates should not overlook the value in pursuing impact litigation that emphasizes the right to education, as it can provide a powerful galvanizing link.

2

Unlawful Discrimination

Among the most troubling aspects of the School-to-Prison Pipeline are the grave disparities in areas such as suspensions, expulsions, and law enforcement referrals for certain identifiable subgroups of youth. Particularly in the current climate of increasing schools' accountability, driven by high-stakes testing and the No Child Left Behind Act, school officials may face increasing pressures to push poor-performing students out of their schools. Those who suffer disproportionately from these practices include students with disabilities, children of color, English language learners (ELLs), and undocumented students, as well as homeless youth and youth in foster care. And, of course, many students will fit into more than one of these categories.

This chapter begins with an analysis of strategies to protect the rights of children of color under both federal and state laws. The second section explores the rights of ELL students and undocumented students. The third section discusses protections for homeless youth and children in foster care. The rights of students with disabilities are discussed in chapter 3.

A. ANTIDISCRIMINATION PROTECTIONS FOR STUDENTS OF COLOR

Studies show that children of color consistently are overrepresented at every point of the School-to-Prison Pipeline, from enrollment in underresourced public schools to suspension and expulsion rates to referrals to disciplinary alternative schools to referrals to law enforcement and the juvenile justice system.

Children of color are more likely than their white counterparts to attend underresourced schools.[1] They also bear the weight of negative school disciplinary policies in disproportionate numbers. From 1973 to 2006, the percentage of African American students enrolled in public schools who were suspended at least once in a given year rose from 6 percent to 15 percent.[2] For African American males in 2003, the risk of suspension was nearly 18 percent; the rate for white males was 7 percent.[3] In most large districts across the nation, middle-school suspension rates for minority students are consistently over 20 percent, and in many cities it is not uncommon for over half the African American male students to have been suspended at least once in a given year.[4] Studies also suggest that children of color are more likely than their white counterparts to be referred to disciplinary alternative programs.[5]

Those racial disparities carry over into and may be exacerbated by arrests and referrals to the juvenile justice system. Students of color are more likely than their white counterparts to be arrested at school.[6] As for disparities in overall arrest rates, in 2003, African American children made up 16 percent of the nation's overall juvenile population but accounted for 45 percent of juvenile arrests.[7] And children of color are far more likely to be detained in the criminal justice system. From 1985 to 1995, detention rates for African American and Hispanic youth increased by 180 and 140 percent, respectively, while the rate for white youth decreased by 13 percent.[8] Children of color represent 34 percent of the nation's total youth population but constitute 62 percent of youth in detention pending adjudication and 66 percent of youth committed to public facilities after disposition.[9] When white youth and African American youth are charged for the same offense, African American youth with no prior admissions are six times more likely to be incarcerated in public facilities than white youth with the same background; Latino youth are three times more likely than white youth to be incarcerated.[10] Notably, studies suggest that African American children are more likely than their white peers to be suspended, expelled, or arrested for the *same kind* of conduct at school.[11]

Federal law prohibits school officials from discriminating against students on the basis of race pursuant to the Equal Protection Clause of the U.S. Constitution[12] and Title VI of the Civil Rights Act of 1964.[13] State laws sometimes provide even greater protections.[14] In the following section, we distinguish between "different treatment" claims (sometimes referred to as "intentional discrimination" or "disparate treatment") and "disparate impact" claims. Different treatment, as the term is used in this book, refers to claims of *intentional* discrimination by school officials or the government. Litigants pursuing these claims are not necessarily required to produce "smoking gun" evidence of animus targeting a racial group; circumstantial evidence should suffice.[15] However, the ultimate question posed in these cases is, did government officials *intend* to discriminate against the group? In contrast, disparate impact refers to the *effects* of a given policy on a targeted group. Even when government actors *do not intend* to target a group, a disparate impact claim relies on the disproportionate *effects* of a given policy on a protected class.[16] The ultimate question posed in these types of claims is, how does the policy impact the education of particular groups of students?

The following subsection begins with an analysis of case law involving claims of different treatment to challenge the discriminatory imposition of discipline and the unjust maintenance of a racially hostile educational environment. The next subsection discusses legal avenues for challenging the disparate impact of other policies that contribute to the School-to-Prison Pipeline, including an analysis of federal administrative complaint mechanisms and the potential for state law claims to address these disparities.

1. DIFFERENT TREATMENT: FEDERAL CLAIMS OF INTENTIONAL DISCRIMINATION

The Equal Protection Clause of the U.S. Constitution and Title VI of the Civil Rights Act of 1964 have been interpreted to require that private plaintiffs prove the existence of discriminatory *intent*.[17] Litigants may use these laws to challenge the School-to-Prison Pipeline in two areas: the discriminatory imposition of discipline and the maintenance of a racially hostile educational environment.

a. Discriminatory Discipline

Advocates seeking to address the pipeline on behalf of children of color should explore the possibility of challenging the discriminatory imposition of school discipline on the basis of race. In *Sherpell v. Humnoke School District No. 5*,[18] a federal court found that an Arkansas school district's discipline system was racially discriminatory and unconstitutional. The court found that teachers referred to Black students using such racist terms as "niggers," "blue gums," and "coons"; furthermore, a former teacher testified about forms of corporal punishment administered to Black students—including one who was left bloodied by a teacher—that were never administered to a white student during her nine years with the district.[19]

Absent "smoking gun" evidence such as the use of racial epithets by school officials, courts consider circumstantial evidence to determine whether officials intended to discriminate on the basis of race when punishing students. This inquiry focuses on whether minority students are punished differently than "similarly situated" white students.[20] Unfortunately, some courts have set a high bar for establishing "similarly situated" students, requiring virtually identical factual circumstances.

For example, in *Parker v. Trinity High School*, a federal district court concluded that two female African American students seeking to enjoin their expulsion after engaging in a fight were unlikely to prevail on the merits of their discrimination claim.[21] Although the plaintiffs identified instances in which white students who engaged in fights were not expelled, the court concluded that those other students were not "similarly situated" to plaintiffs, because the other fights, unlike the one involving the plaintiffs, did not continue after teachers tried to break it up and did not result in injury to teachers.[22] Similarly, in *Heller v. Hodgin*, a federal district court rejected a different-treatment claim raised by a white high school student who had been suspended for cursing in school.[23] In that case, an African American student called the plaintiff a "white ass fucking bitch" at school, and the plaintiff responded by stating that she was not a "white ass fucking bitch."[24] On the basis of these statements, both students were suspended for five days.[25] Rejecting plaintiff's equal protection claim, the court stated, "Even had Plaintiff's punishment been more severe than the other student's, the fact that a different faculty member imposed each student's punishment would have served to insulate the school's actions both from the appearance of and the fact of any discriminatory or vindictive punishment."[26]

But at least one federal district court has been willing to find that students were sufficiently similarly situated to warrant a discriminatory-discipline claim. *Payne v. Worthington Schools* involved a discriminatory-discipline claim raised by two African American students.[27] In that case, a white student told one African American student, "no niggers on the big toy," and held him to the ground; the other African American student came over, and a pushing match ensued wherein one plaintiff ended up hitting the white student.[28] Consequently, the African American student who hit the white student was suspended, while the white student was disciplined in a less severe manner.[29] The court concluded that this incident was sufficient to establish discriminatory discipline and consequently rejected the district's motion for summary judgment.[30]

A lawsuit filed by the American Civil Liberties Union (ACLU) in 2006 provides an example of remedies that might obtain where discriminatory discipline is alleged. In that case, the ACLU filed a class action lawsuit on behalf of a class of Native American students attending a majority-white school district, alleging the imposition of racially discriminatory discipline, in violation of the Equal Protection Clause and Title VI.[31] The complaint alleged that Native American students in the district were three times more likely to be suspended and twelve times more likely to be referred to the Winner City

Police Department than their Caucasian counterparts.[32] At least one-third of these students were suspended during their academic career, and roughly one in five were arrested for violating a school disciplinary rule.[33] The complaint highlighted specific instances in which Native American students were suspended or arrested, while similarly situated white students were not. For example, it described how a Native American student who placed a white student in a headlock and laughingly said he would break his neck was arrested, whereas a white student who told a Native American boy, "I'm going to kill you," and another white student who told a Native American girl that he wanted "to kill Indians" and see her "blood all over" were not arrested.[34]

Although the district consistently denied the allegations raised, the parties agreed to court-ordered mediation in 2007, and the federal district court entered the resulting agreement as a comprehensive Consent Decree with continuing jurisdiction in December of that year.[35] Pursuant to that decree, the district agreed to work with an expert to revise its discipline policies to ensure objectivity and clarity; hire a full-time ombudsperson, nominated by the collective Native American community, to serve as a liaison between Native American families and school officials, especially on disciplinary issues; convene a committee of Native American parents and school officials to review disciplinary incidents quarterly for racial disparities and, where disparities were found and could not be explained, recommend policy changes to reduce such disparities; and convene a separate committee, again including Native American representatives and school administrators, to identify benchmarks for levels of school discipline and racial disparities in discipline that the district would need to meet in order to terminate the court's jurisdiction. The consent decree further provided for training on reducing school disciplinary incidents and issues such as unconscious bias, as well as the development of culturally appropriate curricula in the schools. Finally, the consent decree provided for an independent monitor to conduct periodic site visits to monitor implementation of the agreement's terms.

In addition to litigating different-treatment claims of discriminatory discipline in federal court, advocates may choose to file administrative complaints with the U.S. Department of Education's Office for Civil Rights (OCR) on behalf individuals or classes of students. Even when such administrative complaints are not pursued, advocates should determine whether OCR or another agency has initiated an investigation or issued findings regarding the particular district or school. A finding that the district is not complying with, for example, a resolution agreement that addresses the precise problems alleged may provide useful evidence in a future lawsuit.

b. Racially Hostile Education Environment

The federal prohibition against intentional discrimination on the basis of race also protects against the maintenance of a racially hostile educational environment. In *Davis v. Monroe County Board of Education*,[36] the Supreme Court established that schools may be held liable for maintaining a hostile educational environment characterized by, for example, student-on-student harassment.[37] The *Davis* court held that to succeed in a claim for failure to protect against student-on-student harassment, a plaintiff must establish five elements: (1) the defendant had actual knowledge of the harassment; (2) the harassment is sufficiently "severe, pervasive and objectively offensive"; (3) the harassment "deprive[s] the victims of access to the educational benefits or opportunities provided by the school"; (4) the school was "deliberately indifferent" in its response to this harassment; and (5) the district exercised "substantial control over both the harasser and the context in which the known harassment occurs."[38] Because *Davis* held that "deliberate indifference" constitutes intentional discrimination,[39] it is likely that plaintiffs retain a private right of action to bring these claims even after the U.S. Supreme Court's decision in *Alexander v. Sandoval*.[40]

2. DISPARATE IMPACT: FEDERAL AND STATE AVENUES

Under the "disparate impact" theory, a method of discipline that is racially neutral on its face but has a discriminatory effect may be found unlawful absent sufficient justification, such as educational necessity. Even if a school's action is found to be justified, it still may be unlawful if equally effective, less discriminatory alternatives are available.[41] Advocates should explore challenging the disparate impact of School-to-Prison Pipeline policies on children of color through legal mechanisms at both the federal and state levels.

a. Disparate Impact Claims under Federal Law

As mentioned earlier, disparate impact, without discriminatory intent, does not amount to a violation of the Equal Protection Clause. At the federal level, disparate impact in the education context can be most effectively addressed by Title VI of the Civil Rights Act of 1964. However, the Supreme Court held in *Sandoval* that Title VI does not grant a private right of action for private litigants to bring suit in federal court on the basis of a racially disparate impact absent discriminatory intent.[42] Yet, even after *Sandoval*, administrative regulations interpreting Title VI to prohibit disparate impact may still be enforced by federal agencies. Regulations issued by the Office for Civil Rights for the U.S. Department of Education prohibit recipients of federal funding from

> utiliz[ing] criteria or methods of administration which have the effect of subjecting individuals to discrimination because of their race, color, or national origin, or have the effect of defeating or substantially impairing accomplishment of the objectives of the program as respect individuals of a particular race, color, or national origin.[43]

After several years of what some advocates viewed as anemic enforcement efforts, the U.S. Department of Justice issued a memorandum to all federal agency civil rights directors and general counsels emphasizing the importance of their enforcement of disparate impact regulations.[44] That same memorandum further urges these agencies to submit cases directly to the Justice Department when informal resolution is not possible or the termination of federal funding would be insufficient.[45] This memorandum suggests that federal agencies may be more inclined than in the past to investigate vigorously and to resolve administrative complaints submitted because of disparate impact on the basis of race. Advocates should seriously consider this strategy to reduce racial disparities in the various aspects of the School-to-Prison Pipeline.

b. Disparate Impact Claims under State Law

In addition to considering the filing of federal administrative complaints, advocates should consider filing suits pursuant to state law. At least in some jurisdictions, advocates may be able to file a writ of mandamus[46] to compel compliance with federal disparate impact regulations.[47] Alternatively, they may petition to mandate compliance with federal disparate impact regulations pursuant to a third-party beneficiary claim under contract law, for example, when intergovernmental agreements include nondiscrimination provisions. In the context of Medicaid, which requires states to provide language access,[48] courts have recognized both that these grants have a contractual aspect and that the intended beneficiaries of the programs may have a contractual interest in the service provided by such programs.[49] However, this theory has not yet been tested in the context of enforcing federal disparate impact regulations.

In addition, some states provide their own protections against policies that have a disparate impact on racial minorities.[50] Some of these provisions are referred to as state-level "*Sandoval* fixes" because they were adopted after the U.S. Supreme Court decision. The following subsections provide examples from California, Illinois, Minnesota, and Connecticut. Civil rights attorneys should carefully review laws and regulations in their own state to determine whether state courts or administrative agencies have recognized disparate impact claims or have implicitly suggested that disparate impact claims would be recognized.

(1) California

In response to the threat that *Sandoval* would wholly eviscerate plaintiffs' abilities to obtain legal relief from racial discrimination, California has adopted statutes that permit disparate impact claims under state law.

California Government Code Section 11135 prohibits discrimination on the basis of race, national origin, ethnic group identification, religion, age, sex, sexual orientation, color, or disability in any program or activity that is conducted, operated, or administered by the state or a state agency.[51] Regulations adopted under Section 11135 prohibit the use of "criteria or methods of administration that have the purpose *or effect of*" discriminating on any prohibited basis.[52] California courts have confirmed that this is classic disparate impact language.[53] In 2001, the statute was amended to specifically cover any program or activity "conducted, operated or administered by the state or any state agency."[54] The state legislature also adopted amendments clarifying that the statute can be enforced in a private right of action without prior exhaustion of administrative remedies. In contrast to federal Title VI regulations, the California Government Code expressly provides that Section 11135 and its progeny regulations may be enforced by a civil action for equitable relief.[55]

Although there is little authority addressing the scope and applicability of these provisions, it is likely that California courts would rely heavily on federal precedents under both Title VI and Title VII in evaluating disparate impact claims under Section 11135. As of 2009, there is at least one case pending in California evaluating this type of claim, but not in the context of education or school discipline.[56]

In addition to state statutes, there may also be alternative state-law channels to enforce federal regulations. Although the Supreme Court has limited direct federal jurisdiction to enforce federal regulations promulgated under Title VI, theories to enforce those regulations based on state law have not been foreclosed.[57] In California, for example, two state-law mechanisms provide advocates potential means to enforce federal disparate impact regulations.[58]

(2) Illinois

Section 5(a)(2) of the Illinois Civil Rights Act of 2003 (ICRA) provides that "[n]o unit of State, county or local government in Illinois shall . . . utilize criteria or methods of administration that have the effect of subjecting individuals to discrimination because of their race, color or national origin or gender."[59] The ICRA was enacted in 2003 and applies to conduct subsequent to January 1, 2004.[60]

Despite this promising language, to date there have been very few cases relying on this statute. However, an ICRA claim is currently pending in the federal district court of the Northern District of Illinois in the case of *McFadden v. Board of Education for Illinois School District U-46*. Filed in February 2005 by minority students in Elgin Area School District U-46, the complaint includes allegations that the school district's student-assignment and districting policies impose disproportionate burdens on minority students in comparison to white students in violation of the ICRA.[61] Although the district court has yet to reach the merits of the ICRA claim, the claim has already survived a motion to dismiss, and the court has certified the matter as a class action.[62] As of April 2010, this case remains in discovery.

Moreover, an Illinois state appellate court in *Illinois Native American Bar Association v. University of Illinois*[63] has made clear that the ICRA is explicitly a *Sandoval* fix—no more and no less. Quoting language from the sponsors of the legislation, the court asserted that the disparate impact clause of the ICRA merely creates a state-court cause of action to pursue disparate impact claims that were previously available in federal court under Title VI prior to *Sandoval*.[64] The Court stated, "It is clear from the legislators' comments and from the language in subsection (b) of the statute that the Act was not intended to create new rights. It merely created a new venue in which plaintiffs could pursue in the State courts discrimination actions that had been available to them in the federal courts."[65]

(3) Minnesota

In *State v. Russell*,[66] criminal defendants asserted Minnesota state and federal challenges to a statute imposing more severe penalties for the use of crack cocaine than for powder cocaine, alleging that it had a disproportionately greater impact on African Americans in particular. The court stated that, under Article 1, Section 2, of the Minnesota constitution, entering statistics could subject the law to a stricter analysis.[67] The court then examined the statute under the Minnesota constitution's rational basis test, which differs from the federal standard, and struck down the law.[68] The court noted that the Minnesota test required the following:

(1) The distinctions which separate those included within the classification from those excluded must not be manifestly arbitrary or fanciful but must be genuine and substantial, thereby providing a natural and reasonable basis to justify legislation adapted to peculiar conditions and needs; (2) the classification must be genuine or relevant to the purpose of the law; that is there must be an evident connection between the distinctive needs peculiar to the class and the prescribed remedy; and (3) the purpose of the statute must be one that the state can legitimately attempt to achieve.[69]

The court went on to observe that, "[i]n order to meet this standard, the state must provide more than anecdotal support for classifying users of crack cocaine differently from users of cocaine powder."[70] Finding that the evidence offered in support of the standard was largely anecdotal, and citing evidence undermining the state's assertion that crack users more than cocaine users were likely to be street-level dealers,[71] the court determined that the statute violated Article 1, Section 2, of the Minnesota constitution.[72]

Advocates may find greater success in states, such as Minnesota, where the interpretation of equal protection principles under the state constitution provides more stringent or different scrutiny than the current interpretation under the federal Constitution.

(4) Connecticut

In *Sheff v. O'Neill,*[73] the state's high court found that *de facto* racial segregation among Hartford public schools deprived minority-student plaintiffs of their right to equal educational opportunities under the Connecticut constitution. Article 8, Section 1, and Article 1, Sections 1 and 20, impose an affirmative constitutional obligation on the state to provide substantially equal educational opportunities.[74] Although the court did not require that the plaintiffs prove intentional discriminatory action to enforce these constitutional rights, it found that Connecticut "has not intentionally segregated racial and ethnic minorities in the Hartford public school system."[75]

Advocates should note that in a subsequent case, *Wendt v. Wendt,* a state appellate court rejected the argument that *Sheff* created the basis for a disparate impact theory under the Connecticut constitution, holding that "[t]he court did not intend to allow state constitutional challenges on the basis of disparate impact."[76] However, *Wendt* was an equal protection challenge in the context of the division of marital property, whereas *Sheff* took into consideration the section of the constitution that explicitly references segregation in the educational setting.[77]

Advocates should seek out states with favorable laws and constitutions, which may both provide a fundamental right to education and create an affirmative constitutional duty to provide an equal education.[78]

B. ANTIDISCRIMINATION PROTECTIONS FOR ENGLISH LANGUAGE LEARNERS AND UNDOCUMENTED STUDENTS

Federal statutes and case law also expressly protect the rights of English language learner students and undocumented students to be free from discrimination. This section discusses those rights and protections.

1. ENGLISH LANGUAGE LEARNERS (ELLS)

According to the 2000 U.S. Census, nearly four million school-age children speak a language other than English at home and speak English less than "very well."[79] In 1993–94, English language learner student enrollment was over three million out of approximately forty-five million public school students in total (or 6.7 percent).[80] Ten years later, in 2003–04, ELL students constituted about five million out of approximately fifty million total students (10 percent).[81] Thus, the population of ELL students grew by over 65 percent, although the total public school population grew by only 9.2 percent during this same period.[82]

ELL students, like children of color and the other identifiable subgroups of students discussed in this chapter and in chapter 3, suffer disproportionately from the negative impact of high-stakes testing and pushing out by schools. New York City, for instance, has implemented new criteria for promotion and graduation, without providing adequate assistance to some ELL students and students from immigrant families, such as adequate English language instruction or ensuring that ELL students remain eligible for summer school and after-school enrichment programs.[83] The result has been an increase in dropout rates among ELLs.[84] ELL students now have one of the highest dropout rates in New York.[85] The New York Immigration Coalition reports that in New York City nearly half of ELL students drop out of school each year.

The system also presents problems regarding the participation of immigrant parents in their children's schools and education. Parental involvement is a key factor to a child's success in school, yet many parents of ELL students are unable to participate actively in their children's education.[87] Some schools, for instance, lack a comprehensive policy to translate school documents and fail to provide interpretation services at school meetings and other events.[88] This resulted in the New York Immigration Coalition finding that "New York's failure to provide meaningful language access to parents with limited English proficiency is a violation of the clear letter and intent of state and federal regulation and law."[89]

Federal law, however, provides explicit protections to ELL students against discrimination. Title VI of the Civil Rights Act of 1964 prohibits discrimination on the basis of national origin, and the U.S. Department of Education has interpreted this provision as requiring school districts to assist ELL students to overcome language barriers and ensure they can meaningfully participate in the school district's educational programs.[90] In *Lau v. Nichols,* the Supreme Court rejected a challenge to this agency interpretation and agreed that the failure of San Francisco public schools to provide English language instruction to children of Chinese descent effectively denied them meaningful participation in the system of public education, in violation of Title VI.[91]

Within weeks of the *Lau* decision, Congress enacted the Equal Educational Opportunities Act (EEOA) to codify the Supreme Court's ruling.[92] Section 1703(f) of the EEOA imposes an affirmative duty on state and local educational agencies to take "appropriate action to overcome language barriers that impede equal participation by its students in its instructional programs."[93] Moreover, the U.S. Department of Education's Office for Civil Rights (OCR) has developed relatively robust policies for assessing compliance with *Lau* and Section 1703(f).[94] Like the statutory and regulatory protections for students with disabilities discussed in chapter 3, federal protections for ELL students impose an affirmative duty on states and localities to provide these students with an adequate education. In contrast to the rules for racial minority children generally, these rules prohibit policies that have the *effect* of denying adequate education to ELLs, regardless of the government's *intent* in adopting the policy.

As a result of the EEOA and subsequent case law,[95] ELL students are entitled to an equal education and English language instruction that will enable them to engage in meaningful school participation.

Some courts have demonstrated their willingness to enforce the provisions of the EEOA. For example, the Ninth Circuit held that, in order to find that a school system is complying with the EEOA, three requirements must be met:

> First, courts must be satisfied that the "school system is purs[uing] a program informed by an educational theory recognized as sound by some experts in the field or, at least, deemed a legitimate experimental strategy." Second, "the programs and practices actually used by a school system [must be] reasonably calculated to implement effectively the educational theory adopted by the school." Third, even if theory is sound and resources are adequate, the program must be borne out by practical results.[96]

Similarly, the Seventh Circuit concluded that, in determining whether a state's implementation of a particular policy violates the EEOA, courts must examine evidence regarding the soundness of the educational theory or principles on which the challenged program is based; determine whether programs actually used by the school system are reasonably calculated to implement effectively the educational theory adopted by the system; and determine whether a school's program, despite ostensibly being premised on a legitimate educational theory, nevertheless failed to obtain results that would indicate that the language barriers confronting students were being overcome.[97]

The lack of adequate notice in a language parents can understand makes ELL children especially vulnerable to unfair treatment. Moreover, and of particular relevance to School-to-Prison Pipeline analyses, OCR has further interpreted the Supreme Court's *Lau* decision and Section 1703(f) of the EEOA to require that school districts communicate with parents in a language and manner that parents understand.[98] This interpretation ensures that when ELL students are suspended, for example, their parents do not unknowingly waive their right to notice of the charges against their child, the due process protections afforded to challenge the discipline, or English language instruction after the student is suspended or transferred to an alternative school.

To date, advocates have enjoyed some success in enforcing this provision through administrative complaints filed with OCR. In 2005, for example, the Education Law Center of Pennsylvania filed an administrative complaint with OCR on behalf of Somali refugee students alleging that the Pittsburgh School District violated the rights of these ELLs by failing to develop an adequate system for communicating with them or their parents in the language that they understand and unnecessarily segregating ELL students from students of other backgrounds.[99] To resolve that complaint, the school district agreed to employ a Somali-speaking ombudsperson, implement procedures for assessing and placing students in the appropriate classroom, and, most relevant to the School-to-Prison Pipeline, develop policies ensuring that school and education information, including notices related to school discipline, would be communicated to parents in a language and mode that they can understand.[100]

2. UNDOCUMENTED STUDENTS

Federal law also offers protection for undocumented students, who sometimes face challenges similar to those of ELLs. In 1982, the Supreme Court struck down a Texas state law that effectively barred undocumented children from school by withholding funds from school districts that enrolled such children. In that case, *Plyler v. Doe,*[101] the Court analyzed the statute under the Equal Protection Clause of the Fourteenth Amendment to the U.S. Constitution and held that Texas did not show a "substantial interest" that would justify the denial of education to undocumented students. Specifically, the Court found that undocumented children have the same right to a free public education as U.S. citizens and permanent residents. As a result, public schools and school personnel are prohibited from adopting policies or practices that deny students access to education based on their immigration status.

C. ANTIDISCRIMINATION PROTECTIONS FOR HOMELESS STUDENTS AND CHILDREN IN FOSTER CARE: MCKINNEY-VENTO

Federal law also provides explicit protections for homeless children and youth in foster care through the rights afforded under the McKinney-Vento Act.

According to the U.S. Department of Education, each year, over eight hundred thousand children in the United States experience homelessness.[102] High mobility, precarious living conditions, and deep poverty combine to present significant educational, health, and emotional difficulties. Enrolling, attending, and succeeding in school is a constant struggle. Children in the foster-care system face similar challenges.

Originally enacted in 1987, subtitle VII-B of the McKinney-Vento Act[103] provides federal funds to assist states in ensuring that homeless children and youth "awaiting foster care placement" can enroll, attend, and succeed in public schools.[104] Its provisions apply to all school districts in every state that accepts McKinney-Vento Act funding. Currently, every state, Puerto Rico, and the District of Columbia accept McKinney-Vento funds.[105]

At its heart, the act is designed to ensure access to education and school stability by requiring that "each child of a homeless individual and each homeless youth has equal access to the same free, appropriate public education, including a public preschool education, as provided to other children and youths."[106] In order to meet this goal, the act contains provisions that provide that homeless students and students in foster care may attend either their local school or their school of origin.[107] The right to stay in the school of origin is realized in most cases by the provision of transportation. The McKinney-Vento Act requires school districts to provide or arrange transportation for students attending their schools of origin, at the request of a parent or guardian. If the student is not in the physical custody of a parent or guardian (referred to as "unaccompanied youth" in the statute), a liaison must request transportation on the student's behalf.[108] As long as it is "feasible" and consistent with parental wishes, homeless students are entitled to remain in their schools of origin, regardless of where they live.[109] The law thus recognizes that school stability is an essential part of preventing loss of educational continuity and further disruption in students' lives.

It is important to note that the definition of children eligible under the McKinney-Vento Act includes "children awaiting foster care placement." Although the term "awaiting foster care placement" has not been defined in federal law or regulations, many states and jurisdictions have created their own definitions. For example, Delaware defines "awaiting foster care placement" as *all* children and youth in foster care. Massachusetts and Connecticut have reached state-level agreements between their respective education and child-welfare agencies to include certain children and youth in foster care under the McKinney-Vento Act. Other state and local jurisdictions have chosen informal policies that determine when a child or youth in foster care is eligible under the act. Still, other states (California, Arkansas, Oregon, and Virginia) have enacted legislation, separate from but similar to the McKinney-Vento Act, to address the educational barriers faced by children in foster care.

Furthermore, when seeking to join a new school, students covered under the act must be immediately enrolled and allowed to participate fully in school, even if the students are unable to produce records normally required for enrollment, such as previous academic records, medical records, proof of residency, or other documentation.[110] In order to facilitate this immediate enrollment, SEAs and LEAs must develop, review, and revise policies to remove barriers to enrolling and retaining homeless students in school. States must pay particular attention to barriers related to immunization and medical records requirements; residency requirements; lack of birth certificates, school records, or other documents; guardianship issues; and uniform or dress-code requirements.[111]

In addition to services provided under the McKinney-Vento Act, homeless children are automatically eligible for services under Title I, Part A, of the No Child Left Behind Act, no matter where they live or what school they attend. In fact, LEAs must reserve funds to provide services to homeless students. These services can go beyond those ordinarily provided to other Title I students and should assist homeless students in taking advantage of educational opportunities. Homeless students must also be included in academic assessment, reporting, and accountability systems.[112]

Several prelitigation McKinney-Vento enforcement strategies have proven effective. Perhaps the most effective are the preventive strategies of outreach and education. Many school administrators are unfamiliar with the McKinney-Vento Act's provisions. Therefore, advocates should inform LEA personnel, providers, families, and children about the act's provisions and strategies for implementation. When advocating for individual students, immediate contact with the liaison is essential. The liaison is a critical state-level contact, given the state's large role in enforcing compliance and providing technical assistance.

Litigation may also provide an avenue for redress. Although the act does not include enforcement provisions beyond the dispute-resolution provisions and the monitoring and enforcement duties of SEAs and the U.S. Department of Education, at least one court held that the rights conferred by the act are enforceable in court via 42 U.S.C. § 1983.[113] Even so, most federal appellate courts have yet to address this issue. Thus, advocates should approach McKinney-Vento litigation with extreme caution and only after careful research regarding the manner in which local district and appellate courts have addressed implied rights of action.

Nonetheless, McKinney-Vento Act litigation has been brought to successful resolution in a number of states, including Louisiana, Illinois, Maryland, Alabama, and New York.[114] Notably, however, not all of these lawsuits yielded court rulings with precedential value; instead, they have mainly been used to force favorable settlements and/or policy changes. Some of these cases demonstrate that McKinney-Vento claims have been most successful when filed alongside other claims, such as race-discrimination and right-to-education claims. This strategy can be useful in the pipeline context. For example, in *Boisseau v. Picard*,[115] the NAACP Legal Defense and Educational Fund, Inc. (LDF) filed a lawsuit on behalf of students who were denied access to public schools when the schools placed the students on waiting lists for an indefinite length of time after returning to New Orleans following temporary displacement due to Hurricanes Katrina and Rita in 2005. At the time, many of the students lived in temporary shelters, in temporary trailer parks, or in packed apartments or houses with numerous relatives, while others lived in permanent housing. Therefore, the complaint included an equal protection claim on behalf of all the affected students (arguing that the wait list constituted an outright denial of education) and a McKinney-Vento claim on behalf of the subset of students who were considered "homeless" for purposes of the act. The remedies sought included immediate enrollment and compensatory education for those who had been placed on the wait list. Without a ruling on any motion by the federal court, the parties settled the case with the adoption of a formal policy by the state board of education requiring that students be enrolled in classes within a specified period of time after they register.

D. CONCLUSION

This chapter has explored potential avenues for enforcing the rights of certain subgroups of students—children of color, English language learner and undocumented students, and homeless students and youth in the foster-care system—who are often the most vulnerable to entering the School-to-Prison Pipeline. Whether students have been affected by intentional discrimination or policies and practices that have a disparate effect, the cases and strategies outlined in this chapter may help advocates combat this aspect of the School-to-Prison Pipeline.

3

Students with Disabilities

Children who have special learning or emotional needs are particularly likely to be pushed out of mainstream schools and into the juvenile justice system. Although only approximately 9 percent of students aged six to twenty-one have been identified as having disabilities that impact their ability to learn,[1] a survey of correctional facilities found that nationally approximately 34 percent of youth in juvenile corrections had been previously identified as eligible for special education pursuant to the Individuals with Disabilities Education Act (IDEA).[2] Other studies suggest a disturbing failure among schools in identifying the children who are eligible for additional support and services as required under federal law; this failure to identify and provide the services the child needs to succeed too often results in the child's acting out, being suspended or expelled, and eventually becoming court-involved. One report, for example, suggests that up to 85 percent of children in juvenile detention facilities have disabilities that would make them eligible for special education services, yet only 37 percent had been receiving any kind of services in their school.[3] It is also critically important to note that there is a profound racial dimension regarding the youth with disabilities who wind up incarcerated. Ultimately, compared to white students with disabilities, Black students with disabilities are four times as likely to be educated in a correctional facility.[4]

The first section of this chapter further examines the extraordinarily high and disproportionate rates of school failure and disciplinary removal of students with disabilities, two factors researchers believe contribute to the high rates of incarceration of youth. Also discussed is how the failure to ensure that students with disabilities are afforded their legal rights and procedural protections likely contributes to their disproportionate representation in the pipeline to prison.

The second section sets forth the legal protections available to students with disabilities, focusing in particular on those aspects of the IDEA and Section 504 of the Rehabilitation Act that would be useful to pipeline litigators.

In addition to describing the substantive and procedural rights of students, this section includes a discussion of some of the litigation requirements and restrictions that may shape legal strategies for those seeking court-ordered remedies as well as for those leveraging these statutory requirements in administrative law forums to generate class-based remedies.

The third section uses case studies to illustrate how lawyers seeking comprehensive remedies to the School-to-Prison Pipeline have succeeded using disability law in court and in administrative proceedings. The remedies pursued in these examples also secured school- or district-wide reforms that benefited students with disabilities and their nondisabled peers.

A. WHY ARE SO MANY CHILDREN WITH DISABILITIES CAUGHT IN THE PIPELINE?

A review of the educational outcomes for students with disabilities suggests that our system of public education is not adequately meeting the needs of these students. For example, the U.S. Department of Education's data on graduation rates for students with disabilities indicates that nationally, in 2005, only 54 percent exited school with a diploma.[5]

Moreover, statistics gathered by the Department of Education's Office for Special Education Programs (OSEP) show that in 2006, at least one district in each of forty-six states imposed long-term suspensions on students with disabilities more often than on nondisabled students. In some states, including Virginia, Tennessee, Delaware, Connecticut, Florida, Maryland, and Washington, 19 percent or more of all districts suspended students with disabilities more often than their nondisabled peers.[6] In many jurisdictions, students with disabilities are also far more likely to be placed in disciplinary alternative education programs.[7] There are also concerns about incentives to exclude these students, who tend to perform less well on tests than their nondisabled peers, from classrooms as a result of test-driven accountability.[8]

1. DISCRIMINATION AGAINST STUDENTS WITH DISABILITIES

The patterns of exclusion of students with disabilities align with the long-standing discriminatory exclusion of students with disabilities from school that prompted Congress to create the federal statutory rights and protections that are the focus of this chapter. Until the passage of Section 504 of the Rehabilitation Act of 1973, closely followed by the Individuals with Disabilities Education Act in 1975, it was common practice to treat students with disabilities as second-class citizens, regardless of their race or ethnicity.[9] Commentators on the rights of students with disabilities referred to the "ghettolike" conditions within schools, where students with disabilities were taught in closets and unheated stairwells while the majority of students sat in adequately resourced classrooms.

Rulings in two lawsuits, *Pennsylvania Association for Retarded Children (PARC) v. Commonwealth*[10] and *Mills v. Board of Education*,[11] became codified in the Education for All Handicapped Act, now known as the Individuals with Disabilities Education Act. The heart of these two lawsuits was that the exclusion of students with disabilities was a form of discrimination that violated the Equal Protection Clause of the U.S. Constitution.[12] For example, the assertions of the *Mills* plaintiffs were summarized by Judge Waddy as follows: "They allege that although they can profit from an education either in regular classrooms with supportive services or in special classes adopted to their needs, they have been labelled as behavioral problems, mentally retarded, emotionally disturbed or hyperactive, and denied admission to the public schools or excluded therefrom after admission, with no provision for alternative educational placement or periodic review."[13]

2. THE RACIAL DIMENSIONS OF DISABILITY EXCLUSION

It is important to note that in *Mills v. Board of Education,* the plaintiffs were all African American students with disabilities who were expelled for their behavior and not allowed to return to the public schools in Washington, D.C. Notably, concerns about racial prejudice and inequity in special education placements as well as tracking had been litigated successfully against the D.C. public schools just a few years prior to *Mills* in the case of *Hobson v. Hansen*.[14] As one scholar notes, given the bigoted and historical exclusionary policies surrounding students with disabilities, it should not be surprising that the disability label was used by racists seeking to preserve Jim Crow when they could no longer get away with the explicit use of race as the basis of exclusion.[15] Today, profound racial disparities raise questions of unconscious racial bias which may combine with discrimination on the basis of disability and contribute to the trends described below.[16]

Recent research demonstrates that for minority students, especially Black and Native American students, overrepresentation occurs in referrals for evaluation and identification, and the research suggests that these higher rates of identification reflect deficiencies in the general education class-rooms.[17] The concern, as reflected in the provisions of the IDEA, is not limited to the high levels of identification of minority students as disabled[18] but also to the fact that once they are identified, there is a higher frequency of their placement in overly restrictive special education environments, where students with disabilities are segregated from the mainstream. Racial disparities are most pronounced among those students who are educated in regular schools but in settings that are separate from their nondisabled peers for more than 60 percent of the school day.[19]

Similarly, data on the repeated suspension and expulsion of students with disabilities suggest that districts may subsequently fail to ensure that the behavior does not recur. According to one study, the number of times students are suspended has a negative correlation with whether they graduate from high school.[20] That longitudinal study of Pinellas County, Florida, showed that high numbers of students with disabilities were suspended repeatedly and that Black males receiving special education and free and reduced lunch were the group most frequently subjected to multiple suspensions.[21] Additionally, nationally, the racially disproportionate discipline among students with disabilities suggests that minority students in particular may be denied the procedural protections from school exclusion that should flow to all students with disabilities.[22]

Further, research indicates that children of color who do have disabilities receive vastly unequal supports and services, especially compared to their white counterparts.[23] The poor outcomes for minority students with disabilities casts doubt on the assumptions that the process of special education identification is a scientific and accurate one and that the placement, supports, and services provided to the recipients are producing the intended outcomes.[24]

For minority children, there is a tension between the misuse of special education identification, placement, and discipline as a means of school exclusion, and another equally troubling phenomenon, the failure to identify poor and minority students with disabilities who need high-quality special education and the related procedural protections. Both the misuse of special education to exclude minority students and the failure to identify minority students who need, and then to provide them with, high-quality special education, related services, and procedural protections likely contributes to the more general trend in which children with disabilities are disproportionately punished and, ultimately, incarcerated.

3. FAILURE TO IMPLEMENT THE RIGHTS AND PROTECTIONS IN DISABILITY LAW

The overarching issue affecting students with disabilities of all races, and the suggested focus for pipeline litigation, is the failure to implement the legal rights and protections found in the IDEA and Section 504 described in detail in section B of this chapter. Children with disabilities who do not receive adequate support and services may be more likely to wind up truant, to drop out, or to engage in misconduct as a result. In turn, inadequately served students who are eligible are more likely to end up suspended, to be referred to alternative schools, or to become court-involved. According to the Juvenile Offenders and Victims 2006 Report, preadolescents with learning disabilities are up to three times more likely to join gangs than their nondisabled peers.[25]

Advocates should note that federal and state agencies require detailed reporting on the monitoring and enforcement of the IDEA and collection and maintenance of extensive data regarding the conditions of education for special education students. However, noncompliance with these statutory requirements is endemic in many jurisdictions. For example, the National Council on Disability's report in 2000, a review of federal monitoring reports between 1994 and 1998, shows that "every state was out of compliance with the IDEA requirements to some degree; in the sampling of states studied, noncompliance persisted over many years."[26] Similarly, advocates may find that reports are available that depict noncompliance by a state or district. In several of the case studies highlighted in section C of this chapter, the parties used documented histories of noncompliance with the IDEA to their advantage. In addition to widespread failure to identify and serve large numbers of students with disabilities, evidence also suggests a systemic inadequacy of education and poorly implemented procedural protections for those who have been identified.

In some cases, advocates will find that school officials do not know that students with disabilities have explicit statutory rights that give them additional protections and benefits.[27] In other cases, school officials may neglect the notice requirements under the IDEA and Section 504 such that many students with disabilities and their families do not know they have enforceable rights.[28] Any lack of knowledge of the rights of students with disabilities on behalf of educators, or their parents, is likely to be detrimental to the child's being effectively educated. It is also worth noting that charter schools and public alternative schools are equally subject to federal law protecting students with disabilities.[29] However, according to one survey, in at least five of the twenty-eight states that responded to the survey question, special education services are likely to be put on hold in alternative schools and resumed only once a student returns to his or her regular school; and in at least three states, staff at alternative programs frequently were not informed of whether enrolled students received special education services at their former schools.[30]

The widespread, blatant forms of noncompliance with disability law may be regarded as "low-hanging fruit" for impact litigators seeking to challenge policies contributing to the School-to-Prison Pipeline. However, many attorneys (and judges) who see or represent students with disabilities in court are not fully aware of their clients' legal rights and remedies and may not consider the full scope of obligations that schools have to meet their students' educational and behavioral needs.[31]

B. LEGAL PROTECTIONS AVAILABLE TO STUDENTS WITH DISABILITIES FOR CHALLENGING THE SCHOOL-TO-PRISON PIPELINE

1. OVERVIEW OF FEDERAL RIGHTS AND PROTECTIONS AFFORDED TO STUDENTS WITH DISABILITIES

This section provides a brief overview of the federal statutes and some of the corresponding regulations protecting students with disabilities. The two main purposes are, first, to provide an introduction to advocates new in the field and to define terminology used frequently in the area of special education and, second, to provide the specific legal background most relevant to systemic legal challenges to the School-to-Prison Pipeline.

Litigants should check state laws and regulations to determine whether they afford broader rights than those afforded by these federal laws. Many states incorporate the IDEA provisions into their state laws, which must at a minimum be consistent with the federal requirements. In a number of the case studies described in section C of this chapter, causes of action based on federal law were combined with state-law claims. State law may also contain requirements for schools and districts that are substantively different (i.e., differences in students' access to alternative schools or age of compulsory attendance), have different procedural requirements (i.e., some may not require administrative exhaustion), or contain legal protections for students with disabilities that are greater than the federal statutory provisions.[32]

Three federal statutes are directly relevant to the rights of special education students and the School-to-Prison Pipeline: the Individuals with Disabilities Education Act (IDEA),[33] Section 504 of the Rehabilitation Act of 1973,[34] and Title II of the Americans with Disabilities Act of 1990.[35]

The IDEA provides extensive statutory rights and protections for eligible children having one of a number of disabilities. The law defines "child with a disability" as "a child with mental retardation, hearing impairments (including deafness), speech or language impairments, visual impairments (including blindness), serious emotional disturbance (referred to in [the IDEA] as 'emotional disturbance'), orthopedic impairments, autism, traumatic brain injury, other health impairments, or specific learning disabilities" and "who, by reason thereof, needs special education and related services."[36]

a. The Right to a Free Appropriate Public Education (FAPE)

The essential right guaranteed to eligible students with disabilities by the IDEA is that schools provide a free appropriate public education (FAPE) to students with disabilities in the least restrictive environment to the maximum extent appropriate. The statute defines FAPE to mean "special education and related services that (A) have been provided at public expense, under public supervision and direction, and without charge; (B) meet the standards of the State educational agency; (C) include an appropriate preschool, elementary, or secondary education in the state involved; (D) and are provided in conformity with the individualized education program [IEP] required under section 614(d)."[37]

Although most special education causes of action will arise under the IDEA and the corollary state provisions, two other statutes contribute to the federal statutory scheme. Section 504 of the Rehabilitation Act prohibits any recipient of federal financial assistance from discriminating against any "qualified" individual on the basis of disability, and Title II prohibits discrimination against "qualified" persons with disabilities by public schools, state departments of education, and juvenile correctional facilities—regardless of whether they receive federal funds. These two laws and their respectively promulgated regulations protect students with disabilities from unlawful discrimination as well as impose an array of rights.

Under Section 504 a school must provide a FAPE to every qualified handicapped person. Although it is a distinct law from the IDEA, it directly references the requirements of the IDEA.[38] Section 504 has procedural requirements to ensure that FAPE is "designed to meet the individual educational needs of" students with disabilities "as adequately as the needs of" nondisabled students are met.[39]

Although a student's core substantive right to FAPE is protected by all three statutes,[40] the eligibility requirements differ.[41] Most important, there are more students eligible under Section 504 and Title II than under the IDEA.[42] For example, often students with mild forms of ADHD, students who are HIV positive, and students with physical disabilities or mild emotional disabilities are protected under the broader definition of disability in Section 504 but not pursuant to the IDEA if they do not need special education.

There are also some subtle yet potentially significant differences between the IDEA and Section 504 with regard to procedural protections, as the IDEA provides far more comprehensive and explicit requirements than those pursuant to Section 504 and its implementing regulations. For this reason the remainder of this chapter focuses on the IDEA's requirements and references Section 504 only when the differences are relevant to litigation strategies seeking to obstruct the pipeline.

b. Child Find[43]

(1) Identification

The IDEA requires each state to ensure proactively that that all children with disabilities who live in the state, "including children with disabilities who are homeless children or are wards of the State,"[44] "are identified, located, and evaluated" and that "a practical method is developed and implemented to determine which children with disabilities are currently receiving needed special education and related services."[45]

(2) Evaluation

School districts must determine whether a child qualifies as having a disability by administering a full and individual initial evaluation of the child using a variety of assessment tools and strategies to determine the child's functional, developmental, and academic needs.[46] The child's parent, the state, or the local school district may request the evaluation.[47] When schools seek to evaluate students initially, or make changes to a student's placement or other aspects of the IEP, they must seek the consent of the parents.[48] Additional details regarding parents' participation, parental consent, and revocation of that consent may also prove important in these cases.[49]

(3) Failure to Meet Child Find Obligation

The research cited in the introduction to this chapter indicates that there is a large number of incarcerated children who have special needs but who did not receive special education in their schools. This suggests a systemic failure to evaluate and identify these students in the mainstream public schools.

A district's failure to evaluate and identify a child with disabilities will not excuse it from affording him or her IDEA protections when it can be demonstrated that the district "should have known" that the student had special education needs.[50] The IDEA provides,

> A local educational agency shall be deemed to have knowledge that a child is a child with a disability if, before the behavior that precipitated the disciplinary action occurred—(i) the parent of the child has expressed concern in writing to supervisory or administrative personnel of the appropriate educational agency, or a teacher of the child, that the child is in need of special education and related services; (ii) the parent of the child has requested an evaluation . . . ; or (iii) the teacher of the child, or other personnel of the local educational agency, has expressed specific concerns about a pattern of behavior demonstrated by the child, directly to the director of special education of such agency or to other supervisory personnel of the agency.[51]

c. Individualized Education Plan (IEP)

For a child with a disability to receive FAPE under the IDEA, the child must be educated and receive services pursuant to an "individualized education plan" (IEP) developed by an IEP team that includes the child's parents.[52] Each IEP must be designed to enable the child to "make progress in the general education curriculum."[53] Critically important, courts have interpreted this provision to require that the IEP provide the child with meaningful educational benefit,[54] both academic and behavioral, if the latter is necessary to address the child's disability-related needs.[55] Each IEP must also provide related services, consisting of such developmental, corrective, and other supportive services such as transportation, counseling, and psychological services as may be required to help the student benefit from his or her specialized instruction.[56]

d. Changing a Student's Placement and Protections from Disciplinary Exclusions

(1) "Stay Put" and Disciplinary Exclusions

A student's IEP provides the details of the student's program with regard to special education, supports and related services, and where the student is to receive education and services. From time to time, during the course of the school year the school or parent may seek a change to the program, including the placement of the child. The disputes that arise are often the subject of administrative hearings. In the course of resolving these disputes, there is a federal requirement referred to as *stay put,* which means that no changes may be made unilaterally by the school or district during the pendency of a dispute.[57] However, if the dispute is about a disciplinary exclusion, a school can unilaterally remove a child short term, either suspending the student or educating the student in an interim alternative educational setting for up to ten days without triggering the IDEA's "stay put" protection.[58]

(2) Manifestation Determinations

School authorities are prohibited from suspending or expelling a student with disabilities *beyond ten days* without first conducting "a manifestation determination."[59] This review must be conducted by the school district, with parents and the other members of the IEP team, and include a review of the child's IEP.[60] The IEP team determines "if the conduct in question was found to be caused by, or had a direct and substantial relationship to the child's disability; or if the conduct in question was the direct result of the local educational agency's failure to implement the individualized educational plan (IEP)."[61] If the determination is that the conduct was a manifestation of the child's disability, then except in "special circumstances," the school would be barred from removing the child beyond ten days, and the child would be entitled to return to his or her regular school setting.[62] It is also important to note that these procedural protections can be triggered for a series of shorter suspensions that cumulatively add up to more than ten days.[63]

(3) Exceptions to Procedural Requirements

There are three "special circumstances" or exceptions to these due process protections whereby school officials may remove a child from school for up to forty-five days. The exceptions are for when the student possessed a weapon or illicit drugs or has inflicted serious bodily injury.[64] In such cases students may be removed immediately, and the removal need not wait on the outcome of the manifestation determination.[65]

Advocates worry that schools may circumvent the rigorous protections afforded under the IDEA by simply referring children with special needs to the juvenile courts. This concern was heightened when the 2004 reauthorization of the IDEA added language stating that none of the aforementioned protections "shall be construed to prohibit an agency from reporting a crime committed by a child with a disability to appropriate authorities or to prevent State law enforcement and judicial authorities from exercising their responsibilities with regard to the application of Federal and State law to crimes committed by a child with a disability."[66] Advocates should be aware that referrals to law enforcement not entailing a state or federal crime actually committed by a child would still violate the requirements to provide due process. In such cases, referrals for noncriminal acts would constitute a change in placement that would trigger these procedural protections for the child.[67]

(4) Noncessation of FAPE and Long-Term Disciplinary Exclusion

For suspensions of greater than ten days, the IDEA also offers a critically important substantive right to education for students with disabilities, even when the offense is not deemed a manifestation of the student's disability. Specifically, the IDEA states that "if school personnel seek to order a change in placement that would exceed 10 school days and the behavior that gave rise to the violation of the school code is not determined to be a manifestation of the child's disability," then the school can discipline the child in the same manner and for the same duration as a child without disabilities *except that the school must provide FAPE.*[68] And an IEP team meeting must be held to determine FAPE for the suspended student.[69] This FAPE requirement is often referred to as "noncessation of services."[70]

This noncessation requirement also applies to students with disabilities when they are placed in alternative educational facilities or are incarcerated.[71] Therefore, pursuant to the IDEA, for long-term disciplinary removals, eligible students with disabilities always retain their right to FAPE.

Students with disabilities who are only eligible under Section 504 are not afforded this right to noncessation of FAPE.[72] The difference is rooted in the nature of the statutes. The IDEA provides grant funding to states and districts, and, in exchange, grant recipients must provide special education to all students who are eligible, including the requirement that FAPE is provided even when eligible students are removed from school. Section 504 protects students with disabilities from discrimination on the basis of their disabilities but provides no grants for the delivery of special education. However,

Section 504's antidiscrimination framework does mean that students with disabilities have a right to receive the same education and support that is provided to nondisabled students who are suspended long term.

(5) Protections from Suspensions of Ten Days or Less?
Short-term suspension is another area where the differences in legal frameworks under Section 504 and the IDEA could prove important. Pursuant to Section 504 and the IDEA, suspending a student for less than ten days generally does not require due process protections beyond those afforded to students without disabilities under the *Goss v. Lopez* standard.[73] However, Section 504 does not share the IDEA's explicit statutory exception that effectively limits challenges to short-term exclusions. Disability advocates suggest that there may be cases in which a colorable claim of unlawful discrimination could be brought pursuant to Section 504's protection.[74] For example if a student with Tourette syndrome was suspended (short term) for shouting out something inappropriate, even a short-term disciplinary exclusion for behavior that was clearly a manifestation of the student's disability would strike most as discrimination on the basis of the student's disability. Although a case like this has not been ruled on in court, as a matter of policy, the Office for Civil Rights for the U.S. Department of Education (OCR) has thus far interpreted Section 504 regulations to include a similar ten-day limitation.[75]

e. Functional Behavioral Assessments (FBA) and
   Behavioral Intervention Plan (BIP) Requirements
When the misconduct at issue was in fact a manifestation of the child's disability or resulted from failure to implement the IEP, districts must also conduct a functional behavioral assessment (FBA) and implement a behavioral intervention plan (BIP) for the child.[76] Moreover, even when a weapon, illicit drugs, or infliction of serious bodily harm prompted the child's removal, the overarching rule is that all students with disabilities suspended for over ten days must also "receive, as appropriate, a functional behavioral assessment, behavioral intervention services and modifications, that are designed to address the behavior violation so that it does not recur."[77]

Although federal law does not define a "functional behavior assessment," experts have developed working definitions of the evaluation in light of generally accepted professional standards, and the IDEA does call for the use of research-tested methodologies for students with disabilities, whenever feasible and if appropriate.[78] The IDEA regulations also require that in conducting evaluations of students, school districts must "use technically sound instruments that may assess the relative contribution of cognitive and behavioral factors."[79] Furthermore, the IDEA requires states to self-report on issues of noncompliance in this area, and many do.[80]

f. The Right to Be Educated in the Least Restrictive Environment (LRE)
The law requires states to ensure that each child with a disability is educated in the "least restrictive environment" (LRE) with children who do not have disabilities in the regular classroom to the "maximum extent appropriate."[81] Similar protections are available under regulations promulgated under Section 504, which state that students with disabilities will be educated with nondisabled students "to the maximum extent appropriate to the needs of the handicapped person."[82] Under Section 504, the program must be appropriate and of comparable quality to that provided to nondisabled students.[83]

The LRE requirement is particularly relevant to the School-to-Prison Pipeline because, properly implemented, it could help to limit inappropriate referrals to alternative school, such as referrals made without reviewing the child's behavioral needs. Properly implemented, the LRE requirement can foster a deeper consideration of how a student's needs might be appropriately met within his or her current setting.

Further, the law requires placement decisions to be made based on a student's individual needs[84] and not based on disability category.[85] It is critical that the educational setting of each student with disabilities is determined on an individual basis to maximize the benefits of inclusion, but without watering down the degree of support and services a student may need to participate meaningfully in the general education curriculum. In a well-known case, *Corey H. v. Board of Education,* against the city of Chicago and the state of Illinois, plaintiffs successfully established systemic denial of the right to be educated in the least restrictive environment because a categorical system was used to assign students with disabilities automatically to certain programs and educational settings. Plaintiffs' class prevailed with a significant judgment against the state.[86] It is also worth noting that compliance with the LRE requirements is a priority area for federal monitoring and enforcement.[87]

g. Transition Services[88]
Students with disabilities maintain their right to a free appropriate public education through graduation with a regular diploma or through the school year in which they turn the age of twenty-one, whichever comes first.[89] Before a student with disabilities leaves school, the school must develop a transition plan as part of the student's individualized education plan (IEP),

starting not later than age sixteen.[90] The IEP must be reviewed annually and identify transition services consistent with the student's postsecondary goals or vision to ensure the child can transition to postschool activities such as postsecondary education or employment.[91]

Implementing regulations define transition services to consist of "a coordinated set of activities for a child with a disability . . . to facilitate the child's movement from school to post-school activities, including postsecondary education, vocational training, integrated employment, . . . adult services, independent living, or community participation."[92] The plan must be based on the student's needs, preferences, and interests and must include instruction, related services, community experiences, development of employment objectives, and, if appropriate, acquisition of daily living skills and a functional vocational evaluation.[93]

Given the low graduation rates of students with disabilities, and the strong relationship between dropping out of school and eventually becoming incarcerated, well-implemented transition plans could become an important tool in keeping students with disabilities out of the School-to-Prison Pipeline.

Unfortunately, anecdotal evidence suggests that districts frequently violate these requirements, and the U.S. Department of Education has prioritized this area for monitoring and enforcement.[94] Among the violations, schools fail to develop transition plans in a timely manner, fail to adhere to transition plans, or develop plans that do not reflect the aspirations of the student.[95]

2. LITIGATING DISABILITIES RIGHTS: EXHAUSTION, REMEDIES, COSTS, AND ATTORNEYS' FEES

a. Exhaustion of Administrative Remedies Pursuant to the IDEA

The IDEA requires each state to establish extensive administrative procedures to enforce individual rights guaranteed under the law.[96] Generally, with some exceptions, a litigant must exhaust these administrative procedures prior to filing suit in federal court alleging IDEA violations.[97] Section 504 and Title II, in contrast, do not require litigants to exhaust administrative remedies prior to commencing suit.[98]

However, because of the considerable overlap with Section 504 and Title II of the ADA when the relief sought is available under the IDEA, administrative exhaustion will be required regardless of whether the case is filed under the IDEA or another statute.[99] In other words, if a claim is cognizable under both the IDEA and Section 504 (e.g., alleging an inappropriate denial of

FAPE through improper suspension for a student eligible under the IDEA), a litigant may not circumvent the IDEA's exhaustion requirements by styling the case as a Section 504 lawsuit.[100]

Federal courts recognize three exceptions to the exhaustion requirement. First, litigants need not exhaust when administrative remedies will not provide the relief sought (e.g., hearing officer lacks authority to grant the relief sought).[101] Second, courts may excuse a failure to exhaust administrative remedies prior to filing in federal court when exhaustion would be futile or inadequate.[102] Futility might exist when there is a documented history of the defendant's failure to comply with the IDEA.[103] Third, a court may excuse a failure to exhaust when plaintiffs allege a system-wide failure.[104] Most important, exhaustion requirements can become quite complicated in class actions, and they may vary from one jurisdiction to the next.

b. Issues Regarding Scope of Remedies, Jurisdiction, and Cost Recovery
A detailed exploration of these issues is beyond the scope of this chapter. However, advocates thinking about bringing impact litigation should be aware that there are several important considerations regarding jurisdiction, the ability to recover attorneys' fees and costs of experts, and limits on remedies. Because federal circuits can vary, advocates should carefully research the relevant precedents on available remedies and recovery of costs for each jurisdiction.

It is also worth noting that advocates representing students with special needs should seriously consider partnering with state Protection and Advocacy (P&A) agencies, which have a statutory right to access the client population as well as the right to access otherwise confidential information related to these students if there are allegations of abuse or neglect.[105]

(1) Scope of Remedies
The IDEA states that once an IDEA violation is found, the court is authorized to "grant such relief as the court determines is appropriate."[106] Available remedies may vary depending on whether a lawsuit or administrative complaint is filed. Both the IDEA and Section 504 permit remedies involving compensatory education.[107] Courts have limited compensatory damages to cases involving exceptional circumstances.[108] However, claims for compensatory damages are also commonly brought pursuant to state-law provisions that parallel the IDEA, and the availability of compensatory damages may not be as restricted as in some federal circuits.

The ability to seek money damages may not be available pursuant to the IDEA or administrative claims[109] but may be available pursuant to Section

504 or the ADA if the case is framed as a discrimination case and brought in federal court.[110] Claims of discriminatory treatment under Section 504 may permit money damages[111] but may be limited to claims of intentional discrimination.[112] Therefore, disparate impact challenges brought pursuant to Section 504 may be limited to injunctive relief.

(2) Jurisdiction and Private Right of Action

Jurisdictional issues may arise depending on whether claims are brought in court or administratively. In one case in Pennsylvania, the Commonwealth Court determined that the Department of Education, Special Education Department Process Appeals Review Panel, lacked the authority to require a number of the Saucon Valley School District's personnel to receive training by a special education expert after finding the district violated its FAPE obligation.[113] Advocates should note that though a private right of action to sue pursuant to Section 504 on the grounds of discrimination is well established, recently at least one federal court has held that this private right of action does not allow parents to enforce a 504 regulation that required establishment of procedural safeguards to protect rights of students with disabilities and parents to participate in the educational process.[114]

(3) Attorneys' Fees

If the parents of a child with a disability prevail either at a due process hearing or ultimately on appeal, they may obtain their reasonable attorneys' fees by petitioning either state or federal court.[115] The IDEA also specifies that school districts may now recover attorneys' fees if the parent filed the due process hearing request frivolously or in bad faith to harass the school district.[116] The ability of attorneys to recover their legal fees pursuant to IDEA litigation may be limited because settlement offers need not include attorneys' fees, yet if a settlement offer is rejected and "the court or administrative hearing officer finds that the relief finally obtained by the parents is not more favorable to the parents than the offer of settlement," recovery of fees and related costs will be prohibited.[117] Whether this limitation applies identically in Section 504 cases, where fees are recoverable, is not clear.

Moreover, even when parents prevail on the merits, they are not entitled to recover fees for services rendered by experts.[118] Advocates contemplating impact litigation should conduct a comprehensive review of this shifting legal landscape. Lawyers filing administrative complaints may be able to negotiate for attorneys' fees in the course of settlements but should not assume they are recoverable.

3. UTILIZING DISABILITY DISCRIMINATION CLAIMS IN
PIPELINE LITIGATION

Section 504 of the Rehabilitation Act of 1973 prohibits recipients of federal funding from discriminating on the basis of disability. It applies to students who (1) have "a physical or mental impairment which substantially limits one or more major life activities," (2) have "a record of such an impairment," or (3) are "regarded as having such an impairment."[119]

a. Establishing Individual Discrimination

To establish a prima facie case of disability discrimination under Section 504, the plaintiff must show that he or she is a qualified individual with a disability, that he or she was denied benefits by a public entity receiving federal funds, and that he or she was discriminated against on the basis of disability.[120] A school district's refusal to place any student with a disability in a high-level (Regents) class is one example of a cause of action based on discrimination under Section 504.[121] Section 504 litigation is often filed as part of a case involving the IDEA. However, the Office for Civil Rights (OCR) will accept any complaint under Section 504 provided that the matter is not being litigated in another forum.

b. Federal and Administrative Complaints Pursuant to
Section 504, and "Disparate Impact"

Like Title VI regulations, the regulations implementing Section 504 have an "effects" test, which states that "[a] recipient may not, directly or through contractual or other arrangements, utilize criteria or methods of administration (i) that have the effect of subjecting qualified handicapped persons to discrimination on the basis of handicap, [or] (ii) that have the purpose or effect of defeating or substantially impairing accomplishment of the objectives of the recipient's program or activity with respect to handicapped persons."[122] A similar three-step test is used to determine if an educational policy is discriminatory under a disparate impact theory. First, does the practice or procedure in question have a disproportionate impact based on disability? Second, is the practice or procedure an educational necessity? Third, is there an alternative practice or procedure that would be feasible and achieve the same purpose, with less discriminatory impact?

Plaintiffs looking to pursue a disparate impact cause of action seeking injunctive relief pursuant to Section 504 of the Rehabilitation Act of 1973 have been permitted to assert this claim along with Section 1983 causes of action against state officials acting in their official capacity. However, case law in the area of disparate impact based on disability is sparse, and courts have taken inconsistent approaches. Some courts have stated that the deliberate indifference to the strong likelihood that an action would violate rights could suffice for an inference of intentional discrimination.[123] Other courts require a showing of intentional discrimination or bad faith, in addition to evidence of the denial of a FAPE.[124] Yet other courts have recognized the importance of a disparate impact analysis to Section 504 claims[125] and have even stated that disparate impact claims under Section 504 are cognizable.[126] For example, the Tenth Circuit in *Robinson v. Kansas* explicitly distinguished *Alexander v. Sandoval* as inapplicable to cases brought under Section 504 and Section 1983.[127]

Disparate impact complaints with OCR pursuant to Title VI may prove to be a viable channel for reasons described briefly in chapter 2 on discrimination.[128] Although the legal ground appears to be more solid for disparate impact Section 504 challenges, with both Title VI and Section 504, advocates should remain aware of changes in OCR enforcement policy.

4. UTILIZING IDEA PROVISIONS ON RACIAL AND ETHNIC DISPROPORTIONALITY IN PIPELINE REMEDIES

Concerns about discrimination bias dovetail with two concerns set forth in section A of this chapter about why so many students with disabilities wind up caught in the pipeline to prison. One major concern is that school districts fail to identify minority students with disabilities, and the subsequent denial of special education and services contributes to their demise. The systemic underrepresentation of a racial or ethnic group compared with others might constitute systemic violations of the Child Find provision of the IDEA. Research suggests that such denial often regards language-minority students.[129] Language minorities with disabilities should not have to choose between special education or ELL support, and this failure has been the subject of successful impact litigation as well.[130] Lawsuits on behalf of ELLs could be brought under the Child Find provisions or pursuant to Title VI of the Civil Rights Act of 1964.

Moreover, the IDEA made the "disproportionate representation of racial and ethnic groups in special education" one of three priority areas for monitoring and enforcement. Although often racial and ethnic disproportionality is discussed in terms of overrepresentation of Black and Latino students, the Department of Education's guidance to states makes it clear that states and districts should be addressing instances of minority underrepresentation as well.[131]

Overrepresentation has received more attention than underrepresentation because there is a history of using special education for unlawful racial segregation[132] and because recent data suggest that there continues to be highly disproportionate numbers of Black and Native American students identified in the cognitive disability categories of mental retardation and emotional disturbance, categories that tend to carry the greatest risk of removal to more restrictive settings.[133] Children of color are also far more likely to be disciplined, as described in section A of this chapter.

For these reasons, when advocates are bringing pipeline challenges grounded in disability law, and when they are fashioning remedies to such claims, the IDEA's safeguards against racial disproportionality warrant consideration. The relevant provisions are summarized in the following paragraphs.

One particular enforcement provision requires state educational agencies to intervene in districts when the state has determined that a district has significant racial disproportionality in identification and that the overrepresentation was the result of inappropriate identification.[134] A subsequent provision requires public reporting by the state regarding each district's performance in this regard.[135] A review of a given state's reported findings may reveal actionable violations of the IDEA that the state has already determined caused racial disproportionality in a particular district.

A third provision requires the state to collect, analyze, and report data to the public, but it also calls for data-driven consequences in response to districts that the state has found to have "significant racial or ethnic disproportionality" in identification, placement, or discipline.[136] Notably, the statistical analysis can trigger a reservation of 15 percent of certain IDEA funds for "early intervening services," to be used for students not currently eligible for IDEA supports and services.[137]

A fourth provision conditions eligibility for IDEA funds on a state's providing assurances that it will attend to differences by race and ethnicity in the rate of long-term suspensions and, if appropriate, require revisions by the SEAs and LEAs of policies, procedures, and practices relating to the development of and implementation of IEPs, the use of positive behavioral interventions and supports, and procedural safeguards.[138]

When racial disparities are distinct, attorneys pursuing disability-based challenges to the pipeline should be aware of these statutory obligations. There may be some utility in highlighting profound racial disparities in complaints. And for remedies, advocates might include demands for stronger implementation of these race-conscious IDEA requirements as part of their request for relief and in the course of settlement negotiations.[139]

Although the case studies that follow in section C did not specifically seek to address racial disparities, it is important to note that in each case the challenges were brought on behalf of students with disabilities in predominantly minority school districts and were very sensitive to the issue of racial disparities in their respective districts.

C. CASE STUDIES

1. CHALLENGING CHILD FIND FAILURE IN WISCONSIN: *JAMIE S. V. MILWAUKEE PUBLIC SCHOOLS*

One notable remedy following a federal court ruling against the Milwaukee Public Schools (MPS) and the Wisconsin Department of Public Instruction (DPI) demonstrates the efficacy of impact litigation pursuant to Child Find and other IDEA requirements. Advocates used published discipline data and state and federal monitoring reports produced by oversight agencies in building a thorough case against the state and district.[140] The comprehensive nature of the settlement agreement is a robust example of what can be achieved through impact litigation pursuant to disability law. The settlement included detailed requirements for action plans and programmatic intervention, continued monitoring by experts, and reporting of relevant data broadly, all designed to ensure compliance with regard to the potential special education needs of students who are repeatedly suspended or retained at grade.

The 2007 case *Jamie S. v. Milwaukee Public Schools*[141] was the culmination of litigation originally filed by Disability Rights Wisconsin in 2001, in which the plaintiffs asserted violations of the IDEA, related Wisconsin state statutes, and Section 504. Specifically, the plaintiffs' class action complaint concentrated on (1) the failure to refer children with a suspected disability in a timely manner, (2) the failure to review all relevant data to determine the appropriate needs at the child's initial evaluation, (3) the pattern of improper extensions of mandated time lines, and (4) the use of suspensions during the prereferral process.[142] In addition to the plaintiffs' substantive complaints, the complaint asserted that the Wisconsin DPI, which has implementation and enforcement obligations under the IDEA, failed its Child Find obligations with regard to oversight of the Milwaukee public schools.[143]

The story of Nathan L., one of the class representatives, provides a particularly strong illustration of the connection between violations of disability law and the pipeline to prison. Nathan had been diagnosed with ADHD and had been receiving services under a Section 504 plan while attending school in Florida. Upon his entering MPS, his mother advised school authorities of his diagnosis and that he had a Section 504 plan. Nathan was very disruptive from the outset. His mother met with his teachers and again mentioned the prior Section 504 plan. Nathan was eventually arrested, handcuffed, and hauled into custody after he hit his teacher in the head with a planner. His mother then learned that no Section 504 plan had been put into effect: she was told that "they don't transfer."[144]

Dr. Rogers Adkinson, the plaintiffs' expert who conducted an extensive file review of seventy similarly situated children,[145] testified that Nathan and other children who exhibited a combination of extreme emotional behavior and poor academic performance were subject to discipline and suspension by the district instead of being promptly referred for special education.[146]

The court gave a good deal of attention to the rising use of suspensions and their impact on the process of referral and evaluation.[147] In ruling on the plaintiffs' behalf in all but the claim of insufficient data review[148] and holding that these violations were "systemic in nature," the court specifically held that "MPS imposed suspensions in a manner that improperly impeded its ability to refer children with suspected disabilities for an initial evaluation."[149] In its reasoning, the court also cited expert testimony detailing how the state agency failed repeatedly to effectively correct the district's noncompliance, specifically that DPI would order many corrective action plans and give deadlines, but if MPS failed to meet the deadline, DPI set another deadline.[150]

In February 2008, a comprehensive settlement was reached with DPI. The settlement, which received the court's approval over MPS's objections, included that the implementation of the terms of the agreement and the achievement of the outcomes identified would represent an appropriate and adequate discharge of DPI's oversight obligations.[151] The final settlement also assigned an independent expert to ensure that MPS has a program to address its untimely initial evaluations, the absence of parent participation, and the use of suspension in lieu of making timely referrals in each of its schools.

A settlement narrowly tailored to the findings of violations might have simply sought to ensure that all students evidencing a need for special education and services were promptly evaluated and referred as appropriate. In contrast, this settlement created a broad and comprehensive remedy. The settlement includes systemic monitoring requirements with reporting, as well as a set of evaluations and outcome standards including oversight and outcome measures. It also gives careful consideration to a much broader array of students, including those who exhibit problematic emotional or academic behavior but who may not need specialized instruction and support services under the IDEA. In other words, students in Milwaukee would not necessarily have to be identified for special education to receive behavioral supports and interventions. This is a subtle but important consideration in light of the fact that as a defense, the district had argued that compliance with Child Find requirements would lead to disproportionate identification of students of color, which would, in turn, unfairly stigmatize these children. In dicta in *Jamie S.,* the judge noted that concerns about the stigmatizing effects of special education expressed by MPS in no way diminished the IDEA's statutory Child Find obligations.[152]

One interesting related fact is that in Wisconsin in 2005, just over 6 percent of all Black children identified as eligible for the IDEA were suspended for more than ten days, but only 0.67 percent of white eligible students were suspended long term.[153] Concerns about racial disparities were correctly not allowed to negate the Child Find violations in Milwaukee. At the same time, the agreed-on remedy in the compliance plan addressed outcome standards for attending to the potential needs of suspended and retained students who are *not* identified as students with disabilities and requires that they are referred to a system of early intervention services designed to address in a timely manner the students' academic or behavior issues that resulted in the suspension or expulsion. The emphasis on the early intervention services and application to nondisabled youth could help prevent the overuse of special education referral and evaluation to process all concerns about behavior. As discussed in section B of this chapter, the same kind of early intervention won in the *Jamie S.* settlement is required pursuant to the IDEA when a state identifies a district as having significant racial disproportionality in identification, placement, or discipline.

The *Jamie S.* settlement clearly demonstrates one successful challenge to state and district failures to identify students who may be in need of special education and support services, while providing in the remedy phase serious consideration to related needs of a broader group of students, particularly those in need of some behavioral support but whose needs might not otherwise be addressed in a court order because they lack eligibility. It is important to note, however, that the Milwaukee Public Schools have appealed the decision, and it is not final as it pertains to the district.

2. CHALLENGING DISCIPLINARY AND NONDISCIPLINARY REMOVALS IN NEW YORK: *E.B. V. BOARD OF EDUCATION*

In *E.B. v. Board of Education,*[154] a case that is still pending, children with disabilities and their parents filed an action challenging various aspects of their exclusion from school after suspensions, expulsions, removals, discharges, and involuntary transfers to alternative schools under 42 U.S.C. § 1983, the IDEA, Section 504, and New York State law. This case raises challenges to most types of potentially unlawful pushouts of children with disabilities described earlier and is an example of comprehensive system-wide impact litigation that can be brought in this area. The following two examples of the specific allegations are revealing.[155]

L.B., a seventeen-year-old with learning disabilities, was discharged from school due to truancy. When he tried to reregister, he was referred to a GED program but was denied enrollment to the program for insufficient credits. He missed eight months of school because of this discharge and was never offered a hearing.

I.P. was receiving special education teacher support services for his learning disabilities. After being accused of a suspendable offense, I.P. was referred to two alternative placements, neither of which provided instruction. A month passed, and I.P. did not receive a decision regarding his suspension. At some point, either I.P. or his mother was verbally informed that I.P. had been transferred to another school.

The court certified the class, held that exhaustion of administrative remedies under the IDEA was not required, and denied a motion to dismiss the action. In fact, the court certified six subclasses including children who were suspended, expelled, or otherwise removed or excluded for behavior with adequate notice and who did not receive a free and appropriate public education, including children who did not have IEPs and children who are protected by Section 504. The case remains pending and is in the discovery phase.

3. ALTERNATIVE MODES OF ENFORCING SPECIAL EDUCATION RIGHTS TO CHALLENGE THE PIPELINE: *P.R. V. PALM BEACH PUBLIC SCHOOLS*

Attorneys and advocates need not rely exclusively on filing formal class actions or impact suits in state or federal courts. In many jurisdictions, including the preceding examples, advocates and attorneys have been successful in changing policies and practices through administrative complaints. Moreover, the systemic failure to provide FAPE, LRE, or due process can be framed as a discrimination issue and, depending on the context, may be brought as an administrative complaint as well as in court. Advocates may enforce special education rights administratively by (1) filing an administrative complaint with the federally mandated state complaint resolution system alleging a violation of the IDEA,[156] (2) filing a request for an impartial due process hearing to challenge a special education decision by a district,[157] or (3) filing an administrative complaint with the U.S. Department of Education's Office for Civil Rights alleging a violation of Section 504 or Title II.

Federal regulations expressly contemplate that the state complaint procedure address complaints raising systemic issues.[158] The Southern Poverty Law Center (SPLC) and the Southern Disability Law Center have brought a number of apparently successful challenges to the School-to-Prison Pipeline by bringing class action state administrative complaints raising systemic claims.[159] They have filed administrative complaints with the Louisiana State Department of Education against school districts in Jefferson Parish, East Baton Rouge, Caddo, and Calcasieu, alleging, inter alia, routine suspensions and expulsions of children with disabilities for minor offenses expressly related to their disabilities; segregation of these students in self-contained classrooms or trailers in violation of federal and state regulations; and failure to provide appropriate levels of related services (social work, counseling, and psychological services) and vocational training to emotionally disturbed children.[160] These practices are recognized as having had a pervasive and dramatic adverse impact on these students, the vast majority of whom are typically performing several years behind their grade level and their peers by the time they reach junior high or high school. This in turn contributes to abysmal state and county graduation rates.

One important strategic element common to the SPLC approach is suggested by a recent complaint filed in Palm Beach County. Several organizations joined forces to file a state school-to-prison complaint with the Bureau of Exceptional Children and Student Services. The class consisted of

> all students of the Palm Beach County public school system with emotional/behavioral disabilities, or who manifest behavioral issues, and who have been, or are being, subjected to repeated disciplinary removals totaling more than ten school days (including in-school suspensions, court referrals, out-of-school suspensions, and undocumented, illegal removals from school, e.g. "cool-off removals").[161]

This Palm Beach filing and settlement is also emblematic of how actions can seek remedies that will predictably address racial disparities, without focusing the complaint on allegations of racial discrimination or limiting the complainants to children of color. For example, the complaint points out that ten years ago in Palm Beach County, "Students with disabilities received school related referrals to the juvenile justice system at more than five times the rate of students without disabilities. At that time, more than 80% of the students with disabilities referred to the juvenile justice system were black males."[162] In this and several other ways the advocates raised awareness of the racial injustice underlying the action while keeping the class action centered on the strongest legal claim, the denial of FAPE and due process to students classified with emotional disturbance.

Similar to the Milwaukee class action, the complaint highlighted the district's history of systemic IDEA violations in the placement of special education students in alternative education.

> The IDEA violations included changes in placement without any IEP meetings or parental participation; changes in IEPs to "get" what is provided or absent in the alternative education site, by removing or reducing the frequency and intensity of related services and program accommodations and modifications, and systemic violations of IDEA's disciplinary scheme requiring manifestation determinations and the development of positive behavior intervention plans [citation omitted].[163]

One of the class representatives, P.R., a twelve-year-old, gifted African American male, was also emotionally/behaviorally disturbed. When he made the transition to middle school, the new school did not have a behavior monitoring system, group counseling, crisis intervention support, or deescalation techniques or other modifications and supports to address his needs as delineated in his IEP. Instead, he received nothing but disciplinary removals. By the end of the year he had received ten days of out-of-school suspension and twenty-three days of in-school suspensions, yet he had not been provided any "behavioral services designed to address the behavior violations so they did not recur," as required pursuant to 34 C.F.R. § 300.530(d)(ii). The attorneys alleged systemic violations and successfully gained systemic relief in the settlement. Most notably they sought and gained a systemic program known as Positive Behavior Interventions and Supports (PBIS).[164]

One important aspect of PBIS is that although it gives special attention to the needs of students with disabilities, the intervention involves the training of every member of the school community.[165] PBIS also entails frequent monitoring of office referrals for discipline and setting goals for reducing these referrals.[166]

The Palm Beach settlement emphasized the PBIS intervention and included monitoring the implementation for a minimum of three years. Specifically, "The settlement stipulates that PBCS [Palm Beach County Schools] will contract with an individual or organization (Consultant) with school-based experience and nationally recognized expertise in the development and implementation of district and school-wide PBIS programs and services."[167]

Within the first ninety days, the settlement provides for the review of every student in the class who is receiving less than one hour of related services per week to ensure the appropriate level of services, which PBCS will implement if agreed to by the parent(s).[168] In addition, specific strategies, objectives, and timelines for significantly increasing the access of the defined class of students to regular education class settings must be developed, with measurable benchmarks and outcomes for determining the successful implementation of the strategies and timelines.[169] The settlement also requires implementation of objectives and timelines for "significantly reducing the number of suspensions of students identified" in the defined class. And specifically the settlement provides for a review of "all data . . . relative to referrals, office disciplinary referrals, removals (suspensions and expulsions), truancies, 45-day placements, and restraint incidents for students in the district." Further, the settlement requires revision of the PBCS code of conduct to be consistent with the PBIS discipline protocol, including that suspensions and expulsions are measures of last resort.[170]

The guidance provided by this detailed, comprehensive settlement suggests that these forms of impact litigation are promising ways to challenge the School-to-Prison Pipeline. However, most of these remedies are new and have not yet been proven effective. Neither settlements nor court orders against districts or states are self-enforcing. The most effective plans on paper face numerous obstacles. One significant barrier is that the same personnel that had contributed to the School-to-Prison Pipeline must now implement the remedy. A contributing factor that complicates the efficacy of implementation is that conscious and unconscious forms of bias against students with disabilities, as well as racial and gender bias, may influence the tendency for children in these subgroups to be pushed out of school and onto the path toward prison.

D. CONCLUSION

This chapter has described numerous legal avenues for seeking systemic change on behalf of students with disabilities. The majority of the case studies have involved students with disabilities who were excluded from school on disciplinary grounds. Many of the systemic remedies highlighted, however, have sought remedies that go beyond concerns of adequate process toward seeking preventive and systemic changes at the school or district level intended to improve the quality of education for students with disabilities, as well as for their nondisabled peers. The next chapter describes impact litigation on behalf of students subjected to unjust disciplinary removal, such as harsh zero-tolerance discipline policies, without regard to disability status.

4

Challenging Suspensions and Expulsions

School administrators are resorting more and more frequently to removing students deemed to be "problem children" from their schools through suspensions and expulsions. In 2004, there were nearly 3.3 million school suspensions and over 106,000 expulsions; in some states, the number of suspensions exceeded 10 percent of the number of students enrolled.[1] Rates of suspension have increased dramatically for all students,[2] but the spike has been most dramatic for children of color. African American children have experienced the largest increase in suspension, from 6 percent in 1973 to 15 percent in 2006. The discipline gap between Black children and white children grew from 3 percent to over 10 percent in the same time period; in other words, Black children are more than three times more likely than whites to be suspended today.[3]

Although the necessity of discipline in schools is self-evident, schools in recent years have begun exercising their disciplinary authority to suspend and expel students more frequently and in far more questionable circumstances.[4] Exclusion from the classroom, for even a few days, disrupts a child's education and may escalate misbehavior by removing the child from a structured environment and giving him or her increased time and opportunity to get into trouble. Studies show that a child who has been suspended is more likely to be retained in his or her grade, to drop out, to commit a crime, and to end up incarcerated as an adult.[5] Unfortunately, as described more fully in chapter 1, there is no federal right to attend school and receive an education. But this is not to say that decisions to remove children from school are immune from challenge.

This chapter explores challenges to disciplinary removals of students from classrooms via suspensions and expulsions. The first section describes the rise of zero-tolerance disciplinary policies across the country. The second section explores the possibility of raising procedural due process claims to

challenge school removals and to ensure that the procedures used to suspend or expel students comport with constitutional requirements. The third
section discusses substantive challenges to the punishment itself, not just
the procedures by which the punishment was imposed. The fourth section
discusses the potential for a specific subset of due process challenges, that
school discipline rules may be void for vagueness. The fifth section discusses
challenges to school discipline rules on the grounds that those rules constitute unlawful restrictions on expressive conduct that is protected by the First
Amendment. Finally, the sixth section discusses the emerging trend of automatic suspensions for students who are arrested for off-campus conduct.

As always, although the focus here is on federal constitutional claims,
advocates should refer to state and local laws and regulations to determine
whether they create additional rights. For example, in the procedural due
process context, New York State statute sets forth additional detailed procedural requirements for teacher removals, short-term suspensions of five days
or less, and suspensions of more than five days.[6]

A. THE RISE OF ZERO-TOLERANCE DISCIPLINE POLICIES

The harshest forms of school discipline today result from "zero-tolerance"
rules. States, school districts, and schools across the nation, perceiving an
onslaught of crime and violence in primary and secondary schools,[7] have
embraced such policies that impose harsh penalties across the board. According to the National Center for Education Statistics, during the 1996–97
school year, 91 percent of public schools imposed zero-tolerance policies for
weapons other than firearms, 87 percent of schools reported zero-tolerance
policies for alcohol, and 88 percent had such policies for drugs; 79 percent
of schools had zero-tolerance policies for violence, and 79 percent also had
such policies for tobacco violations.[8]

These policies can be traced to the federal Gun Free Schools Act, enacted
in 1994 in response to highly publicized school shootings and a perceived
surge in school violence.[9] That act mandates that every state enact a law to
require districts to expel from school for at least one year any student who is
determined to have brought a firearm to school.[10] Importantly, the mandate
requires that the state law create an exception to permit school administrators to modify an expulsion on a case-by-case basis.[11]

States and localities have expanded zero tolerance beyond expulsions for
firearms. Zero tolerance now applies to suspension or expulsion of children
from school for everything from weapons to drugs to smoking to fights.

Unlike the federal law, these rules frequently do not permit for case-by-case exceptions. Zero-tolerance rules also impose automatic suspensions for minor offenses such as dress-code violations, truancy, or tardiness.

One of the hallmarks of zero tolerance is the automatic imposition of a predetermined penalty for a given form of misconduct, without consideration of the individual circumstances surrounding the conduct or extenuating circumstances such as the student's age, cognitive capacity, or even the existence of intent. As the American Bar Association observes,

> Thus, zero tolerance policies for students adopt a theory of mandatory punishment that has been rejected by the adult criminal justice system because it is too harsh! Rather than having a variety of sanctions available for a range of school-based offenses, state laws and school district policies apply the same expulsion rules to the six-year-old as to the 17-year-old; to the first time offender as to the chronic troublemaker; to the child with a gun as to the child with a Swiss Army knife.[12]

Whether formally identified as a zero-tolerance policy or not, overly harsh punishment for students may be vulnerable to challenge. First, impact litigators may consider challenging the procedures used to punish students, to ensure they comport with minimum procedural due process requirements. Second, they may consider challenging the propriety of the punishment imposed, either through a substantive due process claim, a vagueness challenge, or a First Amendment challenge.

B. PROCEDURAL DUE PROCESS

Advocates may consider bringing procedural due process claims to ensure that schools provide students with sufficient procedural protections such as a right to notice or a right to an impartial hearing when they are subject to suspensions or expulsions. Procedural due process requires that states provide fair and adequate procedures for determining when it will deprive a person of life, liberty, or property.

In *Goss v. Lopez*, the Supreme Court acknowledged that although there is no federal fundamental right to education, students have a state-created property and liberty interest in attending school, which cannot be taken away without adherence to minimal due process protections.[13] As to a child's property interest in attending school, the Court stated, "Having chosen to extend the right to an education to people . . . generally, [the state] may not withdraw that right on grounds of misconduct absent fundamentally fair procedures to determine whether the misconduct has occurred."[14] As to the liberty interest, the Court reasoned, "Where a person's good name, reputation, honor, or integrity is at stake because of what the government is doing to him, the minimal requirements of the [Due Process] Clause must be satisfied. . . . [C]harges [of misconduct] could seriously damage the students' standing with their fellow pupils and their teachers as well as interfere with later opportunities for higher education and employment."[15] For this reason, the Court held, the state must adhere to minimal due process protections before compromising the reputation of a child by disciplining him or her for alleged misconduct. Thus, focusing on both the student's property interest in receiving an education and his or her liberty interest in not being arbitrarily disciplined, the Court concluded that children subject to suspension or expulsion must be afforded procedural due process to challenge the proposed punishment.[16]

As with all procedural due process issues, once it has been determined that there is a protected property or liberty interest at stake, the critical question is, how much process is due before that interest can be compromised? Due process involves "a flexible concept that varies with the particular situation."[17] The balancing test set forth in *Mathews v. Eldridge* applies to all procedural due process claims; it considers "the private interest that will be affected by the official action; the risk of an erroneous deprivation of such interest through the procedures used, and the probable value, if any, of additional or substitute procedural safeguards; and the Government's interest, including the function involved and the fiscal and administrative burdens that the additional or substitute procedural requirement would entail."[18] The degree of procedural protections afforded thus depends on the degree of the proposed deprivation. In the context of school discipline, a ten-minute time-out from the classroom will enjoy fewer procedural protections than a one-year expulsion, for example. Although school discipline cases rarely employ the *Mathews* balancing test explicitly, that test should always be considered in any procedural due process argument.

Litigants have sought to limit overly punitive discipline decisions by ensuring that students receive the procedural protections to which they are entitled to challenge those decisions. Although there are few procedural protections available to individuals subject to short-term suspensions of ten days or less, advocates have enjoyed some success in systemic challenges to the failure to provide for adequate procedural protections to challenge long-term suspensions and expulsions. In addition, they have enjoyed success in challenging the permissibility of zero-tolerance policies that do not provide for a meaningful opportunity to determine whether the particular punishment imposed is warranted by the child's individual circumstances. It should be noted that pursuant to federal statute under the Individuals with Disabilities Education Act (IDEA)[19] and Section 504 of the Rehabilitation Act,[20] students with disabilities enjoy additional procedural protections to challenge disciplinary removals, discussed in chapter 3. This section, by contrast, is limited to the minimum procedural protections available to the general student population.

1. PROCEDURAL PROTECTIONS FOR SHORT- AND LONG-TERM SUSPENSIONS AND EXPULSIONS

The Supreme Court has established that students have few procedural due process protections to challenge short-term suspensions of ten days or less, but lower courts have extended far greater protections to challenge long-term suspensions or expulsions, such as the right to notice of the charges, the right to an impartial hearing, the right to appeal, and the right to be represented by a private attorney, depending on the jurisdiction.

Goss v. Lopez, which considered only short-term suspensions of ten days or less, held that the student need only "be given oral or written notice of the charges against him and, if he denies them, an explanation of the evidence the authorities have and an opportunity to present his side of the story" to an objective decision-maker.[21] The opportunity to be heard for a short-term suspension need not be fully adversarial; "an informal give-and-take between the student and disciplinarian" is all that is required.[22] In these circumstances, there is no right to counsel, to confront and cross-examine witnesses, or to call defense witnesses.[23] Moreover, in certain circumstances, schools may wait to afford these procedural protections until *after* the suspension, when notice and a hearing prior to suspension are not feasible because of the dangerous nature of the circumstances.[24] Given these limitations, advocates have little room to challenge the procedures available to students subject to short-term suspensions, at least pursuant to federal procedural due process claims.

Nonetheless, *Goss* itself acknowledged that "[l]onger suspensions or expulsions for the remainder of the school term, or permanently, may require more formal procedures"[25] than those afforded to short-term suspensions. The Court has not delineated precisely what those more formal procedures would entail. The absence of guidance from the Supreme Court in this area has provided a ripe area for advocates to expand the procedural protections afforded to students subject to long-term suspensions and expulsions.

In reviewing such challenges, lower courts sometimes revert to the general *Matthews v. Eldridge* balancing test. In doing so, they recognize that a student's interest in continuing his or her education is weighty, particularly when a long-term suspension or expulsion is at issue. Likewise, they acknowledge that a school's interest in maintaining discipline and a safe environment conducive to learning is important. Most of the debate centers on the risk of erroneous deprivation and the value of additional safeguards. This inquiry is extremely fact specific, and courts have reached differing conclusions on similar issues.[26] Experts in the area suggest that, depending on the jurisdiction, the following may be required:

- Notice of the disciplinary action to the student and parents, preferably in writing, specifying the reason for the action
- Right to appeal the decision in a fair, impartial hearing—for example, before the school board, the superintendent, or a hearing officer—in which the facts of the case are evaluated independently
- Right to be represented at the hearing by counsel, especially if the school district is represented by legal counsel
- Reasonable time to prepare for the hearing
- An opportunity to review evidence against the student
- An opportunity to examine witnesses against the student, subject to safety-related confidentiality concerns
- Opportunity to present evidence and witnesses on the student's behalf
- Right to record the proceedings
- Requirement that the hearing entity's decision be based on substantial evidence[27]

Another area potentially ripe for challenge involves the timing of the due process hearing. Because the purpose of procedural due process protections is to provide an opportunity to challenge the denial of a benefit, notice and the hearing generally must be afforded *before* education is denied.[28] But *Goss v. Lopez* acknowledged an exception to this general rule, permitting the immediate removal of a child from school, without prior notice and a hearing, when he or she "poses a continuing danger to persons or property or an ongoing threat of disrupting the academic process."[29] Under these circumstances, the Supreme Court ruled, "the necessary notice and rudimentary hearing" may be delayed so long as it occurs "as soon as practicable."[30] Unfortunately, a jurisdiction may take advantage of this exception. For example, the Washington State Department of Education has issued regulations permitting "emergency expulsions."[31] Districts have used this exception to delay or even deny process even when there was no urgency or time sensitivity. Advocates might explore challenges to such regulations where they exist, pursuant to procedural due process claims.

2. AUTOMATIC OR MANDATORY PENALTIES

Procedural due process claims may also be used to challenge the *meaningfulness* of disciplinary hearings, particularly those involving zero-tolerance policies that, by definition, impose automatic penalties regardless of the circumstances.[32] Suppose a student is subject to expulsion for possessing prescription medicine for a documented medical condition under a zero-tolerance policy mandating expulsion for possession of any controlled substance. A meaningful hearing requires not only a formal hearing to challenge the expulsion—for example, to determine whether or not the medicine constitutes a controlled substance within the meaning of the discipline code—but also a meaningful hearing that actually considers whether the expulsion is warranted, upon consideration of all the extenuating circumstances of the case.[33]

In *Lee v. Macon County Board of Education,* the Fifth Circuit reversed the decision to expel two girls when the school board simply ratified the recommendation of the principal, rather than render an independent decision as required by state statute.[34] In a much-cited passage, the court stated, "Formalistic acceptance or ratification of the principal's request or recommendation as to the scope of punishment, without independent Board consideration of what, under all the circumstances, the penalty should be, is less than full due process."[35] More recently, a district court in *Colvin v. Lowndes County* similarly reversed a zero-tolerance expulsion involving a child who inadvertently brought a knife to school because of the failure to consider independently all the relevant facts and circumstances of the child's case.[36] These cases suggest that automatic punishments, without allowing for the independent consideration of extenuating circumstances, may be vulnerable to challenge.

The case law, though, is inconsistent on this point. Only six years after the Fifth Circuit decided *Lee,* the same court in *Mitchell v. Board of Trustees* upheld the expulsion of two knife-wielding students pursuant to a mandatory expulsion rule.[37] Describing the central legal issue in the case as "whether, as a matter of substantive due process, a student is guaranteed some discretion by the School Board in fixing the punishment for violation of a rule," the court concluded that the student possesses no such right.[38]

Although it is difficult to tease out any unified principle from these cases, taken together, they suggest that, at least sometimes, courts may be willing to strike down the automatic application of a zero-tolerance punishment on procedural due process grounds in the absence of any possibility for independent review of the decision.

C. SUBSTANTIVE DUE PROCESS

Ultimately, procedural due process claims may prove limited: even if all the protections associated with a full-blown criminal trial are afforded to a student, the child will not necessarily be protected against unreasonably harsh or inherently unfair punishments. To raise challenges to the inherent fairness or appropriateness of a suspension or expulsion, advocates may invoke the substantive due process clause.

The Supreme Court case in *Ingraham v. Wright* left open the possibility of substantive due process challenges to the use of corporal punishment.[39] Substantive due process claims to challenge suspensions and expulsions, however, face an uphill battle. In the absence of federal recognition of a fundamental right to education, such claims are subject to rational basis review under federal law, not strict scrutiny.[40] Courts routinely defer to school administrators in reviewing school discipline decisions. In *Wood v. Strickland,* the Supreme Court admonished, "It is not the role of the federal courts to set aside decisions of school administrators which the court may view as lacking a basis in wisdom or compassion."[41] Federal courts thus will not overturn school discipline decisions so long as they are not arbitrary or so disproportionate as to "shock the conscience."[42]

Nonetheless, at least some courts have concluded that certain suspensions and expulsions are so harsh that they do not survive rational basis review. These cases have occurred when the student lacked any intent. In the Sixth Circuit decision in *Seal v. Morgan,*[43] a student challenged his expulsion after school officials found a knife in the family car that the student drove to school.[44] The school offered no evidence that the student knew or should have known of the presence of the knife.[45] In the absence of such evidence, the court concluded that the expulsion was not rationally related to any government interest because "[n]o student can use a weapon to injure another person, to disrupt school operations, or, for that matter, any other purpose if the student is totally unaware of its presence."[46]

Another federal district court decision likewise found school discipline may fail rational basis review. In *Langley v. Monroe County School District*,[47] a student challenged her removal to an alternative school after an open can of beer was found in her car at school. In light of evidence that the student did not know the beer was there, the court rejected the school's motion for summary judgment, ruling,

> Substantive due process violations occur when a law or governmental act is not reasonably related to its end. . . . In light of the fact[s of the case] . . . and the fact that the [school district] has not produced a policy outlining the time period that a student should be sent to alternative school, this court finds that there is a sufficient jury question as to whether [the student's] penalty was rationally related to the school boards [*sic*] interests.[48]

Seal and *Langley* lend some hope for substantive due process claims to challenge suspensions and expulsions, but they suggest that such claims are strongest when students are punished in the absence of knowledge or intent.

Although there is no fundamental right to education under federal law, such a right is guaranteed by several states, as discussed in chapter 1. In those jurisdictions, courts theoretically apply strict scrutiny to review a suspension or expulsion, and some may in fact do so.[49] But a review of the case law shows that even in states that do recognize a fundamental right to education or that apply strict scrutiny to school finance decisions, courts may conclude that a student who misbehaves waives that right and, thus, that strict scrutiny need not be applied.[50] As always, advocates should check local laws to determine whether they afford greater protections for students excluded from schools on the basis of excessively harsh disciplinary policies.

D. VOID FOR VAGUENESS

Advocates may also consider raising void-for-vagueness claims to challenge inappropriate suspensions and expulsions. Students are routinely punished for poorly defined or subjectively assessed conduct such as "insubordination," "disobedience," "inappropriate language or behavior," "verbal assault," "offensive language," or "gang-related activity."[51] Empirical evidence shows that children of color are particularly vulnerable to being punished for subjectively assessed conduct,[52] and courts have acknowledged the risk that these punishments are meted out in a racially discriminatory manner.[53] Impact litigators should consider bringing void-for-vagueness challenges to the application of these kinds of disciplinary rules. This section explores how courts have resolved such challenges

Although frequently brought in conjunction with First Amendment claims, the "void for vagueness" doctrine presents a particular subset of due process and challenges school rules that fail to provide adequate notice as to what conduct is prohibited.[54] As the Supreme Court has said, "It is a basic principle of due process that an enactment is void for vagueness if its prohibitions are not clearly defined."[55] A vague rule is unconstitutional because "[f]irst, it may fail to provide the kind of notice that will enable ordinary people to understand what conduct it prohibits; second, it may authorize and even encourage arbitrary and discriminatory enforcement."[56]

In *Bethel School District Number 403 v. Fraser,* the Supreme Court held that void-for-vagueness challenges may be sustained against school discipline rules.[57] In doing so, however, it cautioned that such rules require far less exaction and precision than in the criminal context: "Given the school's need to be able to impose disciplinary sanctions for a wide range of unanticipated conduct disruptive of the educational process, school disciplinary rules need not be as detailed as a criminal code which imposes criminal sanctions."[58]

Before discussing the cases, however, it is important to understand the difference between as-applied challenges and facial challenges in the void-for-vagueness context. When First Amendment concerns are not implicated, plaintiffs are limited to arguing that a given rule was impermissibly vague *as applied* to their own alleged misconduct.[59] When such an argument prevails, the court probably will strike down the punishment; it will not, however, necessarily strike down the entire rule. If on the other hand, the rule clearly applies to render the plaintiff's conduct punishable, but it is unclear or vague as to whether it would apply to render other forms of potential misconduct punishable, the plaintiff would not have standing to bring the claim. To strike down a disciplinary rule, not just as applied to a particular plaintiff but for all students, a plaintiff must bring a facial challenge to the discipline rule. Unless the First Amendment is implicated because the rule reaches a significant amount of constitutionally protected activity, a facial vagueness challenge requires a plaintiff to show that the rule is unconstitutional in *all* of its application, not just as applied to him or her.[60] Because of the heightened showing necessary, it is sometimes difficult to raise facial challenges to discipline codes on vagueness grounds.

Generally, courts that reject vagueness challenges tend to reason that school rules need not be as precise as criminal laws and that school administrators must retain the discretion necessary to ensure orderly schools. Courts that sustain vagueness challenges tend to reason that, absent clarity as to when conduct is protected and when it is punishable, there will be a chilling effect on First Amendment activity. Unfortunately, it is virtually impossible to tease out a unifying theme to predict in which of these two camps a given case will fall. Rather, the courts are all over the map on this issue.

1. "OBSCENE," "OFFENSIVE," AND/OR "RACIST" CONDUCT

Fraser rejected a void-for-vagueness challenge to a school rule prohibiting "[c]onduct which materially and substantially interferes with the educational process . . . including the use of obscene, profane language or gestures."[61] Pursuant to that rule, school officials suspended a student who gave a student assembly speech using an "elaborate, graphic, and explicit sexual metaphor"[62] to nominate a classmate for student council. The Court reasoned that the student obtained adequate notice that the rule clearly applied to his conduct here, rendering his speech subject to discipline. Importantly, the Court also noted the fact that teachers specifically warned the student, before he gave his speech, that he could be punished.[63]

After *Fraser*, lower courts have varied greatly in the extent to which they will accept vagueness challenges to generic rules prohibiting "offensive," "disobedient," or "racist" behavior. The courts that reject such challenges reason that even vaguely worded prohibitions can be read to have a comprehensible and normative standard of conduct on which students may base their behavior.

On this ground, the Third Circuit in *Sypniewski v. Warren Hills Regional Board of Education* rejected a vagueness challenge to a rule prohibiting "name calling, using racial or derogatory slurs, wearing or possession of items depicting or implying racial hatred or prejudice," and "possession of any written material that is . . . racially divisive or . . . creates racial hatred."[64] Although the court acknowledged that the rule was imprecise, it reasoned, "The policy is not 'vague in the sense that no standard of conduct is specified at all,' but 'in the sense that it requires a person to conform his conduct to an imprecise but comprehensible normative standard.'"[65]

Likewise, a district court in *Coy v. Board of Education of North Canton City Schools* reasoned that a prohibition against "obscenity, profanity, any form of racial slur or ethnic slurs, or other patently offensive language or gesture" and a prohibition against "disobedience," described as "defiant, belligerent, disrespectful, or failing to comply with school rules or directions of [school officials]," gave students fair notice of a "comprehensible normative standard" of conduct to which they would be held.[66] Importantly, though, the court rejected a "catch-all" disciplinary provision permitting school officials to suspend students for "[a]ny action or behavior judged by school officials to be inappropriate and not specifically mentioned in other sections [of the Student Conduct Code]."[67]

Other courts have been willing to require school codes to incorporate more precision into their discipline codes. In *Smith v. Mount Pleasant Public Schools,* involving the prohibition of "verbal assaults," the court expressed concern about the First Amendment implications of the rule and concluded that it was void for vagueness.[68] More recently, in *Miller v. Penn Manor School District,* the district court sustained a vagueness challenge to a school prohibition against "anything that is a distraction," although it rejected a vagueness challenge to a school rule banning messages promoting violence.[69]

2. GANG-RELATED ACTIVITY

Courts are likewise inconsistent in the extent to which they will tolerate school rules banning "gang-related" activity. Generally, courts will strike down such rules on vagueness grounds if they simply prohibit "gang-related activity" or "gang-related apparel" and fail to specify examples of what constitutes gang activity, such as a list of prohibited symbols, colors, or activities.

In *Stephenson v. Davenport Community School District,* the Eighth Circuit invalidated a school rule prohibiting "[g]ang related activities such as display of 'colors,' symbols, signals, signs, etc."[70] Concerned about the First Amendment implications of the rule, the court held that the ban "fail[ed] to provide adequate notice regarding unacceptable conduct and fail[ed] to offer clear guidance for those who apply it. A person of common intelligence must necessarily guess at the undefined meaning of 'gang-related activities.'"[71]

By contrast, in *Fuller ex rel. Fuller v. Decatur Public School Board,* the school rule at issue prohibited "gang-like activity," which was defined as conduct "1) on behalf of any gang, 2) to perpetuate the existence of any gang, 3) to effect the common purpose and design of any gang and 4) or to represent a gang affiliation, loyalty or membership in any way while on school grounds or while attending a school function."[72] The rule further stated that prohibited conduct "include[s] recruiting students for membership in any gang and threatening or intimidating other students or employees to commit acts or omissions against his/her will in furtherance of the common purpose and design of any gang."[73] Emphasizing that the rule set forth specific forms of conduct that would be punished, the *Fuller* court held that the prohibition against gang activity survived a vagueness challenge.[74]

Recently, the American Civil Liberties Union filed two lawsuits challenging a school district's antigang disciplinary policy on vagueness grounds. The challenged policy provides, in full, that "Students are prohibited from wearing or displaying in any manner on school property or at school sponsored events clothing, apparel, accessories, drawings, or messages associated with any gang or social club that is associated with criminal activity, as defined by law enforcement agencies."[75] Violations of this rule result in suspension or expulsion. In the first case, *J.W. v. DeSoto County School District,* an African American twelve-year-old honors student was expelled from his majority-white middle school pursuant to the policy for having pictures on his cell phone of himself dancing in his home.[76] In the second case, an African American student was expelled from his majority-white high school pursuant to the same rule for quietly singing to himself while bopping his head and bumping his fists to the beat while sitting in the bleachers during assembly.[77] Both cases remain pending at the time of writing.

3. OFF-CAMPUS CONDUCT

All other things being equal, courts are also more likely to sustain a vagueness claim when the challenged rule punishes off-campus conduct. In *Packer v. Board of Education of Thomaston,* the Connecticut Supreme Court concluded that a state statute authorizing expulsion for off-campus conduct anytime the conduct "is violative of such policy and is seriously disruptive of the educational process" was void for vagueness as applied to a student who was expelled after being arrested for having marijuana in his car off-campus and after school hours.[78] The court reasoned, "a person of ordinary intelligence, apprised only of the language of [the statute], . . . could not be reasonably certain whether possession of marijuana in the trunk of a car, off the school grounds after school hours, is, *by itself and without some tangible nexus to school operation,* seriously disruptive of the educational process as required by [the statute] in order to subject a student to expulsion."[79]

E. FIRST AMENDMENT

Overly harsh school discipline may also be susceptible to challenge as a violation of the First Amendment when it punishes protected speech or expression. Public schools routinely suspend or expel students for wearing certain clothes, for criticizing school staff, and for off-campus or Internet speech. This section explores the circumstances under which such discipline decisions and policies may be challenged as unlawful restrictions on speech or expressive conduct.

In *Tinker v. Des Moines Independent Community School District*, the Supreme Court famously stated, "It can hardly be argued that either students or teachers shed their constitutional rights to freedom of speech or expression at the schoolhouse gate."[80] However, the Court held that free-speech rights are more limited in the school context than in other contexts because schools must retain the authority to prescribe and control school conduct.[81]

The plaintiff students in *Tinker* were suspended for wearing black armbands in protest of the Vietnam War and were not permitted to return to school until they removed them.[82] Concluding that the students' First Amendment rights had been violated, the Court held that a school may not discipline a student for expressive conduct unless the conduct "materially disrupts classwork or involves substantial disorder or invasion of the rights of others."[83] The touchstone for determining whether a school's discipline decision or policy violates the First Amendment, then, is whether it punishes expressive conduct and whether that expressive conduct is reasonably likely materially or substantially to disrupt school activities.[84]

As in the context of due process vagueness challenges, litigants should consider whether to raise a First Amendment challenge to a school rule as applied to a particular plaintiff or facially. Unique to First Amendment challenges, a plaintiff may raise a facial challenge to a school rule even when the school rule would be constitutional as applied to the plaintiffs' conduct, so long as it would be unconstitutional as applied to a significant amount of other conduct.[85] In other words, a plaintiff may argue that a discipline rule is unconstitutional as applied to him or her, because the conduct for which he or she was punished is constitutionally protected speech. Alternatively, a plaintiff may argue that, regardless of whether his or her own personal conduct was protected by the First Amendment, the discipline rule is invalid because it would punish a significant amount of protected speech.

Although courts frequently reject *as-applied* First Amendment challenges to decisions to suspend individual students for expressive conduct, they sometimes are more likely to sustain facial *overbreadth* First Amendment challenges to the disciplinary rules themselves. For example, although a court may find that a rule prohibiting "offensive language" is valid *as applied* to the conduct of an individual student who criticized a teacher, it nonetheless may well strike down the rule as unconstitutionally overbroad because it ensnares a significant amount of First Amendment–protected speech.[86]

1. OFFENSIVE, OBSCENE, RACIST, HARASSING, OR OTHERWISE INAPPROPRIATE CONDUCT

Almost all schools maintain discipline rules prohibiting offensive, disobedient, obscene, racist, or harassing conduct. Absent content-based restrictions on speech, courts generally reject First Amendment challenges to these rules, reasoning that such rules are necessary to teach students the boundaries of socially acceptable behavior.

In *Fraser,* the Supreme Court held that suspending a student for making a sexually explicit speech during student assembly did not violate the First Amendment.[87] Distinguishing *Tinker* on the ground that the speech did not involve any political viewpoint, the Court held that "the First Amendment does not prevent the school officials from determining that to permit a vulgar and lewd speech such as [at issue here] would undermine the school's basic educational mission."[88]

A more recent exception permitting restrictions on speech promoting drug use was recognized in *Morse v. Frederick.*[89] In that case, the Supreme Court considered a challenge to the disciplining of a student who had unfurled a banner reading "Bong Hits 4 Jesus" at a school-related event.[90] Despite arguments that the school rule to which the student was subject was viewpoint discriminatory, and despite the absence of evidence that the banner disrupted school activities, the Court concluded that the student's suspension did not offend the First Amendment. The majority carved out an exception to ordinary First Amendment jurisprudence in schools for speech promoting drug use. In light of the majority and concurring opinions, this case is limited to the facts presented and should not be interpreted to alter the general prohibitions against viewpoint-discriminatory restrictions in public schools.

Although courts may defer to schools in determining whether punishment in a particular case is warranted, they are more likely to strike down the discipline rules themselves pursuant to facial overbreadth challenges.

In *Saxe v. State College Area School District,* the Third Circuit reviewed a school prohibition against all "verbal or physical conduct based on one's actual or perceived race, religion, color, national origin, gender, sexual orientation, disability, or other personal characteristics, and which has the purpose or effect of substantially interfering with a student's educational performance or creating an intimidating, hostile or offensive environment," including "any unwelcome verbal, written or physical conduct which offends, denigrates or belittles an individual because of any of the characteristics described above."[91] Finding a First Amendment violation, the court stated, "The Supreme Court has held time and again, both within and outside of the school context, that the mere fact that someone might take offense at the content of speech is not sufficient justification for prohibiting it."[92]

Similarly, in *Flaherty v. Keystone Oaks School District,* the district court reviewed a school rule punishing "student[] expression that is abusive, offending, harassing, or inappropriate" in a way that "interferes with the educational program of the schools."[93] Concluding that the policy was unconstitutionally overbroad, the court emphasized that the policy did not limit itself "to those circumstances that cause a substantial disruption of school operations as required under *Tinker.*"[94] The court concluded, "the breadth of the Student Handbook policies are overreaching in that they are not linked within the text to speech that substantially disrupts school operations. Absent said language, [the court] can find no way to reasonably construe the Student Handbook policies to avoid this constitutional problem."[95] Taken together, these cases suggest that litigants would do better to raise facial challenges to the text of discipline codes themselves, rather than challenging the discipline imposed on a particular student.

2. THREATS OR SPEECH INVOLVING VIOLENCE

More common, and more difficult to challenge, are discipline codes that punish threats or threatening behavior. Even outside the school context, "true threats," defined as "those statements where the speaker means to communicate a serious expression of intent to commit an act of unlawful violence to a particular individual or group of individuals," enjoy no First Amendment protection at all.[96] Within public schools, language need not even reach this standard of a "true threat" in order to be punishable; courts routinely uphold punishing students for any speech that involves violence.

In *Boim v. Fulton County School District,* the Eleventh Circuit sustained the suspension of a high school student who wrote in her notebook about a "dream" she had in which she brought a gun to class and shot a teacher.[97] The student had passed the notebook to a classmate but had no intent to give it to the teacher. The court held that the suspension did not violate the First Amendment because the speech, although expressive conduct, "was reasonably likely to . . . cause a material and substantial disruption to the maintenance of order and decorum" at her school.[98]

Likewise, in *LaVine v. Blaine School District,* the Ninth Circuit upheld the expulsion of a high school student who had shown his teacher a poem filled with imagery of violent death and suicide and the shooting of fellow students, even though the court acknowledged that the poem constituted protected speech.[99] District courts routinely reach similar results.[100]

3. SCHOOL DRESS CODES

Content-neutral and viewpoint-neutral school dress-code policies and mandatory uniform policies are routinely upheld against First Amendment challenge. Because these policies are content neutral, they are subject only to intermediate scrutiny. In *Jacobs v. Clark County School District,* the Ninth Circuit upheld a high school's mandatory dress code, in which the stated purposes were to increase student achievement, promote safety, and enhance the school environment.[101] In *Bar-Navon v. Brevard County School Board,* the Eleventh Circuit upheld a dress code prohibiting body piercing, which stated its goal as avoiding extreme dress or appearance that could create a school disturbance, or could be hazardous to students.[102]

One district court case describes the relevant standard as follows. School dress-code regulations will be upheld against First Amendment challenge "(1) [if they] further[] an important or substantial government interest; (2) if [they are] unrelated to the suppression of student expression; and (3) if the incidental restrictions on First Amendment activities are no more than is necessary to facilitate that interest."[103]

In many cases, courts will also sustain content-based restrictions on dress in public schools. For example, in *Barr v. Lafon,* the court upheld a prohibition on clothing displaying the Confederate flag, reasoning that school officials were reasonable in concluding that such displays would disrupt schoolwork and school discipline, especially given the documented history of racial tensions in the school.[104] But content-based restrictions on speech are more vulnerable to attack.[105]

Federal and state courts consistently hold that the reach of school authorities may extend beyond the classroom and schoolyard.[106] But school officials may punish students for out-of-school speech or expressive conduct only when there is a sufficient nexus between the speech or expressive conduct and school activities.[107] Absent evidence that the challenged speech interferes with the rights of others or disrupts school activities, courts generally will not permit schools to punish students for such off-campus speech. For example, in *Klein v. Smith,* the federal district court found that disciplining a student who had made a vulgar gesture to a teacher off school premises and after school hours violated the First Amendment because the connection between the student's gesture and school activities was too attenuated.[108]

Discipline of students for off-campus expressive conduct has increased in importance as schools confront new technologies such as social-networking websites, email, blogs, and text messages. But there should be nothing unique about these modes of communication; the fact that messages appear on the Internet or a cell phone should not alter the analysis as to whether the school may punish such off-campus speech.

Accordingly, in *Killion v. Franklin Regional School District,* the district court overturned the suspension of a student who sent an email ridiculing a staff member, because the district failed to show that the email interfered with the rights of others or disrupted school activities.[109] By way of contrast, in *Doninger v. Niehoff,* the Second Circuit upheld the punishment of a student who posted statements on an independent website calling school administrators "douchebags" for canceling a school event and encouraging classmates to contact the superintendent "to piss her off more," because the language related to an ongoing school dispute that was still being resolved, it misled readers into thinking that the school event was canceled, and it led to a deluge of phone calls and emails to the superintendent.[110]

F. EMERGING ISSUE: AUTOMATIC EXCLUSION FOR OUT-OF-SCHOOL ARRESTS

States, school districts, and schools across the country have taken the additional step of imposing suspensions or expulsions when a student is *arrested* for a crime, including when the alleged crime occurred off-campus and after school hours.[111]

Federal and state courts consistently hold that the reach of school authorities may extend beyond the schoolyard.[112] But automatic exclusions based on off-campus arrests arguably violate due process rights in two ways: (1) arrests do not establish that the student actually committed the alleged crime; and (2) even if the student did commit the alleged conduct, the conduct may not interfere with school functions to warrant school punishment.

Mere arrest does not prove that the student actually committed the alleged conduct. A blanket policy mandating suspension or expulsion for any student who has been arrested fails to provide a forum to establish whether the student actually committed the charged conduct, even when it is undisputed that the arrest actually occurred. Cases involving arrests for minor crimes such as shoplifting are particularly appropriate for such an argument, as schools will find it difficult to persuade a court that the continued presence at school of a student who has been arrested for, but is not necessarily guilty of, a minor crime like shoplifting interferes with or disrupts the educational process. Of course, when an arrest involves allegations of serious misconduct such as acts of violence, schools can more easily justify the suspension or expulsion of a student so accused, even if he or she proclaims innocence. The argument that students should not be denied an education based on unproven charges is likely to fail in these circumstances.

Even if the student actually committed the conduct for which he or she was arrested, the punishment may be impermissible because the conduct is wholly unrelated to school functions. Blanket policies that do not examine the substantive nature of the student's act and consequently punish acts that do not relate to campus health, safety, or welfare may be susceptible to challenge.[113] Additionally, suspensions or expulsions for arrests involving constitutionally protected activity such as expressive conduct are vulnerable to attack.[114]

Blanket policies that automatically punish students for off-campus arrests sweep too broadly and may deny due process rights. Advocates should closely examine such rules and consider raising challenges to those that do so.

G. CONCLUSION

Courts exercise great deference toward school officials in meting out suspensions and expulsions to discipline schoolchildren. However, it does not follow that such disciplinary decisions are immune to challenge. This chapter has discussed potential theories to challenge these suspensions and expulsions from school, utilizing procedural due process, substantive due process, void-for-vagueness, and First Amendment protections. The next chapter will discuss the related issue of referring these children to disciplinary alternative schools and programs.

5

Disciplinary Alternative Schools and Programs

As the number of students suspended and expelled from our nation's public schools grows, policymakers, educators, and communities must decide what to do with these children.[1] Arrangements for alternative education, that is, schools and programs serving at-risk students whose needs are not being met in mainstream public schools for various reasons, may contribute to the School-to-Prison Pipeline in two ways.

First, in some jurisdictions, a suspended or expelled student may have no right to education at all or may be deemed to have waived that right.[2] Consequently, children who are suspended or expelled may receive no instruction for the duration of their punishment. In these circumstances, the *denial* of alternative educational opportunities places children at increased risk of falling behind academically, becoming disengaged from the school environment, dropping out, spending time unsupervised and on the street, and becoming involved in the juvenile or criminal justice systems.

Second, when alternative education is provided but the education or environment is substandard, the *provision* of alternative education may keep children in the pipeline and impose similar risks of disengagement and dropout. Ideally, alternative schools and programs should provide the individualized attention and support needed for a child with behavioral issues to succeed. In many cases, however, these schools or programs operate as little more than holding pens for failing youth.

This chapter explores the rights of youth in the context of disciplinary alternative education schools and programs. It explores strategies for securing the right to alternative education for suspended and expelled youth, while at the same time ensuring that the education provided is of high quality. It is only when both of these conditions are met that children are protected from being further drawn into the School-to-Prison Pipeline.

The first section of this chapter introduces the concept of alternative schools and programs, describing the different types that exist and the students who attend them. The second section addresses the problem in jurisdictions where children do not have access to alternative education while they are suspended or expelled; it explores legal strategies to secure the right to continued education for these disciplined students. The third section describes the right to challenge a district's attempt to transfer a child involuntarily to an alternative placement. The fourth section explores the quality of education and related services in these alternative programs and assesses strategies to ensure that alternative schools and programs meet minimum requirements. Finally, the fifth section discusses barriers to returning to mainstream schools upon completion of a term at an alternative school or program.

A. INTRODUCTION TO DISCIPLINARY ALTERNATIVE SCHOOLS AND PROGRAMS

For the purposes of this book, *disciplinary alternative schools* refers to public education placements for at-risk students whose needs are not being met for various reasons and are thus placed in settings separate from the general education classroom.[3] Advocates should be careful to clarify the difference between disciplinary alternative schools and charter schools. Some, but not all, disciplinary alternative schools are charter schools; likewise, some, but not all, charter schools are disciplinary alternative schools. Charter schools are funded by the local school district and are generally exempt from ordinary state regulations and requirements. Disciplinary alternative schools may operate pursuant to a charter, they may operate pursuant to ordinary district rules, or they may be contracted out entirely to a private for-profit provider.[4]

Most disciplinary alternative schools were developed to serve children suspended or expelled from the mainstream school,[5] although not all children who are suspended or expelled are permitted to attend alternative schools. Children may also be placed in these schools and programs for reasons entirely unrelated to school discipline, such as being new to the district, recently released from juvenile detention, at risk of dropping out, or pregnant.[6] In some cases, the student or the student's family chooses the placement in disciplinary alternative education, and in other cases, the transfer is involuntary.[7]

As of 2000–01, there were over ten thousand public alternative schools and programs in the nation.[8] They may operate as programs within a school, schools with separate facilities, charter schools, juvenile detention centers, or community-based schools.[9] Alternative schools may operate out of trailers behind or near the mainstream public school,[10] or they may be nothing more than an in-school suspension or detention room.

The length of stay at an alternative school or program may span a single day to provide instruction during a child's one-day suspension, or it may last for years and through graduation. In one study, nine of the thirty-one responding states indicated that students in alternative education typically remain in the program for between one month and six months; six states reported that students typically stayed for at least one full academic year; and three states indicated that students typically remained in alternative education through graduation.[11]

Estimates on the number of children enrolled in alternative schools/programs vary greatly; one study places the number at 612,900 students, while another places it at well over one million students.[12] In some jurisdictions, up to 18 percent of the student body may be enrolled in an alternative school or program at any given time over the course of any given school year.[13] Urban districts, districts with high minority student enrollment, and districts with high poverty concentrations are more likely to operate these types of alternative schools and programs.[14]

The extent to which students with disabilities are placed in alternative schools also varies greatly. Some districts enroll no children covered by the Individuals with Disabilities Education Act (IDEA) in their alternative schools and programs, whereas others enroll a vastly disproportionate number of such children.[15] In one district in Texas, almost 50 percent of the students enrolled in the disciplinary alternative education program have been identified as disabled.[16]

Students with special needs may be inappropriately placed in alternative settings because they have not been properly evaluated for disabilities. They may be inappropriately placed because they are not receiving the services to which they are entitled in the mainstream school, causing them to act out and misbehave. Or they might be unlawfully placed in alternative settings because that is the only place in the district that offers the specialized services that the student needs. For more discussion on the rights of students with special needs, see chapter 3.[17] Similarly, children of color are frequently overrepresented in alternative school placements, particularly when placement is related to a disciplinary exclusion from the mainstream classroom.[18]

Alternative schools and programs are frequently exempt from statewide education standards and requirements. Some states provide that teachers need not be certified, while others may permit fewer hours of instruction than mainstream schools. The overall lack of accountability and standards has prompted the California Legislative Analyst's Office to warn that schools and districts may use referrals to alternative schools as a way to avoid responsibility for the progress of low-performing students.[19] Some scholars have described a perception of an increasingly common practice of transferring students to alternative schools as a means of removing from regular school students who have discipline problems or are labeled as troublemakers.[20]

Alternative schools are subject to federal accountability requirements under the No Child Left Behind Act, which mandates progress in standardized-test scores for all public schools in a state, including alternative schools. States are not, however, held accountable for students who have been enrolled in a school for less than a full academic school year. Many students who are placed in alternative settings are placed there for less than a full academic year, exempting the state from being accountable for these students' performance.[21] Nonetheless, at least to the extent that the No Child Left Behind Act does mandate accountability, and, in turn, data reporting, it may provide a powerful tool for advocates, because it requires the collection and reporting of information for students.

B. RIGHT TO ALTERNATIVE EDUCATION FOR SUSPENDED AND EXPELLED YOUTH

Under what circumstances does a student who has been suspended or expelled from a mainstream school have a right to continue to receive instructional services? Under what circumstances must the district enroll that student in an alternative school or program? This section explores arguments to establish a right to alternative education.

1. ARGUMENTS UNDER FEDERAL LAW

As described in chapter 1, the Supreme Court in *San Antonio Independent School District v. Rodriguez* held that there is no fundamental right to education under the federal Constitution.[22] As a result, a denial of education for suspended or expelled students violates substantive due process rights only when it fails rational basis scrutiny.[23] Lower courts have found that the denial of alternative education to students who have been suspended or expelled survives this standard.[24]

In the absence of a substantive due process right to alternative education, litigants might explore procedural due process and equal protection theories when a district or state provides alternative education to some, but not all, similarly situated suspended and expelled students.[25] For example, if a district enrolls suspended students in alternative schools on a first-come, first-served basis, regardless of the length of the suspension or the reason for the suspension, one might argue that there is no rational basis for this unequal treatment. Alternatively, there may be states in which some districts provide alternative education, while other districts do not. Similarly, one might argue that a child is entitled to a hearing to determine whether he or she is entitled to this scarce resource.

Children with disabilities, unlike their nondisabled peers, possess a federal statutory right to alternative educational services when they have been suspended or expelled. Under the federal Individuals with Disabilities Education Act, a child identified as having a disability is entitled to a "free and appropriate education," regardless of whether he or she has been disciplined, and thus may not be denied educational services even after suspension or expulsion.[26] For further discussion on the rights of students with special needs, see chapter 3.

2. ARGUMENTS UNDER STATE LAW

In the absence of a federal right to alternative education for nondisabled children, state law may provide such a right, either under statute or under the state constitution.[27] At the time of this writing, the following states had enacted legislation requiring public school districts to provide alternative education to at least some suspended or expelled students: California,[28] Colorado,[29] Delaware,[30] Kentucky,[31] Louisiana,[32] Minnesota,[33] Mississippi,[34] Nebraska,[35] New Jersey,[36] New York,[37] Rhode Island,[38] and Tennessee.[39]

Even where there is no express statutory right to alternative education, if the state constitution provides for a fundamental right to education, a state court may conclude that the denial of instructional services to suspended and expelled pupils violates that state constitutional right. West Virginia, for example, recognizes a fundamental right to education in its state constitution. Seeking to enforce that right, in *Cathe A. v. Doddridge County Board of Education,* a high school student filed a mandamus petition to secure educational services after he had been expelled for one year for bringing a knife to school.[40] The county board of education offered to send a teacher to the boy's house for four hours a week to provide continuing educational services, but only if the child's mother was willing to pay for the service.[41] On review, the state supreme court held that such an arrangement violated the child's state constitutional right to a free public education.[42]

Likewise, New Jersey's state constitution recognizes a fundamental right to education. In *State ex rel. G.S.,* a child who had been adjudicated delinquent and expelled from school for making a bomb threat challenged the state's refusal to provide him with alternative educational services.[43] Finding that the constitution guaranteed a right to free school instruction for all children until they obtain a high school diploma or reach the age of nineteen, the state superior court ordered the state to provide the expelled child with continuing instruction appropriate to his grade level, through an in-school program, in-home instruction program, or other alternative education facility or program.[44]

But courts in other states that recognize a state constitutional right to education have not been willing to mandate alternative educational services for children who have been suspended or expelled. The Massachusetts state constitution provides a right to education, but the state's highest court, in *Doe v. Superintendent of Schools of Worcester,* clarifying its prior opinion in *McDuffy v. Secretary of the Executive Office of Education,*[45] held that this right is not "fundamental."[46] Consequently, school districts in that state may deny a student who has been suspended or expelled alternative educational services so long as the denial is rationally related to a legitimate state interest.[47] Courts in Georgia,[48] North Carolina,[49] and Wyoming[50] have reached similar conclusions, as has an attorney general opinion in Michigan.[51]

Thus, courts have held that federal substantive due process does not guarantee a right to alternative education. Advocates seeking to secure these rights through state courts pursuant to state rights have enjoyed success in some but not all jurisdictions.

C. DUE PROCESS CHALLENGE TO PLACEMENT IN ALTERNATIVE SCHOOL OR PROGRAM

As alternative schools and programs grow in number, students face a real possibility of being sent to such schools and programs with no opportunity for notice or a hearing. Under what circumstances must a district provide procedural protections such as a hearing before sending a student to an alternative school or program? Successful advocates litigating a right to procedural due process protections to challenge these disciplinary transfers have emphasized (1) the differences, if any, in educational quality in these programs and schools and (2) the disciplinary nature of the transfer, to argue that being sent to an alternative disciplinary school implicates not only a property interest in education but also a liberty interest in not being mistakenly or unfairly disciplined for misconduct.

As discussed more fully in chapter 4, the Supreme Court in *Goss v. Lopez* held that a state must provide certain minimal procedural due process protections before suspending a child, because students have a state-created property interest in education and liberty interest in reputation.[52] Districts have sometimes argued, however, that placement in an alternative school or program does not constitute a suspension or an expulsion implicating protected interests and thus that procedural due process is not required.

As far back as 1977, a federal district judge in Pennsylvania reasoned, "Realistically, I think many if not most students would consider a short suspension a less drastic form of punishment than an involuntary transfer, especially if the transferee school was farther from home or had poorer physical or educational facilities."[53] Under this view, transfer of a student to an alternative school should regularly be attended by full-blown due process procedures, despite claims by a school system that attendance in an alternative school is a "privilege."

Contrary to such reasoning, courts frequently hold that due process is not required, or at least that relaxed due process protections apply, when a district intends to transfer a student to an alternative school rather than deny the student access to all educational services altogether. Districts generally win in such claims when the student fails to show that the alternative program is substantially inferior to regular public schools. In those cases, most federal courts suggest that procedural due process protections are not required because a student has no property interest in attending a particular school.[54]

Some courts have gone so far as to hold that the alternative school must be so inferior to the regular school as to amount to an outright denial of all educational services before procedural due process protections rights are triggered. In the Fifth Circuit decision in *Nevares v. San Marcos Consolidated Independent School District,* a fifteen-year-old student accused of throwing rocks at cars was immediately transferred to an alternative school without a hearing, pursuant to a school regulation requiring such transfer anytime there was "reason to believe" that the child had committed an assault.[55]

The lower court had concluded, pursuant to *Goss,* that the school must provide notice and a hearing before the transfer.[56] First, it reasoned that property interests were implicated because "[a]lthough a student still receives an education at" the alternative school, "it is not comparable to that received at" the regular school.[57] The trial court noted that instruction was provided in only four core courses; lectures were limited; and students generally worked independently from textbooks and only had access to teachers when they encountered a problem in the book, raised their hand, and waited for up to twenty minutes.[58] Second, the court recognized the liberty interests implicated as a result of the stigma attached to attending the alternative school.[59] Concluding that the transfer "is a form of punishment which results in an inferior academic experience and can seriously damage the student's reputation, standing, and future prospects," the district court found that some form of procedural due process must be afforded.[60] Notwithstanding these factual findings, on appeal, the Fifth Circuit reversed, summarily concluding, "[Plaintiff] is not being denied access to public education, not even temporarily. He was only to be transferred from one school program to another program with stricter discipline."[61]

Although a difference in the quality of education offered at an alternative school is important, litigants and courts, unlike the district court in *Nevares*, often fail to address whether one's liberty interest in reputation—as opposed to one's property interest in education—has been infringed. As the Supreme Court articulated in *Goss*, procedural due process is required to prevent arbitrary deprivations of not only property interests but also liberty interests:

> Where a person's good name, reputation, honor, or integrity is at stake because of what the government is doing to him, the minimal requirements of the Clause must be satisfied. . . . If [charges of misconduct against students are] sustained and recorded, those charges could seriously damage the students' standing with their fellow pupils and their teachers as well as interfere with later opportunities for higher education and employment. It is apparent that the claimed right of the State to determine unilaterally and without process whether that misconduct has occurred immediately collides with the requirements of the Constitution.[62]

Advocates should draw attention to the liberty prong of the *Goss* analysis to argue that a student's reputation interest in not being punished for alleged but unproven misconduct remains the same regardless of whether the punishment imposed consists of a suspension or a transfer to a disciplinary alternative program. It is the injury to reputation resulting from being disciplined for alleged misconduct, not the form of the discipline imposed (or the educational impact of that transfer), which triggers the liberty prong of the procedural due process analysis.

Such an argument recently swayed a state court in a case brought by the Juvenile Law Center and Education Law Center of Pennsylvania. In *D.C. v. School District of Philadelphia,* the Pennsylvania Commonwealth Court invalidated, on procedural due process grounds, a law that automatically placed juveniles released from delinquency placement or criminal conviction in alternative schools rather than mainstream schools.[63] Plaintiffs argued that due process protections were necessary under the "stigma plus" test announced in the U.S. Supreme Court case *Paul v. Davis.*[64] In *Paul v. Davis,* involving a challenge to a government flyer accusing the respondent of being a shoplifter, the Supreme Court held that procedural due process protections are triggered when the state harms the reputation of an individual, stigmatizing him or her, *plus* deprives him or her of a state-created property or liberty interest.[65]

In *D.C.,* plaintiffs argued that the placement in alternative schools branded them as "disruptive and not fit to attend regular classes, regardless of whether they actually are."[66] Weighing both sides, the appeals court concluded that the transfer was indeed disciplinary in nature, thus triggering due process rights; it based this determination on the fact that the relevant statutes described the transfers as applying to "disruptive" students and on the district's defense of its position—specifically, that the transfers were necessary to maintain order in regular classrooms.[67] In light of a total absence of opportunity for students to challenge these transfers, the court concluded that the automatic transfers of such students violated due process.[68]

These cases suggest that advocates are more likely to secure procedural due process protections to challenge an involuntary transfer to an alternative school when they can demonstrate that the conditions of the alternative school are significantly inferior to the conditions at the mainstream school and/or when they persuade the court that the transfer sufficiently compromises the student's liberty interest in reputation, not merely his or her property interest in education, to trigger procedural due process protections. Additionally, advocates should note that a decision to change the placement of the child with disabilities, including a transfer from a mainstream school to an alternative school, may only be made by the child's individualized education plan (IEP) team, including the child's parents. For further discussion of the rights of students with special needs, see chapter 3. Similarly, where districts inappropriately funnel children of color into alternative schools, advocates should explore possible discrimination claims. Such challenges are discussed more fully in chapter 2.

D. QUALITY OF EDUCATION IN ALTERNATIVE
SCHOOLS AND PROGRAMS

Conditions and standards in alternative education programs vary greatly. Alternative schools in general were created to serve the particular needs of at-risk youth. Education policymakers and researchers reasoned that these youth would benefit from alternative settings providing small classes, one-on-one interaction with teachers, a student-centered curriculum, and a supportive and personalized school environment.[69] Sadly, though, these very schools and programs targeting at-risk youth frequently offer fewer services and less opportunity to learn than their mainstream counterparts do: they may provide minimal classroom instruction, offer little to no support services, offer no chance to earn a regular high school diploma, and, in some cases, even lack textbooks and teachers. This section discusses potential challenges to conditions in alternative education schools and programs, including their educational adequacy.

In a survey of state departments of education, fourteen of the thirty-four responding states reported that they did not provide physical education, health, art, or music in their alternative schools and programs. Five states indicated that a student who successfully graduates typically receives a GED.[70] In another survey, 9 percent of a sample of public school districts reported that their alternative schools and programs did not provide a curriculum that would lead to a regular high school diploma;[71] 13 percent of districts did not offer academic counseling, 21 percent did not offer career counseling, and 21 percent did not offer crisis or behavioral intervention at their alternative schools.[72]

As described in the preceding section, the federal Constitution does not provide a right to alternative education, much less a right to an adequate alternative education. Although the federal No Child Left Behind Act imposes minimum education standards on all public schools, in the form of standardized-test results, attendance, and graduation rates, states are frequently exempt from accountability for students in alternative schools and programs.[73] State law varies in the extent to which it imposes minimum standards for alternative schools and programs. In jurisdictions that guarantee a fundamental state constitutional right to alternative education, advocates should argue that this right guarantees a minimally adequate education in those schools and programs.

Another avenue for improving the quality of disciplinary alternative schools may be provided by state statute. One-third of all states have no legislative standards for the educational curricula in alternative schools.[74] And several states have created explicit statutory exceptions to state education standards for these settings. In Georgia, which does not guarantee a fundamental right to alternative education, alternative schools for suspended and expelled students may obtain waivers from state educational code requirements, including the minimum hours of instruction time provided and the awarding of course credit in a standard manner.[75] Arkansas exempts alternative schools from state teacher-certification requirements.[76] Ohio permits districts to create and operate "deregulated" alternative schools.[77]

Other states, by contrast, have attempted legislatively to impose standards and accountability on their alternative schools. Twenty-eight states legislatively mandate that alternative schools and programs comply with core-curriculum content standards or standards adopted by the state.[78] Tennessee requires districts to track the operation and performance of alternative schools using academic indicators.[79] Florida requires school report cards for alternative schools.[80] North Carolina requires its state board of education to develop and adopt minimum standards for alternative learning programs.[81] Maryland requires alternative schools to provide certain core curricula to expelled students.[82]

The following cases highlight issues that advocates for quality alternative education might raise.

1. CASE STUDY: *M.H. V. ATLANTA INDEPENDENT SCHOOL DISTRICT*

In March 2008, the American Civil Liberties Union filed a class action suit in *M.H. v. Atlanta Independent School District* against a public school district and a for-profit corporation contracted to administer the district's alternative school, Community Education Partners (CEP).[83]

Plaintiffs alleged, *inter alia,* violations of students' state constitutional and statutory right to an adequate public education. The state constitution in Georgia guarantees children a right to an "adequate public education." Pursuant to state statute, an adequate public education must include a safe learning environment, a sufficient number of teachers and support staff, appropriate classroom instruction and resources, appropriate support services, and basic record-keeping. State statute requires that the instruction provided in these programs "shall enable students to return to a general or career education program as quickly as possible."

To support plaintiffs' claims that these rights were violated, the complaint described the lack of qualified teachers at that school, the minimal provision of classroom instruction, the prohibition against taking textbooks home, a no-homework policy, and the lack of a cafeteria, gym, or library. It also cited the facts that two-thirds of the student body failed to achieve proficiency in reading and that over 90 percent failed to achieve proficiency in math, according to state standardized tests.

In addition to the claim of inadequate public education, the case challenged the district's failure to provide adequate procedural due process rights to students to challenge their placement in the alternative school. It also challenged the violation of Fourth Amendment rights at the school, where in order to enter the building every day, students were required to take off their shoes, to open their mouths and show their tongues, and even to "snap" their bras to demonstrate that they were not hiding contraband.

The case was removed to federal court, and in March 2009, the district court denied both defendants' motions to dismiss.[84] The parties entered into mediation, and the school district decided to decline to renew its contract with Community Education Partners, effective June 30, 2009.[85] After this significant victory, plaintiffs agreed to dismiss Community Education Partners from its suit but to continue to negotiate with the school district for minimum standards for the administration of its alternative school program.

2. CASE STUDY: *C.S.C. V. KNOX COUNTY BOARD OF EDUCATION*

Another class action case, filed by the legal clinic at the University of Tennessee Law School, seeking to enforce a state statutory right to an adequate alternative education, however, met resistance in state court. In *C.S.C. v. Knox County Board of Education,* students who had been subject to a long-term suspension and placed in an alternative school sought to enforce state statutes and regulations requiring, "Alternative schools shall be operated pursuant to rules of the state board of education pertaining to them, and instruction shall proceed *as nearly as practicable* in accordance with the instructional programs at the student's home school."[86]

The alternative school at issue used a computer program to provide subject-matter instruction. The program provided for "facilitators"—licensed and certified teachers—to remain on-site to assist the students in using the computer program. Students attended school in the evenings, three hours a night, four nights a week, and all class time was spent with the computer program.[87] Despite these facts, the lower court rejected plaintiffs' claim, and the Tennessee Court of Appeals affirmed, suggesting that educational and instructional decisions by school boards should be overturned only if arbitrary or unreasonable.[88]

In a similar case, dating from 1979, *Mrs. A.J. v. Special School District No. 1*, the federal district court concluded that the provision of supervised homework during a fifteen-day suspension satisfied the state statutory requirement that school districts provide alternative educational programs to suspended students.[89] The "program" challenged in that case provided the suspended student every day with homework assigned by her regular classroom teacher, which was collected near the end of the suspension and returned to her teacher for grading.[90]

These cases suggest a disturbing reluctance among courts to enforce the educational rights of students sent to alternative schools. But as a greater and greater percentage of schoolchildren are being educated in these schools, and as more states enact legislation imposing minimum standards for them, judicial receptiveness to these claims may improve.

Another common issue arises when alternative schools violate other rights on the ground that they are alternative schools. For example, alternative schools may employ unlawful search-and-seizure policies or deny procedural due process rights prior to suspending or expelling children from the school. Advocates should challenge such violations where they occur. Although children may not possess an affirmative right to attend school, it does not follow that alternative schools may operate free from traditional constitutional restrictions such as the Fourth Amendment or procedural due process.

Another deficiency that may be prevalent in alternative schools is the failure to provide adequate special education services or English language learner (ELL) instruction. As discussed in chapter 3, the federal Individuals with Disabilities Education Act and Section 504 of the Rehabilitation Act require states to provide a free and appropriate public education to students with a disability, regardless of whether they have been suspended or expelled and, by extension, regardless of whether they are placed in an alternative school. Nonetheless, five of twenty-eight state departments of education responding to a survey reported that special education services are likely to be suspended until a student returns to his or her regular school; three states reported that staff at alternative programs are not informed of a child's special education status.[91] And as discussed in chapter 2, the federal Equal Educational Opportunity Act (EEOA) provides affirmative educational rights for ELL students and does not carve out an exception for those students who are placed in disciplinary alternative schools. Advocates who suspect that disciplinary alternative schools serving these populations are failing to provide the federally mandated services to which they are entitled should consider raising challenges pursuant to these federal statutes.

E. RIGHT TO RETURN TO MAINSTREAM SCHOOL

A final concern regarding disciplinary alternative placements involves students' right to return to their regular public school upon completion of the disciplinary term. Most students sent to alternative schools are not sent permanently but rather for a predetermined period, whether for five days or even a full academic year. According to a survey of a sample of school districts, 74 percent of districts permit all alternative students to return to mainstream schools, while 25 percent of districts allow some, but not all, students to return;[92] 1 percent stated that they never permit alternative students to return to mainstream schools.[93]

Even where students are legally entitled to return to their mainstream schools, barriers may exist. Some districts may fail to inform students that they have a right to return. Anecdotal reports indicate that an alternative school in Houston (managed by the private company Community Education Partners) sent letters to all parents informing them that their child would automatically be reenrolled in the alternative school for the following year. Such conduct arguably violates due process rights in failing to provide parents with notice of their right to return the child to a regular school after the term of suspension is complete.

Students may encounter barriers where districts refuse to credit students for coursework completed while at the alternative school. Such refusals may violate state statute and regulations. Regulations from the Georgia Department of Education expressly require that students in alternative schools and programs earn course credits in the same manner as in other schools.[94] Similarly, Maryland regulations require public school districts to treat course credits earned in an alternative education program as credit earned in a mainstream school.[95]

The transition from an alternative school back to a student's base school can be fraught with difficulties, including in course selection and credit, behavior management, and resocialization. Some states require school systems to develop reentry plans for returning students.[96] Advocates should continue to collect facts identifying the extent to which barriers to reentry to mainstream schools exist in their jurisdictions and develop legal theories based on constitutional or statutory law to eliminate them.

F. CONCLUSION

When advocates seek access for students to alternative education in order to challenge the School-to-Prison Pipeline, they should ensure that they include safeguards against the kinds of substandard schools that actually exacerbate the pipeline. Alternative schools were developed with the goal of providing specialized attention and services to at-risk youth; advocates need to make sure that this goal is fulfilled, rather than these schools' providing a dumping ground for failing children.

It is also worth repeating that charter schools and public alternative schools are equally subject to federal disabilities law as ordinary mainstream public schools; the federal rights of special education in these schools are in no way diminished.[97] As discussed in chapter 3, alternative educational programs frequently are incapable of meeting the individualized special education related needs of students with disabilities.

6

Criminalizing School Misconduct

One of the more direct manifestations of the School-to-Prison Pipeline is the policing of K–12 public schools. Schools have begun using law enforcement tactics routinely, including random sweeps, searches of students, drug tests, and interrogations. The National Center for Education Statistics reports that 61 percent of public high schools use random dog sniffs to check for drugs, and almost one-third use at least one other type of random sweep for contraband; 13 percent drug test athletes, and 8 percent drug test students for nonathletic extracurricular activities. More than one in ten public school students aged twelve to eighteen pass through metal detectors at school, and more than half are subject to locker checks.[1] Evidence seized in the course of school searches and statements made during school interrogations may be used against students in court proceedings. Increasingly, widespread zero-tolerance policies, described more fully in chapter 4, frequently mandate police referrals for disciplinary infractions. And school officials and police are sharing and exchanging information about children in new and sometimes questionable ways.[2]

As a result, the number of children arrested or referred to court for school discipline has grown in recent years.[3] In South Carolina, the single most common offense resulting in a juvenile court referral during the 2007–08 year was "disturbing schools."[4] In Florida, during the same time period, 15 percent of all delinquency referrals stemmed from school-related conduct, with 40 percent involving "disorderly conduct" or "misdemeanor assault and battery."[5] In the past several years, there have been several high-profile incidents in which children were arrested at school for questionable reasons.[6] Even juvenile-court personnel have expressed concern that school officials may be relying on the juvenile justice system inappropriately to handle minor school misconduct. For example, the National Council of Juvenile and Family Court Judges has urged collaboration between the justice system and school officials to "[c]ommit to keeping school misbehavior and truancy out of the formal juvenile delinquency court."[7]

Another factor exacerbating the increased criminalization of school misconduct involves the deployment of full-time police officers to patrol K–12 school hallways.[8] Frequently referred to as school resource officers, or SROs, these agents are often sworn police officers employed by the local police department and assigned to patrol public school hallways full-time.[9] In larger jurisdictions, such as Los Angeles and Houston, these officers may be employed directly by the school district. In 2004, 60 percent of high school teachers reported armed police stationed on school grounds.[10]

As with other aspects of the School-to-Prison Pipeline, children of color and students with disabilities are disproportionately impacted by these trends.[11] For example, in Florida, Black youth, who represent only 22 percent of the overall juvenile population, account for 47 percent of all school-based delinquency referrals; youth with special needs account for 23 percent of all school-based referrals.[12] Another study found that in one jurisdiction, African American and Hispanic students account for 24 percent of the student body but 63 percent of school-based arrests; it further found that students of color are more likely to be arrested at school than white students committing the very same infractions.[13]

Improper school-based arrests and referrals to law enforcement have a devastating impact on children. Studies show that being arrested has detrimental psychological effects on the child: it nearly doubles the odds of dropping out of school and, if coupled with a court appearance, nearly quadruples the odds of dropout; lowers standardized-test scores; reduces future employment prospects; and increases the likelihood of future interaction with the criminal justice system.[14] These arrests and referrals also have a negative impact on the larger community. Classmates who witness a child being arrested for a minor infraction may develop negative views or distrust of law enforcement. Juvenile-court dockets and detention centers become crowded with cases that could be handled more efficiently and more effectively by school principals. And the community pays the costs associated with an increase in dropouts, crime, unemployment, and, in extreme cases, the incarceration of children.

This chapter explores the potential for raising affirmative challenges to police practices in schools.[15] Civil litigants considering such challenges, however, should keep several issues in mind. First, although this chapter focuses primarily on federal law, litigants should always explore whether state law is more protective. For example, some jurisdictions provide additional protections to students against searches or questioning pursuant to the state constitution or state statute.[16] Second, litigants must consider the various obstacles to filing civil rights lawsuits, especially in federal court, which include issues of standing—particularly for injunctive relief—and issues of sovereign, absolute, and qualified immunity and federal court abstention.[17] For example, litigants who have been adjudicated delinquent or found guilty and who then wish to challenge civilly the police tactics to which they were subjected may be precluded from doing so unless their delinquency adjudications or convictions have been overturned.[18]

With those caveats in mind, the first section of this chapter explores the scope of students' rights when school officials, for example, principals and teachers, implement policelike searches and seizures and question students about conduct that would expose them to criminal liability. The second section proposes approaches for holding law enforcement officers, including school resource officers, accountable for their conduct in public schools. The third section discusses affirmative challenges to school-specific statutes and ordinances frequently used to criminalize school misconduct.

A. CHALLENGING SEARCHES AND QUESTIONING BY SCHOOL OFFICIALS

In prior generations, school officials were given broad leeway to investigate and punish student misconduct, largely on the theory that school officials retained a tutelary or even parental responsibility over their charges.[19] Under this view, a teacher might look through a student's desk for a cheat sheet during an exam or question a student about missing lunch money; such conduct would be characterized as part of the disciplinary education of the child, necessary to impart the civic responsibility and morals necessary to function in society.[20] But as described in this chapter's introduction, school officials are increasingly referring children to law enforcement for school-based misconduct. Given the increasing potential for subjecting students to criminal liability, limitations on the authority of school officials to search or question students has become increasingly important.[21] This section explores the circumstances under which school officials, for example, principals and teachers, may conduct such searches or questionings. The discussion is limited to conduct by school officials acting alone, rather than in conjunction with or at the behest of law enforcement, which is discussed in the subsequent section.

1. SEARCHES BY SCHOOL OFFICIALS

In *New Jersey v. T.L.O.,* the Supreme Court squarely held that the Fourth Amendment right applies to students who are searched by school officials in K–12 public schools.[22] However, it concluded that given the "special needs" of schools to maintain order and discipline, ordinary standards would be relaxed in this context; consequently, school administrators need only *reasonable suspicion,* rather than probable cause, to search students.[23]

Pursuant to this relaxed standard, a school official may permissibly search a student when (1) there are "reasonable grounds for suspecting that the search will turn up evidence that the student has violated or is violating either the law or the rules of the school" and (2) the scope of the search is reasonable, that is, the "measures adopted are reasonably related to the objectives of the search and not excessively intrusive in light of the age and sex of the student and the nature of the infraction."[24] This holding has generated a large body of case law regarding the circumstances under which different types of searches will be sustained.

Searches of a student's person or belongings such as backpacks or purses require reasonable suspicion of a violation of a crime or school rules, and such searches probably also require individualized suspicion. *T.L.O.* itself involved a challenge to the search of a student's purse, a search that was upheld because the principal had reasonable suspicion to look for cigarettes in the student's purse—a violation of school rules but not criminal law—based on a report by a teacher that the student had been smoking in the lavatory.[25] Because individualized suspicion existed in that case, the Supreme Court did not have occasion to determine whether individualized suspicion would always be required to justify a school search.[26] Lower courts have since held that individualized suspicion ordinarily will be required.[27] They have sustained searches lacking individualized suspicion, however, when there was a particularly serious and immediate threat present at the school. In *Thompson v. Carthage School District,* the Eighth Circuit upheld a generalized search of all male students in grades six through twelve—involving taking off shoes and socks, emptying pockets, and being subjected to pat-downs and metal detectors—when the bus driver had reported fresh cuts on seats of the bus and students had informed the principal that there was a gun at school that morning.[28]

Even absent a serious or immediate threat present at the school, courts are more likely to sustain less intrusive searches of students, including searches of lockers or other school property, metal-detector searches, or the use of drug-sniffing dogs. As for searches of lockers, desks, or other school property, the *T.L.O.* Court declined to determine whether students retain a reasonable expectation of privacy in this context.[29] But lower courts examining this issue have suggested that students have a lesser expectation of privacy in spaces belonging to the school.[30] Some courts have gone so far as to hold that students possess no privacy right in such school property at all and that a locker or desk search does not constitute a "search" within the meaning of the Fourth Amendment because students lack a reasonable expectation of privacy in their lockers, and school officials need no suspicion to conduct such a search.[31] Other courts, however, acknowledge the reality that students view and treat their lockers as private spaces, and accordingly these courts are willing to scrutinize searches of these spaces under a reasonableness standard.[32] In any case, even in jurisdictions where students are held to have no privacy interest in lockers, it does not follow that items stored *inside* lockers, such as book bags and coats, may automatically be searched just because the locker itself is subject to search. At least one court has held that students do not lose their expectation of privacy in a coat or book bag merely because the student places these objects in his or her locker.[33]

As with locker searches or searches of other school property, the Supreme Court has not had occasion to determine the scope of students' rights with respect to metal-detector searches or the use of drug-sniffing dogs in schools. Lower courts, however, have held that the use of metal detectors constitutes a minimally intrusive administrative search requiring no reasonable or individualized suspicion.[34] Schools may subject all students, or a random sample of students, to step through or be wanded by a metal detector as a condition of entering the campus.[35] Where an individual student is singled out to be subjected to a metal detector for law enforcement purposes, however, courts may require reasonable suspicion.[36] As for the use of drug-sniffing dogs, lower courts have concluded that direct dog-sniffs of students' bodies require individualized suspicion,[37] but dog-sniffs of public spaces such as hallways and locker exteriors do not.[38]

Far more intrusive strip searches in public schools, by contrast, are less likely to be upheld. In the recent case *Safford Unified School District No. 1 v. Redding*, litigated by the ACLU Drug Law Policy Reform Project, the Supreme Court invalidated the strip search of a thirteen-year-old student who was accused by a classmate of possessing prescription-strength ibuprofen pills, which were prohibited under the district's zero-tolerance policy.[39] The Court held that the search of the girl's backpack and outer clothing was justified under the reasonable suspicion standard, but requiring her to pull out her underwear was not justified because there was no reason to believe that the alleged painkillers posed a danger to students; "the content of the suspicion failed to match the degree of intrusion."[40] Nor was there sufficient reason to suspect that the girl was hiding the alleged contraband in her underwear, because there was "no evidence in the record of any general practice among students [at the school] of hiding that sort of thing in underwear.[41] In addition to the seriousness of the suspected violation, lower courts prior to *Safford* also considered, in weighing the constitutionality of a strip search, the extent to which school officials take measures to corroborate the suspicion of the student prior to the search[42] and the school's efforts to limit the invasiveness of the search.[43] State case law and statutes may provide further protections against student strip searches. At least seven states have legislated blanket prohibitions on school strip searches: California, Iowa, New Jersey, Oklahoma, South Carolina, Washington, and Wisconsin.[44]

A final area of school searches that has generated significant litigation involves the drug testing of students. The Supreme Court has twice addressed the permissibility of drug tests where the test was limited to students participating in extracurricular activities and both times concluded that individualized suspicion was not required. In *Vernonia School District 47J v. Acton,* the Court upheld a school policy requiring drug testing of all student athletes.[45] The Court relied on the policy's "distinctly *non*punitive" purpose and the fact that test results were "not turned over to law enforcement authorities or used for any internal disciplinary function," distinguishing the drug tests from searches designed to produce evidence for court proceedings.[46] Seven years later, in *Board of Education of Independent School District No. 92 of Pottawatomie County v. Earls,* the Court upheld a school policy of drug testing all middle- and high-school students participating in competitive extracurricular activities.[47] Again, the Court reasoned that the policy did not lead to any law enforcement consequences.[48] Lower courts generally have declined to extend *Acton* and *Earls* beyond the context of drug testing to determine eligibility for competitive extracurricular activities.[49] One notable exception is random drug testing of student drivers, which at least one court has upheld.[50]

This subsection has examined the manner in which school officials may conduct searches and seizures that would violate the Fourth Amendment if conducted outside the school context. The next subsection examines the contours of a student's right to refuse questioning by school officials.

School administrators question students about alleged misconduct and seek admissions of wrongdoing as a matter of course. On the one hand, such questioning may be necessary to ensure safety and avert a dangerous situation in the school; in addition, it serves pedagogical interests in teaching students to accept responsibility for wrongdoing. On the other hand, individuals, including students, have a constitutional right to be free from being forced to make self-incriminating statements.[51]

A case filed by the ACLU Racial Justice Program illustrates the manner in which some districts have conducted student questioning. According to the complaint's allegations, school principals in a rural South Dakota school district routinely forced students to confess to misconduct for the express purpose of prosecuting them in juvenile courts.[52] The principals required students to write out statements on forms entitled "Affidavit" or "Affidavit in Support of Criminal Prosecution" and sign the forms, which were then notarized and forwarded to law enforcement officials.[53] The parties settled the case pursuant to a consent decree, under which the school district agreed (1) to refrain from requiring any student to make any statement, written or otherwise, that may be used against the student in court and (2) to provide *Miranda* warnings to students before questioning them in connection with any incident that would be reported to law enforcement.[54]

Questioning by school officials generally does not amount to a custodial interrogation triggering *Miranda* rights.[55] But even outside the context of custodial interrogations, the Fifth Amendment prohibits government officials from compelling an individual to make self-incriminating statements. This right does not depend on the forum of the questioning or even the identity of the government actor; unlike *Miranda* rights, the right against self-incrimination applies to informal questioning in the principal's office as well as more formal questioning during a disciplinary hearing.[56]

Rather, availability of the Fifth Amendment right against self-incrimination depends on whether the statement exposes the individual to criminal liability or a delinquency petition.[57] Exposure to school discipline is not sufficient. Furthermore, the right is not violated unless or until the statement is actually used against the student in a delinquency or criminal proceeding.[58] Thus, although a student may *assert* the Fifth Amendment right during questioning by school officials to refuse to make statements that would expose the student to a delinquency petition, he or she may not bring an affirmative suit to challenge violation of the right until the statement has actually been used.

As a corollary to the rule prohibiting compelled self-incriminating statements, the government may not punish an individual for asserting the right and refusing to make such statements.[59] In most cases, though, students are unaware of their Fifth Amendment right and fail to assert it during questioning by school officials.

In other contexts, a failure to assert the right constitutes a waiver of the right.[60] But, for children, a majority of jurisdictions employ a "totality of circumstances" test to ascertain whether a juvenile's statement was voluntary rather than compelled in the absence of an assertion of the privilege.[61] The test "includes evaluation of the juvenile's age, experience, education, background, and intelligence, and into whether he has the capacity to understand the warnings given [to] him, the nature of his Fifth Amendment rights, and the consequences of waiving those rights."[62] Courts also evaluate the context of the questioning, including the relationship between the child and the questioner, when determining the voluntariness of a juvenile's statement.[63]

A minority of more protective jurisdictions instead apply the "interested adult rule." This rule requires that any juvenile being questioned must have the "opportunity to consult with, and have present at interrogation, an adult who is informed of the juvenile's rights and is interested in the juvenile's welfare."[64] Even in jurisdictions that have not adopted, or that have even explicitly rejected, such a per se rule, courts still consider the absence of an interested adult as an important factor in weighing the "totality of the circumstances" and conclude that the juvenile's statement was coerced.[65]

With respect to searches and questioning, the role of school officials has changed significantly in the past twenty years. *T.L.O.* was decided in an era quite different from today, when communities relied on school officials to impart values of discipline and civility on their children. Since then, however, school officials have been delegating this duty to law enforcement and the juvenile and criminal justice systems. As acknowledged by the National Council of Juvenile and Family Court Judges, schools are increasingly relying on these outside forces to handle discipline, resulting in a growth in the number of children arrested at school and processed through court for schoolyard misbehavior.[66] The very fact that school officials are relying on the juvenile and criminal justice systems in new and unprecedented ways supports the argument that courts should revisit the dilution of constitutional standards in schools.[67]

B. CHALLENGING THE CONDUCT OF POLICE IN SCHOOLS

It is now commonplace for students to be searched or questioned not only by school administrators but also by police officers acting alone or in conjunction with school officials. As police officers and school-based arrests become more prevalent on K–12 public school grounds, advocates and courts alike should carefully consider the appropriate role and functions of these officers and ensure that children's rights are appropriately protected.

Three cases filed by the ACLU of Northern California illustrate the problems that may arise when police are deployed in public schools. In the Union City School District, school officials worked with police officials to target sixty minority students to be searched, interrogated, and photographed as part of a "gang intervention" effort.[68] In Fairfield, a school resource officer (SRO) and police officers required groups of Latino students to be lined up and photographed for a gang database.[69] In Bishop, a police officer permanently stationed at the school physically threatened and abused students, causing one to lose consciousness.[70]

Should the authority of police officers to search or question individuals differ when such searches or questioning involves a student at a public school? What if they are conducted in conjunction with, or even at the behest of, school officials? Do these standards differ when the police officer is an SRO who works full-time at the school rather than an ordinary police officer who is merely summoned by school officials? Absent Supreme Court guidance on these issues,[71] lower courts have differed significantly in how to resolve them. This section describes some of the leading lower court cases in the area and also explores the potential for new theories to limit the authority of police to search and question students in public schools.

With respect to the questioning of students, at least some cases have held that questioning conducted by school resource officers or police officers alone constitute custodial interrogations triggering *Miranda* rights.[72] Cases diverge, however, when the questioning is conducted by law enforcement *in conjunction* with school officials; some courts consider the extent to which the police officer initiated or participated in the questioning, and others do not.[73]

With respect to searches and seizures of students, when law enforcement conducts searches at the request of or in conjunction with school officials, courts will usually apply the more relaxed *T.L.O.* standard, although they will consider the extent to which an officer initiated or participated in a search of a student to determine whether the more lenient *T.L.O.* standard applies.[74] In

Shade v. City of Farmington, for example, the Eighth Circuit rejected a Fourth Amendment challenge to a search conducted by a teacher and two police officers.[75] Concluding that the *T.L.O.* standard applied, the court emphasized that the teacher and the principal, not the officers, initiated the search and had requested the assistance of law enforcement because they "reasonably believed that a police officer was more capable and better trained to search for a weapon in a student's possession."[76]

What about searches and seizures initiated by and/or conducted by law enforcement officers acting alone, outside the presence of school officials? In these cases, unlike in the cases analyzing the permissibility of the questioning of a student, courts tend to distinguish between outside law enforcement and assigned school resource officers or school liaison officers. With respect to outside police officers, courts are generally clear that officers who enter a public school pursuant to an independent criminal investigation may not circumvent traditional standards solely because the search or seizure occurs at a school; likewise, they cannot circumvent traditional probable cause standards by asking school officials to conduct the search for them or with them.[77] By contrast, courts diverge in their treatment of searches initiated by or conducted by school resource officers and school liaison officers acting alone. Some treat such officers as school officials entitled to the relaxed *T.L.O.* standard, while others treat them identically to ordinary police and subject to probable cause requirements.[78] Advocates should carefully evaluate the facts of each case to determine whether a claim of circumvention can be made.

But treating school resource officers the same as school officials does not comport with the reality that these officers possess and indeed exercise the power to arrest children with great frequency. The fact that a police officer's beat is a school hallway rather than a street corner should not alter the rules to which the officer will be subject, nor should it alter the rights of individuals who are subject to the arrest authority of that officer. Unlike school officials, the primary duty of SROs is not to instill civic values and morality in children through education but rather to provide law enforcement services. As such, courts should be more willing to acknowledge that SROs are, in fact, law enforcement officers and should not permit police to operate with impunity just because they happen to be deployed in a public school.

One approach to push the case law in this direction would be to rely on the Supreme Court case in *Ferguson v. City of Charleston.* In that case, the Court suggested that police involvement in any program whose immediate goal is detection of criminal wrongdoing defeats a "special needs" claim to a relaxed constitutional standard.[79] *Ferguson* involved a hospital program requiring pregnant women to be tested for cocaine use.[80] Hospital staff worked in conjunction with the police to develop the program, and positive test results led to arrest.[81]

The defendants argued that relaxed Fourth Amendment standards applied pursuant to the special needs doctrine, because the ultimate goal of the program was to provide treatment to the women. Rejecting that argument, the Court noted the "immediate objective of the searches was to generate evidence *for law enforcement purposes.*"[82] The Court found this distinction crucial in concluding that the program violated the Fourth Amendment, stating that a contrary conclusion would ensure that "virtually any nonconsensual suspicionless search could be immunized under the special needs doctrine by defining the search solely in terms of its ultimate, rather than immediate, purpose."[83] Litigators should argue that this rationale applies equally in the context of law enforcement programs in schools and that such programs should not be entitled to relaxed standards.

Regardless of the standard applied, courts are more inclined to find that a search or seizure conducted by an SRO is unreasonable in violation of the Fourth Amendment when the officer exercises authority unique to law enforcement, for example, handcuffing a student or arresting the student for resisting a police officer, to enforce school discipline rather than criminal law.[84]

One relatively unexplored avenue for holding SROs accountable to the higher Fourth Amendment standards is to litigate provisions of the documents creating, assigning, or hiring SROs.[85] When these documents limit the SRO's duties to law enforcement, award no disciplinary authority, or ensure that officers receive a certain type of training or credential,[86] third-party beneficiary or other theories should be explored to enforce the terms of the document. Another strategy to improve accountability in SRO programs is to represent the school officials. The New York Civil Liberties Union filed a lawsuit seeking to limit the authority of SROs not on behalf of students but rather on behalf of teachers.[87] But at least one state appellate court has held that, in a conflict between SROs and school officials, the officer's authority outweighs the superintendent's; the case was subsequently reversed on other grounds.[88]

C. AFFIRMATIVE CHALLENGES TO SCHOOL-SPECIFIC CRIMES

As described in this chapter's introduction, an increasing number of students are arrested and referred to court for minor schoolyard misbehavior.[89] In addition to using ordinary criminal laws to arrest and refer children to the courts, states have legislated laws defining crimes specific to the school context.[90] Students are being adjudicated delinquent for various school-specific offenses, most commonly disrupting classes, talking back to teachers, and loitering or trespassing on school grounds. This section explores affirmative challenges to school-specific criminal statutes and ordinances.[91] Two primary theories to be explored are vagueness and free speech.[92]

Vagueness: A school-specific criminal statute will be void for vagueness, in violation of due process, if it fails to provide sufficient specificity as to what kind of conduct is prohibited. As discussed in chapter 4 exploring challenges to school suspensions and expulsions on this theory, the Constitution protects individuals from prosecution under a vague rule for two reasons. "First, it may fail to provide the kind of notice that will enable ordinary people to understand what conduct it prohibits; second, it may authorize and even encourage arbitrary and discriminatory enforcement."[93]

A litigant raising a vagueness claim must show, at a minimum, that the law was impermissibly vague as applied to him- or herself. The Supreme Court has made clear that

> one who has received fair warning of the criminality of his own conduct from the statute in question is [not] entitled to attack it because the language would not give similar fair warning with respect to other conduct. . . . One to whose conduct a statute clearly applies may not successfully challenge it for vagueness.[94]

When no First Amendment concerns are implicated by the statute, a *facial* challenge to the statute—in contrast to an *as-applied* challenge—requires a showing that the law is impermissibly vague in *all applications*.[95] The subsections that follow examine the extent to which statutes and ordinances that prohibit "being disruptive," "talking back," "loitering," "trespassing," or "threatening" provide sufficient notice to schoolchildren as to what kind of conduct will subject them to arrest and criminal prosecution and discuss whether such statutes and ordinances might be vulnerable to a vagueness challenge.

Free speech: A school-specific criminal statute may also be affirmatively challenged when it penalizes activity protected by the First Amendment. Unique to the First Amendment context, a litigant need not show that the statute was impermissibly applied to him- or herself. The overbreadth doctrine, "which is a departure from traditional rules of standing, permits a defendant to make a facial challenge to an overly broad statute restricting speech, even if he himself has engaged in speech that could be regulated under a more narrowly drawn statute."[96] Thus, "the overbreadth doctrine . . .

enables [a litigant] to benefit from the statute's unlawful application *to someone else*."[97]

Certain types of school-specific criminal statutes are ripe for challenge under either or both of these theories. The following subsections analyze how courts have approached challenges to criminal statutes or ordinances that prohibit disrupting the schools, talking back to school staff or faculty, trespassing or loitering on school grounds, and issuing terroristic threats.

1. DISRUPTION OF SCHOOLS

A number of states criminalize the disruption of or disturbance in schools. The Supreme Court sustained this type of statute in *Grayned v. City of Rockford*, which involved a city ordinance prohibiting the willful making of "any noise or diversion which disturbs or tends to disturb the peace or good order of [a] school session or class thereof."[98] Rejecting a vagueness challenge, the *Grayned* Court reasoned, "Although the prohibited quantum of disturbance is not specified in the ordinance, it is apparent from the statute's announced purpose that the measure is whether normal school activity has been or is about to be disrupted."[99] The Court concluded that the statute was sufficiently defined, as it required a "demonstrated interference with school activities."[100] Similarly rejecting the challenge on First Amendment grounds, the Court concluded that the statute was "narrowly tailored to further Rockford's compelling interest in having an undisrupted school session conducive to the students' learning [because it] punishes only conduct which disrupts or is about to disrupt normal school activities."[101] Lower courts have followed suit, permitting the criminalization of disorderly conduct at schools so long as the prohibited acts are shown actually to disrupt or to have the potential actually to disrupt school activities.[102]

Not every court, however, will rubber-stamp statutes that criminalize behavior that is "disruptive" to schools. In an unreported opinion, *In re Williams*, the Ohio Court of Appeals reviewed an ordinance making it a crime to "disrupt, disturb, or interfere with any activity conducted in a school," in an appeal brought by a sixth-grade child who had been adjudicated delinquent for throwing spitballs in class and wanting to enter the girls' bathroom.[103] Invalidating the statute on vagueness grounds, the court reasoned, "there is no guidance as to what constitutes a disruption, disturbance, or interference of school activity. As a result of this vague language, a charge may be filed for something as minor as throwing a spitball to something as serious as assaulting an employee of the school."[104]

The Idaho Supreme Court opinion in *State v. Doe* also expressed discomfort with the use of criminal statutes to maintain order in the classroom.[105] Ten-year-old Doe was adjudicated delinquent under a disruption-of-school statute after standing up in class and asking his teacher for a shotgun so that he could shoot another student who had been bothering him. The statute in question provided that a "person who disrupts the educational process or whose presence is detrimental to the morals, health, safety, academic learning or discipline of the pupils . . . is guilty of a misdemeanor."[106] Rather than review Doe's constitutional challenges to the criminal statute, the court interpreted the statute in such a way as to categorically exempt the behavior of school students, and thus Doe. The court reasoned that because the statute "evidences a legislative purpose of protecting, not prosecuting, students," it does not apply to criminalize the behavior of students.[107]

Historically, courts have been willing to sustain criminal prohibitions against "disruption of school" on the ground that school officials and law enforcement could be trusted to distinguish between serious disruptions that warranted law enforcement intervention and disruptions that happen during the course of any ordinary school day. But as school officials and law enforcement officers demonstrate their inability and unwillingness to exercise this discretion in a reasonable manner, resulting in children's being arrested routinely for minor and entirely predictable childish misbehavior on the playground or in the classroom, advocates should use cases like *Williams* and *Doe* to limit the reach of statutes that would otherwise criminalize all forms of misbehavior at schools.

2. TALKING BACK TO TEACHERS

Some states also criminalize talking back to teachers. In Idaho, it is a misdemeanor to "upbraid[], insult[] or abuse[] any teacher of the public schools, in the presence and hearing of a pupil thereof."[108] Courts are less deferential toward statutes that broadly criminalize talking back to teachers and routinely invalidate them on both void-for-vagueness and overbreadth grounds. As early as 1978, in *McCall v. State*, the Florida Supreme Court reversed the conviction of a student's mother prosecuted under a statute that imposed liability on anyone "who upbraids, abuses, or insults any members of the instructional staff on school property or in the presence of the pupils at a school activity."[109] Invalidating the statute on First Amendment grounds, the court concluded that it was not narrowly tailored to the state's interest in maintaining order in the schools, as it contained "no language tying the prohibited expression to disruption of normal school activities at specific fixed times."[110] More recent cases have followed suit.[111] However, at least five states—Arizona, Arkansas, Idaho, Montana, and North Dakota—still maintain these constitutionally vulnerable statutes.[112]

3. TRESPASSING OR LOITERING ON SCHOOL GROUNDS

States and localities also criminalize trespassing or loitering on school grounds. These laws typically prohibit any person from "loiter[ing] around the [school] premises, except on business, without the permission of the principal or president in charge."[113] As applied to individuals who are not students at the school, these laws generally are upheld against attack,[114] although at least one court has found the term *loiter*, without further definition, to be impermissibly vague.[115] These laws are often applied to students, as when children who have been suspended or expelled from school return to campus to see their friends, although at least one court, in *E.W. v. State*, held that this kind of statute could not be applied to students who were enrolled in the school and who were not suspended or expelled.[116] Although school officials may find case law to defend such statutes, advocates may, at the very least, raise public policy considerations to counsel against such application.

4. TERRORISTIC THREATS

Another common ground for arresting children at school is for making "terroristic threats."[117] A typical state statute will read as follows:

> A person commits the crime of terroristic threats if the person communicates, either directly or indirectly, a threat to: (1) commit any crime of violence with intent to terrorize another; (2) cause evacuation of a building, place of assembly or facility of public transportation; or (3) otherwise cause serious public inconvenience, or cause terror or serious public inconvenience with reckless disregard of the risk of causing such terror or inconvenience.[118]

In the past, courts have generally upheld such statutes against First Amendment overbreadth arguments[119] as well as against due process vagueness challenges.[120] Today, more and more children, of younger and younger ages, are being arrested at school for making disturbing statements such as "I want to kill you" or "I want to bomb the school," rather than their receiving the attention and support that they clearly need. Advocates should continue to push courts to acknowledge the lack of wisdom inherent in hauling a small child to a police station rather than providing him or her with the structured reinforcement and support that schools have historically offered.

D. CONCLUSION

As school officials rely more heavily on police officers and tactics to maintain order in schools, advocates will be increasingly challenged to develop theories to ensure that courts do not impose blanket exemptions to the rights of children on public school campuses. It is our hope that advocates will use the guidance in this chapter to challenge those instances in which school officials overstep their authority and act as agents of law enforcement and also to provide a measure of accountability for police officers who are deployed to patrol K–12 schools.

7

Court-Involved Youth and the Juvenile Justice System

Thus far, this book has explored the ways in which children are drawn into the School-to-Prison Pipeline—through inadequate resources in public schools, discrimination, a failure to provide required services for students with special needs, draconian discipline policies, substandard alternative schools, and overzealous policing of school hallways. These policies and practices intersect with one another and, too often, ultimately culminate in the child's referral to the juvenile justice system. This chapter explores systemic opportunities to enforce the rights of these most in-need children at the back end of the pipeline.[1]

According to the Annie E. Casey Foundation, each year across the nation, "police make 2.2 million juvenile arrests; 1.7 million cases are referred to juvenile courts; an estimated 400,000 youngsters cycle through juvenile detention centers; and nearly 100,000 youth are confined in juvenile jails, prisons, boot camps, and other residential facilities on any given night."[2] A quarter of all children placed in secure confinement after being adjudicated juvenile delinquent were charged with violent offenses; 22 percent were incarcerated as a result of a technical violation, and 6 percent were confined due to a status offense.[3] A growing number of children are being referred to the system directly by their schools: in South Carolina, the single most common offense resulting in a juvenile court referral during the 2007–08 year was "disturbing schools";[4] in Florida, 15 percent of all delinquency referrals stemmed from school-related conduct during the 2007–08 year.[5]

Youth who become involved with the courts have considerably different life chances. As mentioned in chapter 6, a juvenile arrest impacts the likelihood that the child will drop out of school, the child's academic achievement, future employment prospects, and the likelihood of future interaction with the criminal justice system.[6] The life chances of juveniles who are ultimately incarcerated are even worse. Only 12 percent of formerly incarcerated youth have a high school diploma or GED by young adulthood, and less than a third are either in school or a had job one year after release.[7] Far from improving public safety, detention of youth actually increases recidivism.[8] Of youth released from juvenile facilities, 50 to 80 percent are rearrested within two to three years, including those who were not serious offenders prior to their commitment. Half or more of all released youth are later reincarcerated. And increasingly relevant in these budget-strapped times, detention costs the state approximately two hundred to three hundred dollars per child per day.[9]

The juvenile justice system involves a great deal of subtleties and complexities; advocates and scholars have devoted lifetimes to it. This chapter is not intended as an exhaustive list of ideas for systemic reform. Rather, it is our goal to encourage advocates to continue brainstorming possibilities and to provide a starting place for advocates new to the area. The first section of this chapter provides an introductory overview of the salient features of the juvenile justice system. The second section discusses the potential for systemic challenges to the initial referral or arrest of children. In the third section, the chapter explores the rights of incarcerated children, focusing in particular on the right to education. Finally, the fourth section explores the rights of court-involved youth to reenter the mainstream educational system.

A. OVERVIEW OF THE JUVENILE JUSTICE SYSTEM

This section is not intended as an exhaustive account of the juvenile justice system. Rather, its purpose is to provide a brief overview of some of the unique aspects of the system for newcomers to the area, to provide sufficient background for the subsequent sections, which explore the potential for systemic reform to minimize the impact of the School-to-Prison Pipeline for court-involved youth.

In the nineteenth century, advocates driven by the conviction that children are less responsible for their actions than adults are and that children would benefit from treatment and rehabilitation rather than punishment sought to create a separate system for children accused of crimes.[10] As the Supreme Court described,

> The early reformers were appalled by adult procedures and penalties, and by the fact that children could be given long prison sentences and mixed in jails with hardened criminals. They were profoundly convinced that society's duty to the child could not be confined by the concept of justice alone. They believed that society's role was not to ascertain whether the

child was "guilty" or "innocent," but "What is he, how has he become what he is, and what had best be done in his interest and in the interest of the state to save him from a downward career."[11]

As a result of this movement, each state developed a juvenile justice system distinct from the adult criminal system.[12] Initially, these proceedings were viewed exclusively as civil and nonadversarial in nature, where "the rules of criminal procedure were . . . altogether inapplicable. The apparent rigidities, technicalities, and harshness . . . observed in both substantive and procedural criminal law were therefore to be discarded."[13]

Through time, however, it became apparent that the juvenile justice system exposed the accused child to "the worst of both worlds: that he gets neither the protections accorded to adults nor the solicitous care and regenerative treatment postulated for children."[14] Consequently, in *In re Gault,* the Supreme Court held that children in juvenile proceedings are entitled to at least some of the same procedural rights guaranteed to adults in criminal court.[15] Notwithstanding, there remain important differences between the juvenile system and the adult criminal system.

Generally, a child may be referred to the juvenile justice system for a criminal violation or status offense that would not be considered criminal if committed by an adult, for example, curfew violations, truancy, running away, and underage drinking.[16] Upon arrest, the child may be detained for a statutorily prescribed amount of time before a probable-cause hearing is held to determine whether there is sufficient evidence to charge the child formally.[17] At arraignment, the child is formally charged and given an attorney.[18] At this point, the child may be detained pending the adjudicatory hearing.[19] As a result, the child may be detained for months before he or she is adjudicated delinquent.[20] Studies document that juvenile detention, even when limited to the time period prior to the adjudicatory hearing, has negative consequences on youth, including increasing the likelihood of harsher punishments postadjudication, stigma of being labeled as a delinquent, increased likelihood of recidivism, and negative physical and emotional repercussions.[21] Although the child may be detained at each of these different points along the system prior to the adjudicatory hearing, the child may, alternatively, have his or her charges dismissed or have the matter diverted to nonformal means at each of these different points.[22]

During the adjudicatory hearing, children enjoy many but not all of the procedural due process rights associated with criminal trials; the rights afforded to juveniles vary from state to state. The federal constitutional minimum, though, provides for a right to notice of the charges, a right to counsel, a right to confront and cross-examine witnesses, a right against self-incrimination, a right to appellate review, and a right to a transcript of the proceedings,[23] but not a right to a jury trial.[24]

The juvenile court has wide discretion in entering a disposition of the matter. The child may be subject to commitment to a detention facility, placement in foster homes or treatment facilities, probation, or counseling, among other possibilities. In *Schall,* which involved the constitutionality of preadjudication detention, the Supreme Court held that there are circumstances in which detention of a child is permissible even though an adult could not be detained under the same circumstances, pursuant to the court's *parens patriae* authority over juveniles.[25] The Court acknowledged that, like adults, children maintain an interest in being free from institutional restraints; however, because children are always in some form of custody, their liberty interests may be subordinated to the state's interest in "preserving and promoting the welfare of the child."[26] Consequently, courts may detain juveniles not only to ensure their later appearance in court but also to keep them off the streets or to protect them from harm.

The federal Juvenile Justice and Delinquency Prevention Act (JJDPA) prohibits states from placing juveniles in secure detention for status offenses.[27] However, the act creates an exception to this general prohibition: children may be placed in secure detention if the status offense violates a valid court order, such as a condition of probation.[28] Consequently, every year, thousands of children are incarcerated for status offenses, that is, offenses such as truancy or running away, that would not be considered criminal if committed by an adult. In 2006, 6 percent of all youth committed to a juvenile facility pursuant to court-ordered disposition, or 3,635 children, were committed for status offenses.[29]

B. CHALLENGING THE INITIAL REFERRAL OR ARREST

Perhaps the most effective method for addressing the back end of the School-to-Prison Pipeline is to keep youth out of the courts in the first instance. As discussed more fully in the preceding chapter, a growing number of youth in juvenile court are referred to law enforcement for conduct fairly typical of adolescent behavior that, a generation ago, would have been handled informally by school administrators. As a result, juvenile courts spend more time addressing school behavior issues than in generations past. Attempts to address these trends may involve civil challenges to limit school-based arrests, to curb the circumvention of special education laws through court referrals, and to address the racial disparities in juvenile referrals.

The preceding chapter discusses strategies for challenging the criminalization of school misconduct, that is, facial challenges to laws underlying school-based arrests. Impact litigators should probe additional avenues. For example, in New York, the Family Court Act prohibits officers from taking children aged fifteen or younger into custody for noncriminal violations, for example, disorderly conduct or loitering, which do not amount to misdemeanors or felonies.[30] Data disclosed pursuant to a Freedom of Information Act request suggest, however, that school resource officers in New York City schools frequently arrest young children for such minor offenses.[31] Where a jurisdiction provides similar statutory limits to the arrests of children, advocates might consider bringing structural reform litigation to enforce them.

In other jurisdictions, where there are no such statutory provisions but where there are contractual agreements or memoranda of understanding between the police department and public school district that limit the circumstances under which children may be arrested at school, advocates might seek to enforce the terms of these agreements through litigation. Administrators from the juvenile court, the police department, and the public school district in Clayton County, Georgia, have entered into such a cooperative agreement to limit the arrest of schoolchildren for common public-order offenses such as affray and disorderly conduct.[32]

Where no such agreements or statutory protections exist, nonlitigation tools remain available, such as research and public education on patterns of police referrals for minor misbehavior that may indicate a school's failure to supervise children, failure to implement programs to address discipline issues, or inappropriate delegation of disciplinary authority. Alternatively, advocates might seek the passage of legislation or the entry of contractual agreements between police and schools to limit school-based arrests.[33]

2. PREVENTING THE CIRCUMVENTION OF SPECIAL EDUCATION PROTECTIONS

Another area for reform is the use of law enforcement referrals to circumvent federal disabilities law protections. Youth with disabilities are detained disproportionately in the juvenile justice system.[34] School officials may have an incentive to refer children with special behavioral needs to law enforcement rather than providing them with the services, sometimes costly, to which these children are entitled.

Prior to 1997, at least one federal court had ruled that a school's referral of a youth to the juvenile court constituted a "change in placement" triggering due process protections under the Individuals with Disabilities Education Act (IDEA).[35] Other courts had held that the juvenile court lacks jurisdiction in cases involving noncriminal school-related misconduct in which special education procedures had not been followed.[36] Amendments to the IDEA passed in 1997, however, expressly provide, "Nothing in this subchapter shall be construed to prohibit an agency from reporting a crime committed by a child with a disability to appropriate authorities or to prevent State law enforcement and judicial authorities from exercising their responsibilities with regard to the application of Federal and State law to crimes committed by a child with a disability."[37]

Since then, at least two courts have confirmed that federal law does not prevent juvenile courts from exercising jurisdiction over students with disabilities.[38] Nonetheless, where systemic patterns exist of referring special education students to law enforcement, or where other evidence suggests an attempt by districts to use law enforcement referrals to circumvent special education obligations, advocates should consider raising claims of discrimination on the basis of disability pursuant to Section 504 of the Rehabilitation Act or Title II of the American Disabilities Act (ADA) or state statute where such laws offer additional protections.[39] As discussed more fully in chapter 3, some jurisdictions may recognize a disparate impact claim for discrimination on the basis of disability. Alternatively, advocates might consider raising administrative challenges to such disparate referrals of students with disabilities.

3. ADDRESSING RACIAL DISPARITIES IN JUVENILE REFERRALS

A third important area for advocates to address is the persistence of racial disparities in juvenile court referrals. From 1985 to 1995, detention rates for African American and Hispanic youth increased by 180 and 140 percent, respectively, while the rate for white youth decreased by 13 percent.[40] Today, children of color represent 34 percent of the nation's total youth population but constitute 62 percent of youth in detention pending adjudication and 66 percent of youth committed to public facilities after disposition.[41] African American youth represent 16 percent of the total youth population nationwide but constitute 28 percent of all youth arrests and 58 percent of juveniles admitted to adult prisons.[42] When white youth and African American youth are charged for the same offense, African American youth with no prior admissions are six times more likely to be incarcerated in public facilities than are white youth with the same background; Latino youth are three times more likely than white youth to be incarcerated. African American youth are confined on average for 61 days longer than white youth are, and Latino youth are confined 112 days longer than white youth are.[43] Three out of four children who are admitted into adult prisons are children of color.[44]

Legal theories to address racial disparities are discussed in chapter 2. In addition to those strategies, advocates seeking to address racial disparities specifically in the juvenile justice system should explore the possibility of using the federal Juvenile Justice and Delinquency Prevention Act (JJDPA), due for reauthorization at the time of this writing. This act provides federal formula grants to each state, on the condition that the state submit and annually report on a plan to "reduce . . . the disproportionate number of juvenile members of minority groups, who come into contact with the juvenile justice system."[45] Unfortunately, the current act does not provide for a private right of action or other meaningful enforcement mechanism. Nonetheless, the act remains critical to providing access to data on disproportionate minority contact, data that may be used to bolster the types of systemic racial discrimination claims discussed in chapter 2.

C. RIGHT TO EDUCATION FOR INCARCERATED CHILDREN

The frequently substandard conditions in juvenile detention facilities and their consequences on youth have been well documented. According to the Annie E. Casey Foundation, "juvenile correctional facilities have shown a persistent propensity toward shocking and sometimes pervasive abuses against youth."[46] This section explores efforts to secure educational services for incarcerated youth. Without access to education, children have little chance of extracting themselves from the School-to-Prison Pipeline through rehabilitation and of success upon returning to the mainstream education system.[47] The need for adequate education services for this population is particularly acute, given that youth who enter these facilities tend to have a wide range of unmet educational, mental health, medical, and social needs; large numbers of incarcerated juveniles are marginally literate or illiterate and have experienced school failure and retention.[48] First, this section addresses access to educational services for children confined in juvenile facilities; then it explores efforts to secure such services for juveniles incarcerated in adult facilities.

1. EDUCATION IN JUVENILE FACILITIES

According to the U.S. Department of Justice, only 89 percent of residential facilities for juvenile offenders reported that at least some of their youth attended school.[49] Less than three-quarters of these facilities, representing 67 percent of the juvenile offender population in residential placement, reported that all their youth attend schools;[50] 6 percent of juvenile boot camps and 14 percent of group homes reported than none of their youth attended school;[51] and 8 percent of juvenile facilities, housing 11 percent of all juvenile offenders in residential placements, indicated that they performed no educational screening for incoming youth.[52]

As discussed in chapter 1, all states have compulsory attendance laws, and many provide a state right to education either through the state constitution or by statute. However, whether this right extends to children in juvenile correctional facilities varies by state. In Washington State, for example, the state supreme court has held that all school-age children in detention centers are entitled to a right to education both before and after adjudication and disposition.[53] Georgia maintains an anomalous rule, in which court-involved children who are sentenced to probation do not have a right to an education, but children committed to juvenile facilities do enjoy such a right.[54]

Even in jurisdictions that recognize a right to education for detained and incarcerated youth, the right is routinely denied. These denials generally fall into three categories. First, in some facilities there is no system to educate confined youth at all. Or the education program may be characterized by failure to provide minimum hours of education per day; failure to provide adequate numbers of qualified teachers to ensure proper teacher-to-student ratios; or failure to provide adequate space for instruction to take place, as required by state regulations for general education. Second, facilities may offer a GED class as the sole education program. These limited programs may exist even in states that expressly require for delinquent youth a curriculum substantially equivalent to that required under the law for public school students. Third, facilities may structure their programs or operations in a way that a child is forced to choose between attending class or other desirable institutional options such as paid work, recreation, or placement in a less secure facility, for example, camps and shelters. Other examples of disincentives include facilities' failing to maintain academic records and transcripts, thereby preventing juveniles from earning academic credit.

Advocates should determine whether their particular jurisdiction provides a right to education either under constitutional or statutory law or whether statutory requirements exist regarding the minimum educational services that must be provided to incarcerated children.[55] In cases where they do, advocates might bring systemic challenges to enforce these rights. Litigants who have done so in the past generally have included such education claims as part of a larger challenge to overall conditions in juvenile detention facilities.[56] Where such constitutional or statutory protections do not exist, advocates might consider equal protection challenges on behalf of, for example, incarcerated youth who obtain fewer educational services than the general population, fewer than youth incarcerated in other facilities, or none at all.

According to some estimates, a third of all incarcerated children have been identified as being disabled.[57] As discussed in chapter 3, children with special needs—those with learning disabilities or behavioral or emotional disorders—unlike children without disabilities, enjoy a right to a free and appropriate education (FAPE) under federal law pursuant to the Individuals with Disabilities Education Act (IDEA) and Section 504 of the Rehabilitation Act.[58] The IDEA mandates the provision of FAPE for all children between the ages of three and twenty-one, expressly including children who are wards of the state; indeed, the Department of Education regulations implementing the IDEA expressly provide that its requirements apply to "State and local juvenile and adult correctional facilities."[59]

Notwithstanding these clear dictates, juvenile detention facilities frequently fail to provide the requisite services to their disabled populations. As mentioned earlier, some have no system in place to assess a student's educational needs. They may fail to develop individualized education plans (IEPs), and advocates have reported that some facilities simply use "form" or boilerplate IEPs for all their students, without accounting for the unique needs of the individual child. Other failures may include a failure to implement IEPs once they have been drafted, a failure to provide a qualified teaching staff, and the use of waiting lists for particular services or classes. They may also often fail to provide the required transition plans that would permit the child to succeed upon transitioning outside the facility. Violations of due process requirements, including rights to notice, timely assessments and IEP development, and the right of appeal, may also occur. And the right of parents to participate in their children's education is routinely abrogated. Consequently, since 1975, advocates have filed over twenty class actions against juvenile correctional facilities, alleging violations of special education rights pursuant to the IDEA and Section 504; again, many of these cases have included such claims within a larger challenge to overall conditions in juvenile detention facilities.[60] Many have succeeded in obtaining extensive settlements and consent decrees to secure these and other rights.[61]

2. EDUCATION FOR CHILDREN IN ADULT FACILITIES

On a typical day, approximately seven thousand children are held in adult jails; in a given year, forty-one hundred children are committed to adult prisons.[62] Children confined in adult facilities, whether in adult jails pending adjudication or in adult prisons after being transferred to the adult criminal system and convicted, face even greater barriers to educational services than do children in juvenile correctional facilities. Unsurprisingly, adult facilities simply tend not to offer standardized secondary educational curricula for their incarcerated populations.

As mentioned earlier, states vary in the extent to which they grant a right to education for any youth, much less incarcerated youth. Although some states statutorily mandate minimum educational standards to be provided in juvenile correctional facilities, these standards do not necessarily apply to adult correctional facilities.[63] And, as interpreted by the Department of Education's regulations, there are several exceptions to the applicability of IDEA special education requirements in adult correctional facilities. First, individuals aged eighteen through twenty-one are not eligible for a free and appropriate education if they were not identified as having a disability or did not have an IEP prior to incarceration.[64] Second, otherwise-eligible children convicted as adults and confined in adult prisons may not participate in general assessment programs, such as standardized achievement or school "accountability" tests.[65] Third, these children are not entitled to transition planning and services if their IDEA eligibility would end before they are released from prison.[66] Finally, IEP teams for these children may modify placements, notwithstanding the least restrictive environment or IEP, "if the State has demonstrated a bona fide security or compelling penological interest that cannot otherwise be accommodated."[67] For these reasons, systemic challenges to secure the educational services—both general education and special education—for youth in adult facilities face greater difficulties than those for youth in juvenile correctional facilities.

The case law suggests a greater willingness to provide general and special education services for juvenile pretrial detainees in adult facilities than for juveniles incarcerated in adult facilities after conviction. In January 1993, the Legal Assistance Foundation and the Northwestern University Legal Clinic filed a class action lawsuit on behalf of twenty-three school-age pretrial detainees held in adult county jail in Chicago, in *Donnell C. v. Illinois State Board of Education.*[68] Plaintiffs alleged that they were denied access to regular and special education services during their detention or were provided educational services that were vastly inferior to those offered nondetainees, in violation of substantive due process rights and equal protection under the U.S. Constitution, as well as under the IDEA and Section 504 of the Rehabilitation Act. Denying defendants' motion to dismiss, the district court found that plaintiffs' allegations that only about 40 percent of special-needs detainees were receiving services and that instruction lacked educational basics of reading and math were sufficient to state a substantive due process violation.[69] It further held that there was no rational basis for denying educational services to these children, thus sustaining plaintiffs' equal protection claim.[70] This success suggests judicial willingness to require education services for children pending trial or an adjudicatory hearing.

By contrast, courts have been less inclined to require the provision of educational services to children incarcerated in adult facilities after conviction. In *Brian B. v. Commonwealth of Pennsylvania Department of Education,*[71] the Juvenile Law Center filed an equal protection suit on behalf of a state-wide class of school-age children incarcerated in adult county prisons and jails. Pursuant to state statute, convicted juveniles in adult *county* facilities— mostly nonviolent offenders—who were under the age of seventeen were entitled to no more than five hours, and as little as one and a half hours, of educational programming per week; school-age offenders aged seventeen to twenty-one were entitled to no education at all while incarcerated. By contrast, convicted juveniles sent to adult *state* facilities—those who had committed murder or other serious crimes—retained their right to education. Affirming the district court's rejection of plaintiffs' motion for a preliminary injunction, the Third Circuit concluded that there was a rational basis for the difference in treatment between convicted juveniles in county facilities versus state facilities.

In *Tunstall v. Bergeson,*[72] the Washington Supreme Court considered the right to education for convicted children incarcerated in state prisons. Reversing the trial court's grant of summary judgment to the inmates, the higher court concluded that individuals younger than eighteen retain a right to education but that the right was satisfied through compliance with the Department of Corrections' regulations providing limited educational programming, which provided far fewer services than the basic education and special education statutes governing the state's public school systems.[73] The court found no equal protection violation because the Department of Corrections' education programs, which were vastly inferior to those afforded at public schools, were rationally related to the state objective of meeting the inmates' unique educational needs. The court also held that the rational basis test, rather than strict scrutiny, applied because state law did not infringe on a fundamental right, and the inmates' incarceration and juvenile status did not place them in a suspect class.

Together, these cases suggest that children convicted under the criminal justice system may have a right to an education while they are incarcerated in adult facilities, but that right may be severely limited and may differ substantially from the educational rights of children in the juvenile justice system and the public school system.

D. RIGHT TO EDUCATIONAL REENTRY

Another area of concern identified by advocates and experts contributing to the School-to-Prison Pipeline involves barriers for court-involved youth— whether they were incarcerated or not—to reentering the mainstream educational system. In New York City, for example, two-thirds of high-school-age offenders released from state custody do not return to school.[74] In Kentucky, nearly 95 percent of school-age adjudicated youth fail to transition back into mainstream or alternative schools.[75]

The U.S. Department of Justice's Office for Juvenile Justice and Delinquency Prevention has described the problem as follows:

> [T]he criminal justice and education systems often seem to work at cross-purposes. Judges mandate school attendance, but the community lacks an effective system for reenrolling students. The justice system releases young offenders from custody during midsemesters and summers, when schools are least equipped to admit new students. Many court-involved youth perform below grade level and have histories of truancy and suspension. They require a disproportionate rate of special education services and often feel alienated from school. If the special needs of these youth are not met, they are at risk of dropping out of school and returning to the justice system, at considerable social and financial cost.[76]

Even worse than the lack of coordination between agencies for timely and appropriate placement, schools and districts sometimes outright refuse to enroll court-involved youth. Some districts have developed system-wide policies of funneling children into disciplinary alternative schools upon their release from custody; in other jurisdictions, school administrators have exercised their discretion simply to reject enrollment applications from delinquent youth. This section describes litigation efforts to challenge such policies and minimize the barriers that adjudicated youth face when they attempt to return to the mainstream educational system.

1. JURISDICTION OF FAMILY COURTS TO ORDER PUBLIC SCHOOL SERVICES

Several cases have sought to challenge districts' refusal to enroll or reenroll a court-involved youth even when the juvenile court orders school attendance as a condition of the child's probation or release. These cases have been framed as a question of the juvenile court's authority over school districts, and their outcomes have varied.

In West Virginia, in *Philip Leon M. v. Greenbrier County Board of Education,* a fifteen-year-old boy who brought a firearm to school was expelled and then adjudicated delinquent. As a condition of probation, the juvenile court ordered that the student attend school regularly, but the school district refused to provide him with any educational programming during his expulsion.[77] A virtually identical situation arose in *State ex rel. G.S.* in New Jersey, where a student who served as a lookout for a false bomb threat to the school was expelled and then adjudicated delinquent. Again, as a condition of probation, the juvenile court ordered him to attend school regularly, but the school district refused to reenroll him.[78] In both cases, the reviewing court concluded that the district was required to provide alternative education to the student, enabling him to comply with the terms of his probation as ordered by the juvenile court.

In contrast, in *In re Jackson,* a North Carolina court concluded that the juvenile court lacked jurisdiction to order a local school district to provide a delinquent student with any educational services at all.[79] Likewise, in *In re R.M.,* the Wyoming court affirmed a school district's refusal to reenroll two students, notwithstanding an order by the juvenile court that the district provide educational services to the students.[80]

These cases, all brought in state courts, suggest significant differences by state in whether family and juvenile courts may order school districts to provide educational services to delinquent youth.

2. AUTOMATIC REFERRALS TO ALTERNATIVE SCHOOL: *D.C. V. SCHOOL DISTRICT OF PHILADELPHIA*

State laws and regulations may also erect barriers to an adjudicated delinquent's return to the mainstream educational system. In the landmark case *D.C. v. School District of Philadelphia*, the Juvenile Law Center and Education Law Center of Pennsylvania challenged a state law that (1) automatically placed all students returning from juvenile delinquency placements in a transition center for up to four weeks prior to enrollment in a public school and (2) automatically assigned children adjudicated delinquent for certain crimes to a disciplinary alternative program rather than a regular classroom.[81]

As to the four-week placement in the transition center, the court concluded that the measure survived challenge because of the "seriousness of reintegrating large numbers of students returning from juvenile placements."[82] However, as to the ultimate placement of students in a disciplinary alternative school, the court agreed that the absence of any opportunity to challenge the placement violated students' procedural due process rights. First, the court rejected the district's claim that the placement constituted a merely administrative decision.[83] Recognizing that the transfer was, in fact, disciplinary in nature, the court held that liberty and property interests were implicated, thus triggering the need for procedural due process protections.[84]

Second, the court concluded that the hearing that the child in the case received when she was adjudicated delinquent did not satisfy the requirement for a hearing to challenge her placement in the alternative school.[85] The court reasoned that the issue to be considered—the child's fitness for the regular classroom at the time of her release from placement—was not considered during the juvenile adjudication.[86] The court noted that this "decision turns on factors that could not be known at the time of the juvenile adjudication," including "whether the student performed in an exemplary manner during juvenile placement or otherwise does not pose a threat to the regular classroom setting."[87] Thus, the Pennsylvania court concluded that a temporary assignment for up to four weeks to a transition center was permitted, but the automatic and permanent transfer of a delinquent student to a disciplinary alternative school, without an opportunity to challenge the placement, violated procedural due process rights. This case, while upholding temporary placements to assess returning delinquent youth, may serve as a useful model for future efforts to challenge the refusal to reintegrate adjudicated delinquents into mainstream schools.

3. FAILURE TO TRANSITION STUDENTS ADEQUATELY INTO PUBLIC SCHOOLS: *J.G. V. MILLS*

Advocates for Children and the Legal Aid Society brought a similar suit, *J.G. v. Mills*, in December 2004, challenging the failure to adequately transition court-involved students into mainstream New York City public schools upon their release.[88] Plaintiffs alleged violations of state education law and the federal IDEA, along with procedural due process violations stemming from (1) the failure to reenroll these students into community schools in a timely manner, (2) the failure to provide credit for course work completed during detention, (3) the reenrollment of these students in the wrong class or wrong grade, and (4) the failure to evaluate and provide special education and related services to the portion of the plaintiff class who were students with disabilities.[89]

On July 6, 2006, the magistrate judge recommended that the district court deny plaintiffs' motion for a preliminary injunction.[90] As to the first issue relating to prompt enrollment, the magistrate agreed that students maintain, pursuant to New York law, a property interest in prompt reenrollment upon release from court-ordered settings.[91] Importantly, however, in reaching this conclusion the magistrate relied heavily on the City's representation that it had recently adopted measures designed to address the problem, including removing principals' discretionary authority to reject admission for court-involved students, establishing enrollment centers with dedicated staff responsible for tracking and enrolling students released from court-ordered settings into public schools, developing new procedures for students' automatic placement into mainstream school rolls upon their release and reducing the likelihood that a student's name would get lost, providing Know Your Rights materials to court-involved youth, providing notice of the right to return to his or her previous school and the right not to be involuntarily transferred into a non-diploma-granting or GED program, and creation of a Family Court Liaison to facilitate the transition from court-ordered settings to public schools.[92] In jurisdictions where districts have not adopted such measures, courts may find that students' rights have been violated.

With respect to plaintiffs' claims regarding errors and delays in the calculation of credits, the magistrate concluded that it was unlikely that plaintiffs could establish pursuant to New York law a property right to credit for course work completed during detention, much less a right to *timely* calculation of credits.[93]

Addressing plaintiffs' third claim, relating to a right to be assigned to an appropriate class and pursue a diploma upon discharge from a court-ordered setting, the magistrate opined that although state law creates a property right to take diploma-track courses and obtain a diploma by the end of high school, this right was not violated, notwithstanding the fact that it might take an adjudicated student more than four years to complete high school given the interruption resulting from adjudication.[94]

Finally, with respect to the claims that delays in reenrollment infringed on a protected liberty interest, the magistrate recommended that the district court dismiss this argument, concluding, "although plaintiffs may indeed bear some degree of stigma as a result of that removal [from their community school by the juvenile court], there is no reason to conclude that a delay of even one month before a student is reenrolled gives rise to more than the minimum *additional* harm to reputation."[95] The magistrate's report and recommendations provide a useful guide to advocates by identifying the methodology by which courts might evaluate claims by court-involved students denied reentry into mainstream schools. First, courts will look to state and local laws and regulations to determine the extent to which property interests exist for students reenrolling in mainstream schools, for accurate and timely credit calculations, and for access to appropriate diploma-track courses. Second, the report suggests that courts may be unlikely to find a liberty, as opposed to property, interest in timely enrollment into public schools.

Notwithstanding the setback issued by the magistrate, the plaintiffs succeeded in obtaining a comprehensive settlement agreement, filed with the court on October 7, 2008, requiring the state to develop a field memorandum for all districts regarding students returning to public schools from court-ordered placements and to provide technical assistance and training to districts for transfers of credits from court-involved settings and reenrollment, as well as to provide on-site monitoring and periodic desk audits to ensure compliance with legal requirements.[96]

In addition to relying on procedural due process rights to challenge the failure to transition court-involved youth into mainstream schools, advocates should explore state laws granting a right to transition. Recognizing the importance of transitioning youth from court-ordered placements into the mainstream community, the federal No Child Left Behind Act awards grants to provide services for students released from court-ordered settings to transition into regular public schools.[97] Consistent with the goals of that federal program, several states have enacted legislation to facilitate the transition.[98] Advocates should explore whether these laws provide a claim to challenge district and state failures to ensure that court-involved students receive the services and access to public education to which they are entitled.

E. CONCLUSION

This chapter has explored the potential for impact-litigation challenges on behalf of children at the back end of the School-to-Prison Pipeline, those youth who become involved in the juvenile or criminal justice systems, and in particular, those who become detained or incarcerated. These are the youth who by definition are at risk and who have been most severely impacted by the pipeline, and they are the youth for whom advocacy may be most immediately critical. It is our hope that readers will find this chapter useful to ensure that each of these children has the opportunity to fulfill his or her full potential.

Conclusion

This book has sought to describe what happens to children at each of the different entry points on the School-to-Prison Pipeline, from the front end of the pipeline, including inadequate and inequitable access to resources, all the way to the back end of the pipeline, including the various barriers confronting court-involved youth who seek to continue their education and eventually reenter the mainstream school system. By analyzing theories and strategies to challenge disturbing trends at each of these entry points through impact litigation, the book has sought to provide an arsenal of resources for advocates seeking to stem the pernicious impact of the pipeline, particularly for our most at-risk youth.

That said, throughout the book, we have noted the limitations of impact litigation to stem the pipeline. In some cases, courts have refused to intervene, even when constitutional or statutory violations have been found. In other cases, doctrinal barriers to relief have been erected. Finally, sometimes advocates have simply lacked the resources, either to bring systemic litigation or to adequately monitor and enforce legal victories.

For these reasons, we encourage all advocates—including members of the bar, the bench, and the legal academy, community members, government officials, and legislators—to identify alternative strategies to protect the rights of these students and to ensure equal educational opportunities for all. Indeed, in many of the case studies profiled throughout this book, advocates initiated impact litigation in conjunction with alternative strategies including grass-roots organizing, legislative lobbying, and policy advocacy, to name a few. In other situations, litigation may not be able to be initiated at all, and advocates will need to rely on these alternative strategies exclusively.

For example, a lawsuit against a particular district for failing to provide a free and appropriate public education as required under the Individuals with Disabilities Education Act for a specific subgroup of students with disabilities with disproportionate suspension rates might be brought at the same time as a distinct lawsuit more generally redressing the high school push-out rate of all students before they reach the maximum age for compulsory education. Each of these lawsuits might complement a general move to increase direct representation of individual students of color in a district or state. Moreover, these distinct legal approaches may be pursued as part of an even broader impact advocacy strategy that could include state litigation for failing to provide an adequate education along with a grassroots awareness and media campaign designed to help communities throughout the state raise these issues at local school board meetings. In the meantime, advocates may also pursue a legislative amendment to the state's definition of "adequate education" or related administrative remedies with the state's board of education. Most advocates agree that pursuing litigation in isolation limits its impact over time. Nonlitigation strategies such as grass-roots activism and state and federal legislative initiatives can develop and build momentum from a successful litigation. Additionally, impact litigation may be coupled with direct legal representation for maximum effect.

It has not been our intent in this book to provide an exhaustive how-to guide to litigate the most damaging aspects of the School-to-Prison Pipeline, much less to set forth the various nonlitigation methods that might be employed. Rather, our goal has been to identify the harms that befall our most at-risk youth, to identify some of the legal strategies that have succeeded in the past, and to issue a call to advocates of different stripes to continue bringing these cases, to brainstorm alternative strategies, and to work together to ensure that children of all backgrounds have a chance at obtaining a high school diploma rather than a criminal record.

Notes

NOTES TO THE INTRODUCTION

1. Drum Major Institute, A Look at the Impact Schools (2005), http://www.drumma-jorinstitute.org/pdfs/impact%20schools.pdf (finding that the New York City Schools labeled as most dangerous are also large, severely overcrowded, and underfunded); National Center for Schools and Communities, Fordham University, Equity or Exclusion: the Dynamics of Resources, Demographics, and Behavior in the New York City Public Schools (2003), http://www.ncscatfordham.org/binarydata/files/EQUITY_OR_EXCLU-SION.pdf (noting correlation between student behavior and level of teacher experience and teacher qualifications and other resources at school).

2. Committee on School Health, American Academy of Pediatrics, *Out-of-School Suspension and Expulsion,* No. 5, 112 Pediatrics 1206, 1207 (2003). *See also* Johanna Wald & Daniel J. Losen, *Defining and Redirecting a School-to-Prison Pipeline,* 99 New Directions for Youth Dev. 9, 11 (2003).

3. Parents and advocates have expressed suspicion that the rise in disciplinary suspensions is attributable, at least in part, to pressures exerted by high-stakes testing accountability such as that required under the No Child Left Behind Act. Empirical evidence provides some support for this suspicion. *See* David N. Figlio, *Testing, Crime, and Punishment,* 90 J. Pub. Econ. 837 (2005) (documenting evidence that schools respond to high-stakes testing by selectively disciplining their students because they have an incentive to keep high-performing students in school and low-performing students out of school during the testing window in order to maximize aggregate test scores).

4. The data from 1973 were obtained from Children's Defense Fund of the Washington Research Project, *Suspensions: Are They Helping Children?* (1975). Data from 2006 were obtained from the U.S. Department of Education's Office for Civil Rights. A full analysis of these data will be published this year. Daniel J. Losen & Russell J. Skiba, Southern Poverty Law Center, *Suspended Education: Urban Middle Schools in Crisis* (forthcoming 2010) (on file with the authors); *see also* U.S. Department of Education, Office for Civil Rights, Times Series CD-ROM, 2000 Elementary and Secondary School Survey: National and State Projections (2006).

5. Losen & Skiba, *supra* note 4.

6. *Id.*

7. *Id.*

8. *Id.*

9. Howard N. Snyder, Office for Juvenile Justice and Delinquency Prevention, *Juvenile Arrests 2003,* OJJDP Juvenile Justice Bulletin 9 (Aug. 2005), http://www.ncjrs.gov/pdffiles1/ojjdp/209735.pdf.

10. *See* American Civil Liberties Union, Missing the Mark: Alternative Schools in the State of Mississippi (Feb. 2009) (documenting racial disparities in referrals to disciplinary alternative schools); American Civil Liberties Union, Hard Lessons: School Resource Officer Programs and School-Based Arrests in Three Connecticut Towns (Nov. 2008) (documenting racial disparities in school-based arrests, even when controlling for offense); Russell J. Skiba, Zero Tolerance, Zero Evidence 11–12 (2000), http://www.indiana.edu/~safeschl/ztze.pdf; Russell J. Skiba et al., The Color of Discipline: Sources of Racial and Gender Disproportionality in School Punishment (2000), http://www.indiana.edu/~safeschl/cod.pdf; The Advancement Project & the Civil Rights Project at Harvard University, Opportunities Suspended: The Devastating Consequences of Zero Tolerance and School Discipline Policies 6–7 (2000), http://www.advancementproject.org/publications/opportunity-to-learn.php; *see also* NAACP Legal Defense and Educational Fund, Inc., Dismantling the School-to-Prison Pipeline 5-6 (2005), http://www/naacpldf.org/content/pdf/pipeline/Dismantling_the_School_to_Prison_Pipeline.pdf.

11. Sue Burrell & Loren Warboys, Office for Juvenile Justice and Delinquency Prevention, *Special Education and the Juvenile Justice System,* OJJDP Juvenile Justice Bulletin 1 (July 2000), http://www.ncjrs.gov/pdffiles1/ojjdp/179359.pdf.

12. Mary M. Quinn et al., *Youth with Disabilities in Juvenile Corrections: A National Survey,* 71 Exceptional Children 339, 342 (2005), http://www.neglected-delinquent.org/nd/docs/mquinn0305.pdf.

13. Thomas D. Snyder et al., U.S. Department of Education, Digest of Education Statistics 2007 230–31 (2008), http://nces.ed.gov/pubs2008/2008022.pdf.

14. Committee on School Health, American Academy of Pediatrics, *supra* note 2, at 1207; Daniel J. Losen, *The Color of Inadequate School Resources: Challenging Racial Inequities That Contribute to Low Graduation Rates and High Risk for Incarceration,* 38 Clearinghouse Rev. J. of Poverty Law & Policy 616, 625 (2005) (*citing* Russell Skiba et al., *Children Left Behind: Series Summary and Recommendations,* Educ. Policy Briefs (Ind. Youth Serv. & Ctr. for Evaluation & Educ. Policy) (Summer 2004), http://www.ceep.indiana.edu/projects/PDF/PB_V2N4_Summary.pdf. *See also* Johanna Wald & Daniel J. Losen, *Out of Sight: The Journey through the School-to-Prison Pipeline, in* Invisible Children in the Society and Its Schools 23, 33 (Sue Brooks ed., 3d ed. 2007); Wald & Losen, *supra* note 2, at 11; Advancement Project & Civil Rights Project, *supra* note 10, at 13; American Bar Association & the National Bar Association, Justice by Gender (2001), http://www.abanet.org/crimjust/juvjus/justicebygenderweb.pdf.

15. *See* Camilla A. Lehr et al., Univ. of Minn., Institute on Community Integration, Alternative Schools: Policy and Legislation across the United States: Research Report 1, at 5 (2003), http://ici.umn.edu/alternativeschools/publications/Legislative_Report.pdf (finding that by 2003, forty-seven states and the District of Columbia had legislation regarding alternative schools or programs); Oleg Silchenko, Education Commission of the States, State Policies Relating to Alternative Education (2005), http://www.ecs.org/clearinghouse/65/77/6577.pdf (providing state-by-state summaries of legislation related to alternative education).

16. *See* Camilla A. Lehr et al., Institute of Community Integration, Alternative Schools: Findings from a National Survey of the States, Research Report 2, 15–16 (2004), http://ici.umn.edu/alternativeschools/publications/alt_schools_report2.pdf; Brian Kleiner et al., Nat'l Ctr. for Educ. Statistics, Public Alternative Schools and Programs for Students at Risk of Education Failure: 2000–01 27 (2002), http://nces.ed.gov/pubs2002/2002004.pdf.

17. The doctrine of *in loco parentis* refers to the authority of a parent or guardian to transfer parental duties to another person, such as a school official for the duration of the school day. Although the parameters of such a temporary relationship to the children under the care and control of school authorities are not formally spelled out, this doctrine has often been cited as the basis for children having far fewer rights when under the supervision of school authorities than they would anywhere else. *See* Betsy Levin, *Educating Youth for Citizenship: The Conflict between Authority and Individual Rights in the Public School,* 95 Yale L.J. 1647 (1986). Levin argues that *in loco parentis* should no longer hold sway legally as it is no longer relevant "where students and teachers do not know each other, where teachers are often of a different race than their students, where a single high school can have the same population as a small town." *Id.* at 1680.

18. The National Center for Education Statistics reports that 61 percent of public high schools use random dog sniffs to check for drugs, and almost a third (30 percent) use at least one other type of random sweep for contraband. Thirteen percent of public high schools across the nation drug test athletes, and 8 percent drug test students for nonathletic extracurricular activities. More than one in ten (11 percent) public school students ages twelve to eighteen pass through metal detectors at schools, and more than half (53 percent) are subject to locker checks. Rachel Dinkes et al., National Center for Education Statistics et al., Indicators of School Crime and Safety: 2007 113, 116 (2007), http://nces.ed.gov/pubs2008/2008021.pdf.

19. In 2004, 60 percent of high school teachers reported armed police stationed on school grounds. Paul Hirschfield, *The Uneven Spread of School Criminalisation in the United States,* 74 Criminal Justice Matters 28 (2008). According to the National Center for Education Statistics, almost 70 percent of public school students age twelve to eighteen reported in 2005 that police officers or security guards patrol their hallways. Dinkes et al., *supra* note 18, at 60.

20. One juvenile court judge in Massachusetts, for example, reported that he handles more school discipline in his courtroom today than in his former position, as a public school principal. American Civil Liberties Union, Race and Ethnicity in America: Turning a Blind Eye to Injustice 149 (2007), http://www.aclu.org/pdfs/humanrights/cerd_full_report.pdf; *see also* The Advancement Project, Education on Lockdown: The Schoolhouse to Jailhouse Track 15 (Mar. 2005), http://www.advancementproject.org/reports/FINALE-OLrep.pdf (documenting growth in the number of school-based arrests in select jurisdictions); Children's Defense Fund, America's Cradle to Prison Pipeline 125 (2007), http://www.childrensdefense.org/child-research-data-publications/data/cradle-prison-pipeline-report-2007-full-highres.html (noting a tripling in the number of school-based arrests in one jurisdiction).); Nat'l Council of Juvenile & Family Court Judges, Juvenile Delinquency Guidelines: Improving Court Practice in Delinquency Cases 151 (2005), http://www.ncjfcj.org/images/stories/dept/ppcd/pdf/JDG/juveniledelinquencyguidelinescompressed.pdf ("It is critical for juvenile delinquency court judges to demonstrate judicial leadership and engage school systems to collaborate with the juvenile delinquency court to . . . [c]ommit to keeping school misbehavior and truancy out of the formal juvenile delinquency court.").

21. *See In re* Gault, 387 U.S. 1 (1967).

22. *Cf.* Schall v. Martin, 467 U.S. 253 (1989).

23. *See, e.g.,* Brian B. v. Commonwealth of Penn. Dep't of Ed., 230 F. 3d 582 (3d Cir. 2000); Donnell C. v. Illinois State Bd. of Educ., 829 F. Supp. 1016 (N.D. Ill. 1993); Tunstall v. Bergeson, 5 P. 3d 691 (Wash. 2000); D.B. v. Clark County Bd. of Educ., 469 S.E. 2d 438 (Ga. Ct. App. 1996); Donnell C. v. Illinois State Bd. of Educ., 829 F. Supp. 1016 (N.D. Ill. 1993).

24. In New York City, for example, two-thirds of high-school-age offenders released from state custody do not return to school. Cora Roy-Stevens, Office for Juvenile Justice and Delinquency Prevention, Overcoming Barriers to School Reentry 1 (Oct. 2004), http://www.ncjrs.gov/pdffiles1/ojjdp/fs200403.pdf. In Kentucky, nearly 95 percent of school-age adjudicated youth fail to transition back into mainstream or alternative schools. Ronald D. Stephens & June Lane Arnette, Office for Juvenile Justice and Delinquency Prevention, From the Courthouse to the Schoolhouse: Making Successful Transitions 1 (Feb. 2000), http://www.ncjrs.gov/pdffiles1/ojjdp/178900.pdf.

25. He Len Chung et al., MacArthur Foundation, Juvenile Justice and the Transition to Adulthood (Feb. 2005), http://www.transad.pop.upenn.edu/downloads/chung-juvenile%20just%20-formatted.pdf.

26. Peter E. Leone et al., The National Center on Education, Disability and Juvenile Justice, School Failure, Race, and Disability: Promoting Positive Outcomes, Decreasing Vulnerability for Involvement with the Juvenile Delinquency System 4 (Oct. 15, 2003), http://www.edjj.org/Publications/list/leone_et_al-2003.pdf.

27. Federal Advisory Committee on Juvenile Justice, Annual Recommendations: Report to the President and Congress of the United States 3 (Aug. 2007), http://www.facjj.org/annualreports/ccFACJJ%20Report%20508.pdf.

28. *See* Charles Hamilton Houston Institute for Race & Justice, No More Children Left behind Bars: A Briefing on Youth Gang Violence and Juvenile Crime Prevention 7–12 (2008), http://chhi.podconsulting.com/assets/documents/publications/NO%20MORE%20CHILDREN%20LEFT%20BEHIND.pdf; Alliance for Excellent Education, Saving Futures, Saving Dollars: The Impact of Education on Crime Reduction and Earnings (2006), http://www.all4ed.org/files/SavingFutures.pdf; Arthur Blakemore & Dennis Hoffman, *The Economics of Dropouts: The Complexities of Uncovering the Real Costs of the Loss of "Human Capital"* (Nov. 7, 2003) (unpublished manuscript, on file with the authors).

NOTES TO CHAPTER 1

1. This does not assume that equalizing school finances would cure all resource concerns or that higher expenditures always yield results. Funding levels are relevant, but how the money is spent and the effectiveness of policies and practices also matter. Neither are improved resources for schools the complete answer, nor are inadequate resources to blame for every student that winds up behind bars.

2. Drum Major Institute, A Look at the Impact Schools (2005), http://www.drummajorinstitute.org/pdfs/impact%20schools.pdf (finding that the New York City Schools labeled as most dangerous are also large, severely overcrowded, and underfunded); National Center for Schools and Communities, Fordham University, Equity or Exclusion: The Dynamics of Resources, Demographics, and Behavior in the New York City Public Schools (2003), http://www.ncscatfordham.org/binarydata/files/EQUITY_OR_EXCLUSION.pdf (noting correlation between student behavior and level of teacher experience and teacher qualifications and other resources at school).

3. *See* Henry Levin et al., The Costs and Benefits of an Excellent Education for America's Children 13 (2007), http://www.cbcse.org/media/download_gallery/Leeds_Report_Final_Jan2007.pdf.

4. *Id.* at 14.

5. *See* James Heckman, *Report Challenging Federal Pre-K Ideas Gets Sharp Rebuttal,* Education Week, Apr. 9, 2008, at 13.

6. *See* Levin et al., *supra* note 3.

7. For a more thorough review of the parameters of the "right to education," *see* James Ryan, *Standards, Testing, and School Finance Litigation,* 86 Tex. L. Rev. 1223 (2008).

8. 347 U.S. 483, 493 (1954).

9. *See* Stuart Biegel, *School Choice Policy and Title VI: Maximizing Equal Access for K–12 Students in a Substantially Deregulated Educational Environment,* 46 Hastings L.J. 1533, 1541 (1995). Recently, the discussion of a constitutionally protected right to an education as connected to citizenship has received renewed attention. *See* Goodwin Liu, *Education, Equality, and National Citizenship,* 116 Yale L.J. 330 (2006).

10. 347 U.S. at 493, 495 n.12.

11. *Id.* at 495.

12. *See, e.g.,* Michael Rebell, *Educational Adequacy, Democracy and the Courts, in* National Research Council, Achieving High Educational Standards for All 221 & n.16 (2002), http://www.schoolfunding.info/resource_center/research/adequacychapter.pdf (citing Peter Enrich, *Leaving Equality Behind: New Directions in School Finance Reform,* 48 Vand. L. Rev. 101, 120–21 (1995)).

13. 411 U.S. 1 (1973).

14. *Id.* at 4–5.

15. *Id.* at 6.

16. *Id.* at 37.

17. *Id.* at 58–59. For a complete description of subsequent litigation in Texas, *see* Albert Kauffman, *Texas School Finance Litigation: Great Progress and Some Regression, in* A Quality Education for Every Child: Stories from the Lawyers on the Front Lines 111 (David Long et al. eds., Washington D.C., 2009).

18. *Id.*; 411 U.S. at 36.

19. The right to a "free appropriate public education" for students with disabilities pursuant to federal statutes is described in detail in chapter 3 on special education.

20. 20 U.S.C. § 6302.

21. Title I of the ESEA is set forth as a grant to the states-based program whereby each state must submit a plan to the U.S. Secretary of Education in order to be eligible for funding. Each state's plan must include a detailed description of how it will satisfy the requirements of the act. *See* 20 U.S.C. 6311(a).

22. *See, e.g.,* 20 U.S.C. § 6311(b)(2)(A)(ii); *see also* letter from Jacquelyn C. Jackson, Director, Student Achievement and School Accountability Programs, to Chief State School Officers (October 12, 2004), http://www.ed.gov/policy/elsec/guid/stateletters/uofc-ssos.html (further explaining how the accountability requirements do not apply to schools that do not receive Title I funds).

23. Elementary and Secondary Education Act of 1965, 20 U.S.C. §§ 6301–7941 (2002).

24. 20 U.S.C. § 6316 (b)(1).

25. *See* Association of Community Organizations for Reform Now v. New York City Bd. of Educ., 269 F. Supp. 338, 347 (S.D. N.Y. 2003); National Law Center on Homelessness and Poverty, R.I., v. New York, 224 F.R.D. 314, 320–21 (E.D. N.Y. 2004) (distinguishing provisions of NCLB that have no private right of action from provisions of the McKinney-Vento Act that do, in part because McKinney was passed originally as a distinct act and was later added to the ESEA). *See also* Alliance for Children, Inc., v. City of Detroit Pub. Sch., 475 F. Supp. 2d 655, 657–59, 663, 671 (E.D. Mich. 2007).

State laws, however, may allow challenges to state implementation of NCLB. *See infra* chapter 3 (discussing possibility of using writs in state court to enforce federal statutes).

26. Federal regulations require states to establish an administrative complaint process and disseminate information on how to file a complaint of a violation of NCLB provisions. 34 C.F.R. §§ 299.10 (a), (b)(1), 299.11–.12 (2009).

27. *See* Molly S. McUsic, *The Future of Brown v. Board of Education: Economic Integration of the Public Schools,* 117 Harv. L. Rev. 1334, 1345–46 & n.72 (2004); James E. Ryan, *The Influence of Race in School Finance Reform,* 98 Mich. L. Rev. 432, 456 (1999).

28. *See, e.g.,* Pauley v. Kelly, 255 S.E. 2d 859, 867 (W. Va. 1979); State v. Rivinius, 328 N.W. 2d 220, 228 (N.D. 1982); Horton v. Meskill, 376 A. 2d 359, 372–73 (Conn. 1977). *But see, e.g.,* Lujan v. Colo. State Bd. of Educ., 649 P. 2d 1005, 1018 (Colo. 1982) (en banc); Bd. of Educ., Levittown Union Free Sch. Dist., v. Nyquist, 57 N.Y. 2d 27, 43 (1982); Meyers *ex rel.* Meyers v. Bd. of Educ. of San Juan Sch. Dist., 905 F. Supp. 1544, 1568–69 (D. Utah 1995); Skeen v. State, 505 N.W. 2d 299, 301 (Minn. 1993); Wall *ex rel.* Reichley v. N. Penn Sch. Dist., 626 A.2d 123, 126 (1993); Brigham v. State, 692 A. 2d 384, 386–87 (Vt. 1997); Phillip Leon M. v. Greenbrier County Bd. of Educ., 484 S.E. 2d 909, 910 (W. Va. 1996); Campbell County Sch. Dist. v. State, 907 P. 2d 1238, 1245–46 (Wyo. 1995).

29. Idaho Schs. for Equal Educ. Opportunity v. Evans, 850 P. 2d 724, 733–34 (Id. 1993); Comm. for Educ. Rights v. Edgar, 641 N.E.2d 602, 605 (Ill. App. Ct. 1994), *aff'd,* 672 N.E. 2d 1178 (Ill. 1996); Feaster v. Portage Pub. Sch., 534 N.W. 2d 242, 246 (Mich. Ct. App. 1995), *rev'd on other grounds,* 547 N.W. 2d 328 (Mich. 1996); Shaw *ex rel.* Kolesnick v. Omaha Pub. Sch. Dist., 558 N.W. 2d 807, 813 (Neb. 1997); City of Pawtucket v. Sundlun, 662 A. 2d 40, 60 (R.I. 1995).

30. Abbott *ex rel.* Abbott v. Burke, 575 A. 2d 359 (N.J. 1990).

31. Edgewood Indep. Sch. Dist. v. Kirby, 777 S.W. 2d 391 (Tex. 1989).

32. For a detailed analysis of these cases, *see* Albert Kauffman, *Texas School Finance Litigation: Great Progress, Some Regression*; and Paul Tractenberg, *Beyond Adequacy: Looking Backward and Forward through the Lens of New Jersey,* in Front Lines, *supra* note 17.

33. The actual number is subject to change, but one organization, Access—located at Teachers College, Columbia University, and directed by Michael A. Rebell—tracks state lawsuits regarding methods of funding public schools. *See* http://www.schoolfunding.info/states/state_by_state.php3.

34. For a good description of the way such litigation efforts unfolded in New Jersey, *see* Tractenberg, *supra* note 32, at 364–68.

35. This chapter encourages potential litigators to review the status of the right to education in any state they are considering litigation, but it does not address overarching legal strategies for resource cases. For a more comprehensive review and commentary on strategies, *see* Ryan, *supra* note 7; Michael A. Rebell, *Adequacy Litigation: A New Path to Equity?* 141 PLI/NY 211 (2004).

36. *See, e.g.,* Michael Rebell, *Introduction, in* Front Lines, *supra* note 17, at 5.

37. *See generally* Front Lines, *supra* note 17 (providing an excellent variety of examples and lessons learned by litigation in fifteen states).

38. 615 N.E. 2d 516, 552–53 (Mass. 1993).

39. McDuffy v. Secretary of the Executive Office of Education, 415 Mass. 545 at 621 (1993).

40. Hancock v. Comm'r of Educ., 822 N.E. 2d 1134 (Mass. 2005).

41. 443 Mass. 428 at 433–35.

42. *See, e.g.,* Alan Jay Rom, *"McDuffy Is Dead: Long Live McDuffy!": Fundamental Rights without Remedies in the Supreme Court of Massachusetts,* St. John's J. L. Comment. 111, 158–59 (2006); *but see* Michael Weismand and Rachel Lipton, *A Quest for Educational Equity in Massachusetts: The Case of Hancock v. Driscoll, in* Front Lines, *supra* note 17, at 204 (noting that the chief justice left "a last glimmer of hope" by writing, "Nothing I say today would insulate the Commonwealth from a successful challenge under the education clause in different circumstances.").

43. *See* DeRolph v. State, 780 N.E. 2d 529 (Ohio 2002). The Ohio court first ruled in 1997 that Ohio's school system violated the state constitution. *See* DeRolph v. State, 677 N.E. 2d 733 (Ohio 1997).

44. Nos. CV-90-883-R, CV-91-0117-R, 1993 WL 204083 (Cir. Ct. Ala. Mont. County, Apr. 1, 1993); *see* Appendix to Opinion of the Justices, No. 338, 624 So. 2d 107 (Ala. 1993) (reprinting Alabama Coalition, 1993 WL 204083).

45. *Ex parte* James, 713 So. 2d 869, 879–82 (Ala. 1997), *vacated in part sub nom.,* Siegelman v. Ala. Ass'n of Sch. Bds., 819 So. 2d 568 (Ala. 2001).

46. *Id.* at 879–82.

47. *Ex parte* James, 836 So. 2d 813, 819 (Ala. 2002).

48. *Id.*

49. *See, e.g.,* Lewis E. v. Spagnolo, 710 N.E. 2d 798, 804 (Ill. 1999) (affirming lower court's dismissal of education adequacy claim against state and district with prejudice on the grounds that the question of the level of quality in the education system was solely for the legislature to decide); *see also* Gould v. Orr, 506 N.W. 2d 349, 354 (Neb. 1993) (dismissing a claim against both state and district defendants for failure to state a cause of action).

50. *See* Lobato v. State of Colorado, 2009 WL 3337684, at *1 (Colo. 2009).

51. *Id.* at *2–3.

52. *Id.* at *13.

53. Coalition for Adequacy and Fairness in School Funding v. Chiles, 680 So. 2d 400, 408 (Fla. 1996) (per curiam).

54. See Jon Mills & Timothy Mclendon, *Setting a New Standard for Public Education: Revision 6 Increases the Duty of the State to Make "Adequate Provision" for Florida Schools,* 52 Fla. L. Rev. 329, 331 (2000).

55. In *Crowley v. Pinellas County Sch. Bd.,* No. 00-005661-C1-021 (Fla. Cir. Ct., July 2004), in which the district was the only defendant, the court held that there was a private right of action to challenge a district under Article IX of the Florida state constitution, but only for bringing systemic challenges.

56. A recent compilation gives an excellent overview of how these cases were brought and argued. *See* Front Lines, *supra* note 17.

57. *See* Access, *supra* note 33.

58. One example of such an effort to incorporate remedies specific to School-to-Prison Pipeline issues into a larger statewide adequacy lawsuit is the brief filed by the Civil Rights Project, on the suggestion of Professor Charles Ogletree, in the *Hancock* litigation. Brief of Amicus Curiae in support of plaintiffs Julie Hancock et al., the Civil Rights Project at Harvard, 2004 WL 3250222 (Mass., August 26, 2004).

59. *See supra* notes 3–6 and accompanying text.

60. *See* Daniel J. Losen, *The Color of Inadequate School Resources: Challenging Racial Inequities That Contribute to Low Graduation Rates and High Risk for Incarceration,* 38 Clearinghouse Rev. J. of Poverty Law & Policy 616, 629 (2005).

61. Kenji Hakuta, Decent Schs. for Cal., English Language Learner Access to Basic Educational Necessities in California: An Analysis of Inequities (no date), http://www.decentschools.org/expert_reports/hakuta_report.pdf (expert testimony by Professor Kenji Hakuta from Stanford University describes the educational opportunities for English language learners); *see also* Jeannie Oakes, Decent Schs. for Cal., Education Inadequacy, Inequality, and Failed State Policy: A Synthesis of Expert Reports Prepared for Williams v. State of California 1, http://www.decentschools.org/expert_reports/oakes_report.pdf.

62. Campaign for Fiscal Equity v. State, 719 N.Y.S. 2d 475, 492 (Sup. Ct. 2001); *see also* Abbott *ex rel.* Abbott v. Burke, 575 A. 2d 359, 399 (N.J. 1990) (comparing teacher ratios, the average experience of instructional staff, and their average level of education, in poor versus rich districts).

63. Campaign for Fiscal Equity, 719 N.Y.S. 2d at 550–51. For related discussions, *see* M. Karega Rausch & Russell Skiba, *Unplanned Outcomes: Suspensions and Expulsions in Indiana,* Educ. Policy Briefs 6 (Ind. Youth Serv. & Ctr. for Evaluation & Educ. Policy) (Summer 2004), www.ceep.indiana.edu/projects/PDF/PB_V2N2_UnplannedOutcomes. pdf; Daniel J. Losen et al., Exploring the Link between Low Teacher Quality and Disciplinary Exclusion (paper delivered at the School to Prison Pipeline Conf., Harvard Univ. Law School, May 2004) (on file with the authors).

64. *See* Russell Skiba, Ctr. for Evaluation & Educ. Policy, The Disciplinary Practices Survey: How Do Indiana's Principals Feel about Discipline? (2004), http://www.iub. edu/~safeschl/ChildrenLeftBehind/pdf/2c.pdf; *see also* Rausch & Skiba, *supra* note 63.

65. *See, e.g.,* Md. State Bd. of Educ. v. Bradford, 875 A. 2d 703, 708 (Md. 2005).

66. A review of right-to-education cases since 1989 (current as of 2006) indicates that nearly every court that considered student outcomes, as opposed to inputs only, acknowledged dropout or graduation rates as evidence of inadequacy. *See, e.g.,* Bradford, 875 A. 2d at 708; Hancock v. Driscoll, No. 02-2978, 2004 Mass. Super. LEXIS 118 (Super. Ct. 2004); Hoke County Bd. of Educ. v. State, 599 S.E. 2d 365, 381 n.10 (N.C. 2004); Campaign for Fiscal Equity, Inc., v. State, 801 N.E. 2d 326, 328 (N.Y. 2003); Opinion of Justices (No. 338), 624 So. 2d 107, 137 (Ala. 1993); Abbott, 575 A. 2d at 363. *McDuffy v. Secretary of Executive Office of Education,* 615 N.E. 2d 516 (Mass. 1993), in fact, relied on graduation rates to doubt the primacy of standardized test scores. This suggests that among the many factors considered by courts to determine adequacy, graduation rates is among the most important.

67. State and district defendants are likely to argue that these indicators result from individual student choice, bad behavior, or poor upbringing. In other words, the blame, they may argue, lies in the child or his or her family, not in the school system. Consequently, advocates should take care to frame such data as reflecting school dysfunction to avoid an indictment of children or their parents.

68. *See, e.g.,* Durant v. State, 566 N.W. 2d 272 (Mich. 1997).

69. *See* Hoke County Bd. of Educ., 599 S.E. 2d at 387–88 & n.15 (involving adequacy claim on behalf of "at-risk" students, identified to include those who enter school from a disadvantaged background including membership in a racial minority).

70. *See supra* text accompanying notes 44–48.

71. *Id.*

72. *See* Opinion of Justices, No. 338, 624 So. 2d 107, 110–67 (Ala. 1993) (Appendix, reprinting Alabama Coalition for Equity v. Hunt, No. CV-90-883-R (Ala. Cir. Ct. Montgomery County, Apr. 1, 1993)).

73. *Id.* at 125.

74. *Id.* at 124.

75. *Id.* at 141–42. The court was particularly concerned with the absence of meaningful transition programs, the lack of individualization in instruction, and poor teacher training and development. *Id.*

76. *Id.* at 165–66.

77. *Ex parte* James (*In re* Alabama Coalition for Equity v. James), 836 So. 2d 813, 819 (Ala. 2002).

78. Lobato v. State of Colorado, 2009 WL 3337684 (Colo., Oct 19, 2009).

79. *Id.*

80. Durant v. State, 566 N.W. 2d 272 (Mich. 1997).

81. *Id.*

82. *Id.* at 283–84.

83. *Id.* at 291.

84. In the *Durant II* suit, the court followed different reasoning than under *Durant I* in dismissing the plaintiffs' claims that the state had failed to correct the situation in future funding. See Durant v. State, 605 N.W. 2d 66 (Mich. Ct. App. 2000).

85. Complaint, Bradford v. Md. State Bd. of Educ., No. 94340058 (Md. Cir. Ct., filed Dec. 6, 1994).

86. *See* Md. State Bd. of Educ. v. Bradford, 875 A. 2d 703, 709 (Md. 2005).

87. See Consent Decree, http://www.aclu-md.org/aTop%20Issues/Education%%20 Reform/1996_Consent_Decree.pdf.

88. *See, e.g.,* Jonathon Kozol, Savage Inequalities: Children in America's Schools 83–132 (1991) (contrasting the quality of education of schools in Riverdale and South Bronx within the same school district).

89. Office for Civil Rights, 2000 Annual Report to Congress, How OCR Does Its Work, http://www.ed.gov/about/offices/list/ocr/AnnRpt2000/edlite-doeswork.html. OCR has not yet, however, issued the guidance. Nonetheless, litigators may want to explore the possibility of filing administrative complaints with OCR pursuant to Title VI on the grounds of resource inequity. For a discussion of Title VI disparate impact claims, *see* Losen, *supra* note 60, at 629.

90. *See* Consent Decree, Rodriguez v. LAUSD, No. C-611-358 (Ca. Super. Ct., Aug. 25, 1992); *see also* Jesse Hahnel, *Intra-District Funding Inequalities: Rodriguez v. LAUSD* (unpublished manuscript, on file with the authors).

91. *Id.* For a brief overview of equal protection analysis, see section B.

92. Crowley v. Pinellas County Sch. Bd., No. 00-005661-C1-021 (Fla. Cir. Ct., July 2004).

93. Complaint, Case No. 502008-CA-007579 (Fla. Cir. Ct., filed Mar. 13, 2008), http://www.aclu.org/racialjustice/edu/34507lgl20080318.html.

94. Order Granting Defendants' Motion to Dismiss Plaintiffs' Class Action Complaint, Schroeder v. Palm Beach County School Board, Case No. 502008CA007579 (Fla. Cir. Ct., July 28, 2008).

95. *See* Bradford, 875 A. 2d at 709; *but see* Campaign for Fiscal Equity, Inc., v. State, 801 N.E. 2d 326, 343 (N.Y. 2003) (rejecting state's cross-claim against district upon holding that state's own actions imposed liability, but stating that both the board of education and the city are "'creatures or agents of the State'" and that "the State remains responsible when the failures of its agents sabotage the measures by which it secures for its citizens their constitutionally-mandated rights"; citation omitted); *see also* Gould v. Orr, 506 N.W. 2d 349 (Neb. 1993).

96. No Child Left Behind Act of 2001, Pub. L. 107-110, § 5131(c), 115 Stat. 1425 (2002). NCLB is the "short title" for the Elementary and Secondary Education Act of 1965 as amended and reauthorized in 2002.

97. *See* Brief for Appellant, Hancock v. Comm'r of Educ., 822 N.E. 2d 1134 (Mass. 2005) (No. SJC-09267).

98. *See* Hancock v. Comm'r of Educ., 822 N.E. 2d 1134, 1138-1141. The State had established "objective competency goals and the means to measure progress toward those goals." *Id.* at 1143-45.

99. Lobato v. State of Colorado, 218 P.3d 358, 364 (Colo. 2009).

100. For further articulation of similar concerns, *see* Ryan, *supra* note 7, at 1223.

101. David N. Figlio, *Testing, Crime, and Punishment,* 90 J. Pub. Econ. 837, 839 (2005).

102. *Id.*

103. Joseph B. Tulman, *Disability and Delinquency: How Failures to Identify, Accommodate, and Serve Youth with Education-Related Disabilities Leads to Their Disproportionate Representation in the Delinquency System,* 3 Whittier J. Child & Fam. Advoc. 3, 76 (2003), http://www.law.udc.edu/resource/resmgr/facultydocs/tulman_disability_delinquenc.pdf.

104. 457 U.S. 202 (1982). *See infra* chapter 2 for further discussion of this case.

105. 334 F. Supp. 1257 (E.D. Pa. 1971).

106. 348 F. Supp. 866 (D.C. Cir. 1972).

107. *See* Mark G. Yudof et al., Educational Policy and the Law 692 (2002).

108. The Individuals with Disabilities Education Act recounts this history in its findings section, which states,

> (2) Before the date of enactment of the Education for All Handicapped Children Act of 1975 (Public Law 94-142), the educational needs of millions of children with disabilities were not being fully met because—
> (A) the children did not receive appropriate educational services;
> (B) the children were excluded entirely from the public school system and from being educated with their peers;
> (C) undiagnosed disabilities prevented the children from having a successful educational experience; or
> (D) a lack of adequate resources within the public school system forced families to find services outside the public school system.

20 U.S.C. § 1401(c).

109. Individuals with Disabilities Education Act of 1970, Pub. L. 91-230 (1970), codified at 20 U.S.C. §§ 1400 *et seq.*

110. 414 U.S. 563 (1974).

111. *Id.* at 568–69.

112. Equal Educational Opportunity Act of 1974, Pub. L. 93-380, 20 U.S.C. §§ 1701 *et seq.*

113. *See* 20 U.S.C. § 1706; *see also* Castaneda v. Pickard, 648 F. 2d 989, 1010 (5th Cir. 1981) (holding that a state violates the EEOA if even an adequately funded program "fails, after being employed for a period of time sufficient to give the plan a legitimate trial").

114. Alan L. Rupe & John Robb, *Montoy v. Kansas: The Fight for Educational Equity and Adequacy for All Kansas Kids in the Home of Brown v. Board of Education, in* Front Lines, *supra* note 17, at 303.

115. 419 U.S. 565 (1975).

116. *See* Seal v. Morgan, 229 F. 3d 567 (6th Cir. 2000) (finding that expulsion of student violated substantive due process).

117. *See* Davis *ex rel.* LaShonda D. v. Monroe County Bd. of Educ., 526 U.S. 629, 664 (1999) (noting that some state constitutions create a fundamental right to education and therefore impose a continuing obligation to educate students who are suspended or expelled); *see also* David J. D'Agata, *Alternative Education Programs: A Return to "Separate but Equal"?* 29 Nova L. Rev. 635, 653–55 (2005).

118. *In re* R.M., 102 P. 3d 868 (Wyo. 2004) (holding that strict scrutiny is the appropriate test to apply to determine whether education must be provided to expelled students); *see, e.g.,* Cathe A. v. Doddridge County Bd. of Educ., 490 S.E. 2d 340, 343 (W. Va. 1997) ("fundamental right" to education triggers "strict scrutiny" when state action expelling student infringes on that right).

119. Keith D. v. Ball, 350 S.E. 2d 720 (W. Va. 1986) (finding that expulsion of students did not abridge fundamental state right to education because disruptive conduct by student forfeits that right); *but see* Cathe A., 490 S.E. 2d at 343 ("fundamental right" meant "strict scrutiny" triggered, yet earlier precedent that required state-funded alternative education for expelled students was modified to be a case-by-case determination).

120. *See* State *ex rel.* G.S., 749 A. 2d 902, 903, 906–07 (N.J. Super. Ct. Ch. Div. 2000) (declining to find a "fundamental" right to education, but nonetheless holding that state constitution guarantees the right to free school instruction, including for students who have been adjudicated delinquent and expelled).

121. 653 N.E. 2d 1088, 1095 (Mass. 1995).

122. Examples include the following: North Carolina: In *In re* Jackson, 352 S.E. 2d 449 (N.C. Ct. App. 1987), the North Carolina Court of Appeals interpreted the state constitution to grant a right to education but concluded that the right "may be constitutionally denied when outweighed by the school's interest in protecting other students, teachers, and school property, and in preventing the disruption of the educational system." *Id.* at 455. It thus reversed the lower court's conclusion that the right to education required a school district to provide alternative educational services to suspended students. *Id.* Michigan: Frank J. Kelley, Attorney General State of Michigan, Opinion No. 6271 (1985),

http://www.ag.stste.mi.us/opinion/datafiles/1980s/op06271.htm (interpreting state constitutional provision creating free public schools as not requiring a board of education to provide alternative education to suspended or expelled students, except those students eligible for services under the Handicapped Children Act).

123. *See* Office of the Public Advocate for the City of New York & Advocates for Children, Pushing Out At-Risk Students: An Analysis of High School Discharge Figures (2002), http://www.advocatesforchildren.org/pubs/pushout-11-20-02.doc; *see also* Elisa Hyman, *School Push-Outs: An Urban Case Study,* Clearinghouse Rev. J. of Poverty Law & Policy 684, 685 (Jan.–Feb. 2005), http://www.advocatesforchildren.org/pubs/2005/sch-pushouts.pdf.

124. *See* Second Amended Class Action Complaint for Injunctive, Declaratory and Other Relief, at 13–14, Ruiz v. Pedota, No. 03-CV-0502, 2004 U.S. Dist. LEXIS 50 (E.D. N.Y. Jan. 6, 2004); *see also* Hyman, *supra* note 123, at 686. The case materials are available online at http://www.Advocatesforchildren.org/litigation/litdocs/pushoutdocs/.

125. Ruiz v. Pedota, No. 03-CV-0502, 2004 U.S. Dist. LEXIS 50 (E.D. N.Y. Jan. 6, 2004).

126. *Id.*

127. N.Y. Educ. Law § 3202(1) (McKinney 2008).

128. *See* Second Amended Complaint, Entitlement to Instruction and Intervention Services under New York State Law and Regulations, *supra* note 124, at 7–9.

129. *Id.*

130. *Id.*

131. *See* R.V. v. New York City Dep't of Educ., 321 F. Supp. 2d 538, 553 (E.D. N.Y. July 17, 2004); Tamar Lewin, *City Settles Suit and Will Take Back Students,* N.Y. Times, Jan. 8, 2004, at B3.

132. Hyman, *supra* note 123, at 688.

133. ACLU et al., Dignity Denied: The Effect of "Zero Tolerance" Policies on Students' Human Rights (2008), http://www.aclu.org/pdfs/humanrights/dignitydenied_november2008.pdf; *see also* Dignity in Schools Campaign, http://www.dignityinschools.org/.

134. Convention on the Rights of the Child, Nov. 20, 1989, 1577 U.N.T.S. 3.

135. International Convention on the Elimination of All Forms of Racial Discrimination, Dec. 21, 1965, 660 U.N.T.S. 195.

136. International Covenant on Economical, Social and Cultural Rights, *opened for signature* Dec. 16, 1966, 993 U.N.T.S. 3 (entered into force Jan. 3, 1976).

137. All three resolutions of the ABA along with supporting reports are currently available at http://www.cleweb.org/latest/ABA.118B.RighttoRemaininSchool.pdf.

138. *See, e.g.,* Jeannie Oakes et al., Grassroots Organizing, Social Movements, and the Right to High-Quality Education (2006), http://www.law.berkeley.edu/files/oakes-rogers-blasi_paper.pdf.

139. *Id.* at 2.

140. *Id.*

141. *Id.* at 22.

1. Johanna Wald & Daniel J. Losen, *Out of Sight: The Journey through the School-to-Prison Pipeline, in* Invisible Children in the Society and Its Schools 26 (Sue Brooks ed., 3d ed. 2007); Daniel J. Losen, *The Color of Inadequate School Resources: Challenging Racial Inequities That Contribute to Low Graduation Rates and High Risk for Incarceration,* 38 Clearinghouse Rev. J. of Poverty Law & Policy 616, 625 (2005); Russell Skiba et al., *Children Left Behind: Series Summary and Recommendations,* Educ. Policy Briefs (Ind. Youth Serv. & Ctr. for Evaluation & Educ. Policy) (Summer 2004).

2. The data from 1973 were obtained from Children's Defense Fund of the Washington Research Project, Suspensions: Are They Helping Children? (1975). Data from 2006 and 2003 were obtained from the U.S. Department of Education's Office for Civil Rights. A full analysis of these data will be published this year. Daniel J. Losen & Russell J. Skiba, Southern Poverty Law Center, Suspended Education: Urban Middle Schools in Crisis (forthcoming 2010; on file with the authors); *see also* U.S. Department of Education, Office for Civil Rights, Times Series CD-ROM, 2000 Elementary and Secondary School Survey: National and State Projections (2006); U.S. Department of Education, OCR Elementary and Secondary Education Survey: 2002; Daniel J. Losen & Christopher Edley, Jr., *The Role of Law in Policing Abusive Discipline Policies: Why School Discipline Is a Civil Rights Issue, in* Zero Tolerance: Resisting the Drive for Punishment in Our Schools 230, 231 (William Ayers et al. eds., 2001); Wald & Losen, *supra* note 1, at 26; The Advancement Project and the Civil Rights Project at Harvard University, Opportunities Suspended: The Devastating Consequences of Zero Tolerance and School Discipline Policies 6–7, 13 (2000), http://www.advancement-project.org/publications/opportunity-to-learn.php. *See* Gary Sweeten, *Who Will Graduate? Disruption of High School Education by Arrest and Court Involvement,* 23 Just. Q. 462, 473, 478–79 (2006); The Advancement Project, Education on Lockdown: The Schoolhouse to Jailhouse Track 12 (Mar. 2005), http://www.advancementproject.org/reports/FINALEOL-rep.pdf ; Terence P. Thornberry et al., *The Causes and Correlates Studies: Findings and Policy Implications,* 9 Juvenile Just. 3, 12 (Sept. 2004); Jeff Grogger, *Arrests, Persistent Youth Joblessness, and Black/White Employment Differentials,* 74 Rev. Econ. & Stat. 100, 105–06 (1992).

3. Losen & Skiba, *supra* note 2.

4. *Id.*

5. Am. Civil Liberties Union, Missing the Mark: Alternative Schools in the State of Mississippi (Feb. 2009); Texas Appleseed, Texas' School-to-Prison Pipeline: Dropout to Incarceration: The Impact of School Discipline and Zero Tolerance 50 (2007).

6. Mark A. Greenwald, Florida Department of Juvenile Justice, Delinquency in Florida's Schools: A Four Year Study 5 (2009); Am. Civil Liberties Union, Hard Lessons: School Resource Officer Programs and School-Based Arrests in Three Connecticut Towns (Nov. 2008); Judith A. Browne, Advancement Project, Derailed: The Schoolhouse to Jailhouse Track 18–20, 23 (2003) (documenting disparities by race and special education status in school-based arrests in select jurisdictions).

7. Howard N. Snyder, Office for Juvenile Justice and Delinquency Prevention, Juvenile Arrests 2003 9 (Aug. 2005), http://www.ncjrs.gov/pdffiles1/ojjdp/209735.pdf; NAACP Legal Defense and Educational Fund, Inc., Dismantling the School-to-Prison Pipeline 6 (2005), http://www.naacpldf.org/content/pdf/pipline/Dismantling_the_School_to_Prison_Pipeline.pdf.

8. James Bell & Laura John Ridolfi, W. Haywood Burns Institute, Adoration of the Question: Reflections on the Failure to Reduce Racial & Ethnic Disparities in the Juvenile Justice System (Dec. 2008); Bart Lubow & Dennis Barron, Office of Juvenile Justice and Delinquency Prevention, Fact Sheet: Resources for Juvenile Detention Reform (November 2000).

9. National Council on Crime and Delinquency, And Justice for Some: Differential Treatment of Youth of Color in the Justice System (Jan. 2007).

10. *Id.*

11. *See* Russell J. Skiba, Zero Tolerance, Zero Evidence 11–12 (2000); Russell J. Skiba et al., The Color of Discipline: Sources of Racial and Gender Disproportionality in School Punishment (2000); NAACP Legal Defense and Educational Fund, Inc., *supra* note 7, at 6.

12. U.S. Const. amend. XIV.

13. Civil Rights Act of 1964, §§ 601, 602, 42 U.S.C. § 2000d.

14. *See* section A(2)(b) of this chapter.

15. *See* Rogers v. Lodge, 458 U.S. 613, 618 (1982) (citing Arlington Heights v. Metropolitan Hous. Dev. Corp., 429 U.S. 252, 266 (1982)).

16. *See* Ricci v. DeStefano, 129 S. Ct. 2658, 2672 (2009). The Department of Education's Assistant Secretary for Civil Rights "is responsible for ensuring that institutional recipients of Federal financial assistance do not discriminate against [those in a protected class such as] American students, faculty, or other individuals on the basis of race, color, national origin, sex, disability, or age." U.S. Gov't Manual 1998–1999, Office of the Fed. Registrar, Dep't of Ed. 247 (1999), http://frwebgate.access.gpo.gov/cgi-bin/getdoc. cgi?dbname=1998_government_manual&docid=177653tx_xxx-37.pdf.

17. Alexander v. Sandoval, 532 U.S. 275, 285 (2001) (requiring proof of discriminatory intent to sustain Title VI claims in a federal court by reading the statute to prohibit a private right of action to enforce disparate impact claims); Washington v. Davis, 426 U.S. 229 (1976) (holding that claims of equal protection violations require discriminatory intent).

18. 619 F. Supp. 670 (D. Ark. 1985).

19. *Id.* at 673, 678.

20. A showing of race discrimination

> [i]n general [] requires that the other incidents' circumstances be "reasonably comparable" to those surrounding [plaintiff's] [] suspensions, and that "the nature of the infraction and knowledge of the evidence by [school] [] officials [be] sufficiently similar to support a finding of facial inconsistency." The test is whether a prudent person, looking objectively at the incidents, would think them roughly equivalent and the protagonists similarly situated.

Dartmouth Review v. Dartmouth Coll., 889 F. 2d 13, 19 (1st Cir. 1989) (quoting Albert v. Carovano, 851 F. 2d 561, 573–74 (2d Cir. 1988)).

21. 823 F. Supp. 511 (N.D. Ill. 1993).

22. *Id.* at 519–20.

23. 928 F. Supp. 789 (S.D. Ind. 1996).

24. *Id.* at 792.

25. *Id.* at 793.

26. *Id.*

27. No. C2-99-830, 2001 WL 506509, at *8 (S.D. Ohio, Apr. 25, 2001).

28. *Id.*

29. *Id.*

30. *Id.*

31. Complaint at 18–20, Antoine v. Winner Sch. Dist., No. Civ. 06-3007 (D.S.D., filed Mar. 24, 2006).

32. *Id.*

33. *Id.*

34. *Id.*

35. Consent Decree at 2–3, Antoine, No. Civ. 06-3007 (D.S.D., filed Dec. 10, 2007).

36. 526 U.S. 629 (1999).

37. *Id.* at 643. Although *Davis* involved a Title IX claim of sexual harassment, *id.* at 632–33, courts apply the *Davis* deliberate-indifference test to Title VI racial harassment. *See* Saxe v. State College Area Sch. Dist., 240 F. 3d 200, 206 n.5 (3d Cir. 2001) ("Although both *Franklin* and *Davis* dealt with sexual harassment under Title IX, we believe that their reasoning applies equally to harassment on the basis of the personal characteristics enumerated in Title VI and other relevant federal anti-discrimination statutes."); Monteiro v. Tempe Union High Sch. Dist., 158 F. 3d 1022, 1032–33 (9th Cir. 1998) (applying Title VI to student-on-student racial harassment). Courts treat racially hostile environment claims under the deliberate-indifference framework in the same manner regardless of whether they were brought under Title VI or the Equal Protection Clause. *See, e.g.,* Gant v. Wallingford Bd. of Educ., 195 F. 3d 134, 140 n.5 (2d Cir. 1999) (holding that the deliberate-indifference standard applied in an equal protection context but noting (without deciding) that some aspects of the *Davis* holding—such as the requirement that harassment be so severe, pervasive, and objectively offensive so as to deprive victims of educational opportunities—might be limited to that statutory context); Crispim v. Athanson, 275 F. Supp. 2d 240, 247–48 (D. Conn. 2003) (applying deliberate-indifference test to an equal protection claim for racially hostile educational environment).

38. Davis, 526 U.S. at 646, 650.

39. *Id.* at 643.

40. Alexander v. Sandoval, 532 U.S. 275, 286, 293 (2001); *see* Bryant v. Indep. Sch. Dist. No. I-38 of Garvin County, 334 F. 3d 928, 932–34 (10th Cir. 2003) (applying *Davis* test to racially hostile educational environment after *Sandoval*); *but see* Almendares v. Palmer, 284 F. Supp. 2d 799, 806 & n.5 (N.D. Ohio 2003) (noting in dicta that unlike the Tenth Circuit, the Sixth Circuit has not yet ruled on whether deliberate indifference may constitute intentional discrimination after *Sandoval*).

41. *See* Yick Wo v. Hopkins, 118 U.S. 356, 374 (1886).

42. For several years since *Sandoval* was decided, policymakers have proposed a legislative "fix" to restore the private right of action for disparate impact claims under Title VI, including the Civil Rights Restoration Act introduced in Congress in 2008. S. 2544, H.R. 5129, 110th Cong. (2008).

Outside of the context of race, advocates should note that disparate impact challenges are still possible through Section 504 of the Rehabilitation Act and Title IX, through both litigation and administrative agency complaints. These contexts were not addressed by the Supreme Court's ruling in *Sandoval*.

43. 34 C.F.R. § 100.3(b)(2). Section 602 of Title VI authorizes federal agencies to adopt regulations and guidance to implement Title VI and to effectuate the purpose of Section 601.

44. *See* Memorandum from Loretta King, Acting Assistant Attorney General, U.S. Dep't of Justice, to Federal Agency Civil Rights Directors and General Counsels 3 (July 10, 2009) (on file with the authors).

45. *Id.*

46. *See, e.g.,* U.S. v. Boutwell, 84 U.S. 604 (1873) (describing function and scope of writs of mandamus); State ex rel. Westchester Estates, Inc., v. Bacon, 399 N.E. 2d 81 (Ohio 1980); Huffman v. State, 813 So. 2d 10 (Fla. 2000); Hennessey v. City of Bridgeport, 569 A. 2d 1122 (Conn. 1990); Los Angeles Taxpayers Alliance v. Fair Political Practice Comm., 14 Cal. App. 4th 1214 (Cal. Ct. App. 1993) (finding the writ available to compel administrative agency to act in a manner consistent with the statute it is charged to enforce); Timmons v. McMahon, 235 Cal. App. 3d 512, 517–18 (Cal. Ct. App. 1991) (holding that the writ may issue to compel agency to correct a policy interpreting a law or regulation in a manner inconsistent with the statute agency is enforcing).

47. Miller v. Woods, 148 Cal. App. 3d 862, 880–81 (Cal. Ct. App. 1983) (finding that violations of the Federal Rehabilitation Act of 1973 provide, in part, basis for issuance of writ); King v. Martin, 21 Cal. App. 3d 791, 794 (Cal. Ct. App. 1971) (noting federal statutory and regulatory language requiring timeliness for welfare hearings provides adequate basis for writ).

48. *See* Jane Perkins, Ensuring Linguistic Access in Health Care Settings: Legal Rights and Responsibilities, National Health Law Program 27–28 (2003). Other contracts with state Medicaid agencies also contain similar provisions and should be available under a state's public records act.

49. Barnes v. Gorman, 536 U.S. 181, 186–87 (2002); Bennett v. Ky. Dep't of Educ., 470 U.S. 656, 670 (1985).

50. *See* Adira Siman, *Challenging Zero Tolerance: Federal and State Legal Remedies for Students of Color,* 14 Cornell J. L. & Pub. Pol'y 327 (2005).

51. *See* Cal. Gov't Code § 11135(a).

52. Cal. Code Regs. tit. 22, § 98101(i) (2010) (emphasis added).

53. *See, e.g.,* Committee Concerning Community Improvement v. City of Modesto, No. CV-F-04-6121, 2007 WL 2408495, at *8 (E.D. Cal. Aug. 21, 2007) ("In addition, intentional discrimination is not required for proof of a § 11135 claim, which may be proved by disparate impact."); *see also* Darensburg v. Metro. Transp. Comm'n, 611 F. Supp. 2d 994 (N.D. Cal. 2009) (holding that prima facie case of disparate impact discrimination under state statute prohibiting discrimination in state-funded programs requires plaintiff to show (1) the occurrence of certain outwardly neutral practices and (2) a significantly adverse or disproportionate impact on minorities produced by the defendant's facially neutral acts or practice).

54. *See* 2001 Cal. A.B. 677.

55. Section 11139 of the Code states, "This article and regulations adopted pursuant to this article may be enforced by a civil action for equitable relief." *See also* Blumhorst v. Jewish Family Servs. of Los Angeles, 126 Cal. App. 4th 993, 1002 (2005) (stating that "the Legislature did create a private cause of action for civil rights discrimination by the amendments to section 11139").

56. In *Darensburg v. Metropolitan Transportation Commission,* a coalition composed of California bus riders and labor and civil rights advocates brought a federal class action against the Metropolitan Transportation Commission alleging federal and state civil rights law violations based on MTC's denial of equitable funding to patrons of color. The coalition alleged that MTC's discriminatory behavior was reflected in the level of public subsidies it provided to transit users. Disproportionately, white and affluent passengers received a per-passenger subsidy of $6.14 and $13.79, respectively, for each ride they take. Riders of color, who constitute 80 percent of the total number of patrons and who are also 60 percent transit dependent, on the other hand, received a public subsidy of only $2.78. The litigation sought equity in the funding and services available for low-income minority transit-dependent riders. On March 27, 2009, the U.S. District Court found that plaintiffs made a prima facie showing that MTC's transit-expansion program had a disparate impact on bus riders of color, but it ultimately ruled against the plaintiffs based on the rationale that MTC's competing goals warranted its practices. On April 23, 2009, the plaintiffs appealed the U.S. District Court's decision to the 9th Circuit Court of Appeals, and the matter remains pending. *See* Darensburg v. Metro. Transp. Comm'n, 611 F. Supp. 2d 994 (N.D. Cal. 2009). *See also* Public Advocates, *Work in Transit,* http://www.publicadvocates.org/ourwork/transportation/index.html.

57. *See* Alexander v. Sandoval, 532 U.S. 275, 287 (2001) (holding private plaintiffs cannot enforce disparate effect regulations against state defendants using original jurisdiction of federal court but holding that "[r]aising up causes of action where a statute has not created them may be a proper function for common-law courts" (quoting Lampf, Pleva, Lipkind, Prupis & Petigrow v. Gilbertson, 501 U.S. 350, 365 (1991)). One potential argument that plaintiffs may face in attempting to use state vehicles for enforcement of Title VI regulations is that the regulations themselves are invalid because they exceed the breadth of the statute. However, as long as the regulations are published, an entity that is bound by current regulations arguably should not be able to raise a defense that the regulation was an improper or illegal exercise of power. This is particularly true under circumstances in which compliance with federal laws and regulations is a condition of a contract or grant and states are charged with administering monies in a manner that is consistent with the interpretation of the federal agency grantor.

58. Although not all of the California state-law theories are available to advocates in other states, some similar remedies may be available. *See* Perkins, *supra* note 48, at 27–30; Jane Perkins et al., *Enforcing Language Access Rights,* Clearinghouse Rev. J. Poverty Law & Policy (Sept.–Oct. 2004), http://www.healthlaw.org/library/item.76299.

59. 740 Ill. Comp. Stat. 23/5 (2004).

60. *Id.; see also* Nicol v. Lavin, No. 03-cv-6688, 2004 WL 1881786, at *7 (N.D. Ill., Aug. 13, 2004).

61. No. 05-cv-760, 2005 WL 453090 (Feb. 7, 2005).

62. *See* McFadden v. Bd. of Ed. for Ill. Sch. Dist. U-46, No. 05-cv-760, 2008 WL 4877150 (N.D. Ill., Aug. 8, 2008)

63. 856 N.E. 2d 460 (Ill. App. 2006)

64. *Id.* at 467.

65. *Id.*

66. 477 N.W. 2d 886 (Minn. 1991), *questioned by* State v. Clausen, 493 N.W. 2d 113 (Minn. 1992), on other grounds.

67. *Id.* at 888 n.2. "Among the many statistics provided to the trial court were those show-ing that of all persons charged with possession of cocaine base in 1988, 96.6% were black. Of all persons charged with possession of powder cocaine, 79.6% were white." *Id.* at 887.

68. *Id.* at 888.

69. *Id.* (quoting Wegan v. Village of Lexington, 309 N.W. 2d 273, 280 (Minn. 1981); Guilliams v. Comm'r of Revenue, 299 N.W. 2d 138, 142 (Minn. 1980)).

70. *Id.* at 889.

71. *Id.* at 889–90.

72. *See id.* at 891. *See also* Siman, *supra* note 50, at 358–59 ("[I]t appears that Minnesota courts would likely subject policies that result in disparate impact to a higher level of scrutiny than the federal courts.").

73. 678 A. 2d 1267 (Conn. 1996).

74. Conn. Const. art. 8, § 1 ("There shall always be free public elementary and second-ary schools in the state. The general assembly shall implement this principle by appropriate legislation."); *id.* art. 1, § 1 ("All men when they form a social compact, are equal in rights; and no man or set of men are entitled to exclusive public emoluments or privileges from the community."); *id.* art 1, § 20 ("No person shall be denied the equal protection of the law nor be subjected to segregation or discrimination . . . because of religion, race . . .").

75. Sheff, 678 A. 2d at 1274.

76. 757 A. 2d 1225, 1244 (Conn. App. Ct. 2000).

77. *See id.* (noting that the *Sheff* court held as it did "because it relied in part on the 'independent constitutional significance' of the word 'segregation' in article first, § 20, of our state constitution and the affirmative constitutional obligation to provide a substan-tially equal educational opportunity under article eighth, § 1" (quoting Sheff, 678 A. 2d at 1267)). Two other states, Hawaii and New Jersey, also have an explicit prohibition on segregation in their constitutions. *See* Sheff, 678 A. 2d at 1282 n.29 (discussing Haw. Const. art. 1, § 9, and N.J. Const. art. 1, para. 5, which explicitly prohibits segregation in public school education). As the *Sheff* court noted, no court has undertaken the question of whether this clause of the New Jersey constitution would prohibit *de facto* segregation.

78. *See* Siman, *supra* note 50, at 361–62.

79. U.S. Dep't of Educ., Office of English Language Acquisition (OELA), Language Use, English Ability, and Linguistic Isolation for the Population 5 to 17 Years by State: 2000 (2000), http://www.census.gov/population/cen2000/phc-t20/tab02.pdf.

80. U.S. Dep't of Educ., Office of English Language Acquisition (OELA), The Grow-ing Numbers of Limited English Proficient Students (2005), http://www.ncela.gwu.edu/policy/states/reports/statedata/2003LEP/GrowingLEP_0304_Dec05.pdf.

81. *Id.*

82. *Id.*

83. *See* Advocates for Children of New York and the New York Immigration Coali-tion, Report from the Front Lines: What's Needed to Make New York's ESL and Bilingual Programs Succeed 12–26 (Feb. 7, 2001), http://www.advocatesforchildren.org/pubs/2005/eslbilingual.pdf.

84. *Id.* at 26; Advocates for Children of New York and the New York Immigration Coalition, Creating a Formula for Success: Why English Language Learner Students Are Dropping Out of School, and How to Increase Graduation Rates 4 (June 2002), http://www.advocatesforchildren.org/pubs/2005/elldropout.pdf.

85. New York Immigration Coalition, Getting It Right: Ensuring a Quality Education for English Language Learners in New York 22 (Nov. 2008), http://www.thenyic.org/templates/documentFinder.asp?did=967.

86. *Id.* at 8.

87. New York Immigration Coalition, Denied at the Door: Language Barriers Block Immigrant Parents from School Involvement (Feb 19, 2004), http://www.thenyic.org/templates/documentFinder.asp?did=79.

88. Advocates for Children of New York and the New York Immigration Coalition, Creating a Formula for Success, *supra* note 84, at 7, 42–44; *see also* Advocates for Children of New York and the New York Immigration Coalition, Report from the Front Lines, *supra* note 83, at 8, 14 n.12 ("In order for parents to participate in their children's education, those parents who are ELLs must have interpretation services offered to them so they can speak with school personnel about their child's academic progress.").

89. New York Immigration Coalition, *supra* note 87.

90. Memorandum from the Dep't of Health, Educ., & Welfare Regarding Language Minority Children (May 25, 1970), http://www.ed.gov/about/offices/list/ocr/docs/lau1970.html.

91. 414 U.S. 563, 566 (1974), abrogation recognized in *Alexander v. Sandoval,* 532 U.S. 275 (2001); *see also* Castaneda v. Pickard, 648 F. 2d 989 (5th Cir. 1981).

92. Equal Educational Opportunity Act of 1974, Pub. L. 93-380, 20 U.S.C. §§ 1701 *et seq.*

93. 20 U.S.C. § 1703(f).

94. These policies may be found at http://www.ed.gov/about/offices/list/ocr/ellresources.html.

95. *See, e.g.,* Castaneda, 648 F. 2d at 1009 (noting that when Congress enacted the EEOA it intended that "schools made a genuine and good faith effort . . . to remedy the language deficiencies of their students.")

96. Flores v. Arizona, 516 F. 3d 1140, 1146 (9th Cir. 2008) (internal citations omitted; alterations in original). The lower court in *Flores* struck down the state's funding scheme for ELL students, finding that the funding level resulted in too many students per classroom, too few classrooms, an insufficient number of qualified instructors, and inadequate tutorial programs and teaching materials, in violation of the EEOA. *See* Flores v. Arizona, 480 F. Supp. 2d 1157 (D. Ariz. 2007). The Ninth Circuit affirmed. Flores, 516 F. 3d at 1180. The U.S. Supreme Court reversed the Ninth Circuit's decision and remanded to the district court to determine whether the school district's compliance with the ELL provisions of the No Child Left Behind Act satisfied its obligations to take "appropriate action" under the EEOA. *See* Horne v. Flores, 129 S. Ct. 2579, 2607 (2009).

97. Gomez v. Illinois State Bd. of Educ., 811 F. 2d 1030, 1041–42 (7th Cir. 1987).

98. *See* Letter from U.S. Dep't of Educ., Office for Civil Rights, to Superintendent of Joint Technical Educ. Dist., regarding OCR Case Number 08041022-D (June 21, 2004), http://www.ed.gov/about/offices/list/ocr/letters/evit08041022-d.html; Memorandum from the Dep't of Health, Educ., and Welfare, Office of the Sec'y, Identification of Discrimination and Denial of Services on the Basis of National Origin (May 25, 1970), http://www.ed.gov/about/offices/list/ocr/docs/lau1970.html.

99. Complaint to the Office for Civil Rights Concerning English Language Learners in the Pittsburgh Public Schools (May 16, 2005), http://www.elc-pa.org/pubs/downloads/litigation/lit-Somali%20OCRComplaint_Final__Final__l5-13-05.pdf.

100. Education Law Center, *Agreement Reached to Improve Educational Opportunities for Somali Bantu Students in Pittsburgh* (May 18, 2006), http://www.elc-pa.org/pubs/downloads/litigation/ell-Press%20Release%20Settlement%20Ed%20Law%20Center%20OCR%20(FINAL)%205-18-06.pdf; Joe Smydo, *City Schools Settle Complaint Filed for Somali Refugees,* Pittsburgh Post-Gazette, May 23, 2006, http://www.elc-pa.org/pubs/downloads/litigation/ell-Post%20Gazette%205-23-06.pdf; Emily Breon, *School Districts Denying Refugee Students Equal Access to Education,* Kids Counsel (Fall 2008), http://www.kidscounsel.org/kidscounsel%20news%20oct%2006.pdf.

101. 457 U.S. 202 (1982).

102. U.S. Department of Education, *Education for Homeless Children and Youths Grants for State and Local Activities,* http://www.ed.gov/programs/homeless/index.html.

103. McKinney-Vento Homeless Assistance Act, Pub. L. 100-77 (1987).

104. 42 U.S.C. § 11432 *et seq.*

105. The McKinney-Vento Act defines "homelessness" broadly as lacking a "fixed, regular, and adequate nighttime residence," including youth living in cars, parks, bus stations, or other public or private locations not typically used for sleeping, as well as children and youth who are sharing the housing of others due to a loss of housing, economic hardship, or a similar reason; living in motels, hotels, trailer parks, or campgrounds due to the lack of alternative adequate accommodations; staying in shelters; or awaiting foster care placement. 42 U.S.C. § 11434A(2).

The act requires every local educational agency (LEA) to designate a liaison to coordinate implementation of the law. The liaison's duties include ensuring that school personnel and other entities and agencies identify homeless children and youth; homeless children and youth enroll in school and have opportunities for academic success; homeless children, youth, and families receive educational services for which they are eligible, including preschool services; students receive transportation services; public notice of rights are posted; parents and guardians are involved; and enrollment disputes are mediated. 42 U.S.C. § 11432(g)(1)(J)(ii), (g)(6)(A). At the state level, every state educational agency (SEA) must establish an Office of State Coordinator for the Education of Homeless Children and Youth. This office is charged with critical responsibilities with respect to the implementation of the act, including developing and carrying out a state plan, engaging in wide-ranging coordination and collaboration activities, collecting information regarding the success of programs, and ensuring the compliance of all LEAs in the state. 42 U.S.C. § 11432(d)(2), (f).

Every state must establish procedures to resolve McKinney-Vento disputes promptly. The McKinney-Vento Act requires schools to give parents written notice of the substance of disputes and procedures for appeals. When disputes are pending, students must be admitted immediately into the school in which they seek to enroll. 42 U.S.C. § 11432(g)(3)(E).

In order to ensure that children and youth in homeless situations benefit from the stability, diversity, opportunities, and resources of mainstream schools, the McKinney-Vento Act also prohibits segregating students experiencing homelessness based solely on their housing status. 42 U.S.C. § 11432(e)(3)(A). The law thus acknowledges that separating children who are homeless from their housed peers increases the stigma associated with homelessness, causes unnecessary educational and social disruption, and deprives children of the full-range of educational opportunities to which they are entitled.

106. 42 U.S.C. §11431(1).

107. *See generally* 42 U.S.C. § 11432(g)(3)(A). The act defines the school of origin as the last school the student attended before losing permanent housing or the school in which the student was last enrolled. 42 U.S.C. § 11432(g)(3)(G).

108. 42 U.S.C. § 11432(g)(1)(J)(iii).

109. 42 U.S.C. § 11432(g)(3). The U.S. Department of Education clarified the meaning of "feasible" in its Guidance on the McKinney-Vento Act. The Guidance states that whether it is feasible for a student to remain in the school of origin "should be a student-centered, individualized determination," considering such factors as "the age of the child or youth; the distance of a commute and the impact it may have on the student's education; personal safety issues; a student's need for special instruction . . . ; the length of anticipated stay in temporary shelter or other temporary location; and the time remaining in the school year." U.S. Dep't of Educ., Education for Homeless Children and Youth Program 14 (July 2004), http://www.ed.gov/programs/homeless/guidance.pdf.

110. 42 U.S.C. § 11432(g)(3)(C).

111. 42 U.S.C. § 11432(g)(1)(H), (I).

112. 34 C.F.R. § 200.6(d); 20 U.S.C. §§ 6313(c)(3)(A), 6315(b)(2)(E); U.S. Dep't of Educ., *supra* note 109, at 27–29. On a related note, although children who are homeless have a higher incidence of learning disabilities and emotional disturbances, they often do not receive the special education and related services to which they are entitled. *See* Better Homes Fund, Homeless Children: America's New Outcasts 23–24 (1999). The Individuals with Disabilities Education Improvement Act of 2004 (IDEA) amendments and its implementing regulations address many of the barriers to special education faced by homeless students. They also contain provisions to ensure SEAs and LEAs implement both IDEA and the McKinney-Vento Act in a coordinated manner. A summary of IDEA provisions related to homelessness can be found at http://www.serve.org/nche/downloads/briefs/idea.pdf.

113. *See* Lampkin v. District of Columbia, 27 F. 3d 605, 612 (D.C. Cir. 1994).

114. *See, e.g.,* Patricia Julianelle, Project HOPE-Virginia, Office on the Education of Children and Youth Experiencing Homelessness, Litigation Related to the McKinney-Vento Act (Spring 2008), http://www.nlchp.org/content/pubs/Litigation_related_to_McKinney-Vento1.pdf (citing Boisseau, et al., v. Picard, et al., No. 2:07-565 (E.D. La. 2007) (favorable settlement); National Law Center on Homelessness & Poverty, et al., v. New York State, et al., No. 04 0705 (E.D. N.Y. 2004); Bullock, et al., v. Board of Education of Montgomery County, et al., No. 2002-798 (D. Md. 2002); Doe v. Richardson, No. 98-1165-N (M.D. Ala. 1998)).

115. No. 2:07-565 (E.D. La. February 1, 2007). The complaint is available at http://www.naacpldf.org/content/pdf/boisseau/BoisseauVPicard_NOLA_Complaint.pdf.

NOTES TO CHAPTER 3

1. This figure, drawn from the U.S. Department of Education, represents the number of students aged six through twenty-one served under Part B of the IDEA, divided by the number of students aged six through twenty-one in the population, multiplied by one hundred. Data Accountability Center, Office for Special Education Programs, *Table 1-15: Students Ages 6 through 21 Served under IDEA, Part B, as a Percentage of Population, by Disability and State: Fall 2007,* https://www.ideadata.org/TABLES31ST/AR_1-15.htm.

2. Mary M. Quinn et al., *Youth with Disabilities in Juvenile Corrections: A National Survey*, 71 Exceptional Children 339 (2005); *see also* Sue Burrell & Lauren Warboys, *Special Education and the Juvenile Justice System*, OJJDP Juvenile Justice Bulletin 1 (July 2000).

3. Southern Poverty Law Center, *SPLC Launches "School to Prison Reform Project" to Help At-Risk Children Get Special Education Services, Avoid Incarceration* (Sept. 11, 2007), http://www.splcenter.org/news/item.jsp?aid=282.

4. David Osher et al., *Schools Make a Difference: The Overrepresentation of African American Youth in Special Education and the Juvenile Justice System, in* Racial Inequity in Special Education 98 (Daniel J. Losen & Gary Orfield eds., 2002) [hereinafter Racial Inequity]. Children with emotional disturbances are particularly at risk, as they are thirteen times more likely than other students with disabilities to be arrested while in school. *Id.* at 97.

5. For the ten states with the lowest percentages, including Indiana, Virginia, Ohio, Texas, Louisiana, South Carolina, Mississippi, Georgia, Nevada, and Alabama, the rates range between 14 and 42 percent. *See* LSU Health Services Center, Human Development, http://www.accountabilitydata.org/National%20and%20State%20Data/National%20Maps/2009/Diploma%20Rate%2006-07.pdf (listing data in rank order for several consecutive years). The rankings are also available at https://www.ideadata.org/StateRankOrdered-Tables.asp#partb.

6. The research, conducted by Daniel Losen, entailed a straightforward review of OSEP monitoring letters made available online by the Department of Education at http://www.ed.gov/fund/data/report/idea/partbspap/index.html. This site posts a response letter from each state including a table with the percentage of districts identified pursuant to indicator 4.a, which requires each state to report the percentage of districts with a significant discrepancy in the rates of suspensions of more than ten days and expulsions for children with disabilities versus children without disabilities in a school year. The numbers quoted were derived by compiling the data from each state's posted table.

7. Alternative educational programs frequently are incapable of meeting the individualized special-education-related needs of students with disabilities. *See, e.g.,* Camilla A. Lehr et al., University of Minnesota, Alternative Schools: Findings from a National Survey of the States, Research Report 2, at 19 (2004).

8. *See generally* Beth Harry & Janette Klingner, Why Are So Many Minority Students in Special Education? Understanding Race & Disability in Schools (2006) (discussing how NCLB accountability seemed to add a greater incentive to identify and remove students).

9. The IDEA recounts this history in its findings section, which states, "Before the date of enactment of the Education for All Handicapped Children Act of 1975 (Public Law 94-142), the educational needs of millions of children with disabilities were not being fully met because (A) the children did not receive appropriate educational services; (B) the children were excluded entirely from the public school system and from being educated with their peers; (C) undiagnosed disabilities prevented the children from having a successful educational experience; or (D) a lack of adequate resources within the public school system forced families to find services outside the public school system." 20 U.S.C. § 1400.

10. 334 F. Supp. 1257 (E.D. Pa. 1971).

11. 348 F. Supp. 866 (D.D.C. 1972).

12. *See* Mark G. Yudof et al., Education Policy and the Law 693 (2002) ("[T]he judicial successes in *Mills* and *PARC* spawned substantial popular and scholarly attention and similar lawsuits in more than thirty states. This litigation campaign was designed to demonstrate that the disabled have a constitutional entitlement to an appropriate education; it was also meant to persuade a broader public that the disabled deserved to be more equitably treated. In the Rehabilitation Act (Section 504) . . . and the Education for All Handicapped Children Act . . . Congress attended to these claims.").

13. Mills, 348 F. Supp. at 868.

14. 269 F. Supp. 401 (D.D.C. 1967), *aff'd sub nom.*, Smuck v. Hansen, 408 F. 2d 175 (D.C. Cir. 1969) (en banc).

15. Thomas Hehir, *Eliminating Ableism in Education,* 72 Harv. Educational. Rev. 1–32 (2002).

16. There is a good deal of evidence to support that racial overrepresentation, in part, may be due to unconscious racial bias. *See* Daniel J. Losen & Gary Orfield, *Introduction, in* Racial Inequity, *supra* note 4, at xxi–xxviii.

17. According to the National Research Council's book *Minority Students in Special and Gifted Education,* "a key factor in addressing disproportion in special and gifted education is support for minority student achievement in general education." National Research Council, Minority Students in Special and Gifted Education 169 (M. Suzanne Donovan & Christopher T. Cross eds., 2002) [hereinafter NRC]. The law is informed by a wealth of research that supports the conclusion that what is regarded as an individual's deficit may actually reflect an inadequate opportunity to learn. *See generally* Jim Ysseldyke, *Reflections on a Research Career: Generalizations from 25 Years of Research on Assessment and Instructional Decision Making,* 67 Exceptional Children 295, 309 (2001). As the NRC stresses in the executive summary, "The same child can perform very differently depending on the level of effective or ineffective classroom management. In practice, it can be quite difficult to distinguish internal child traits that require the ongoing support of special education from inadequate opportunity or contextual support for learning and behavior." NRC, *supra,* at 3, 197–204. Recent research by Klingner and Harry suggests that the quality of instruction in the regular education classroom probably contributes to a higher frequency of special education referrals, yet the qualitative studies suggest that evaluators rarely analyze whether deficiencies in instruction are an issue. *Id.* at 170–71 (citing Klingner and Harry study).

18. Nationally, in 2004, Black public school children, compared to whites, were approximately three times as likely to be labeled "mentally retarded" and twice as likely to be labeled "emotionally disturbed." Data Accountability Center, *IDEA Part B Child Count* (2004), Table 1-18, http://www.ideadata.org/tables28th\ar_1-18.xls.

19. In this highly restrictive category of educational placement (sometimes referred to as "substantially separate"), the data reveal racially disparate risks for removal for all nonwhite students with disabilities as follows: Hispanics, 20.8 percent; Asian/Pacific Islanders, 22.5 percent; and Blacks, 24.5 percent; yet the figure for whites is only 12.6 percent. *See* www.ideadata.org; *see also* Edward Garcia Fierros & James W. Conroy, *Double Jeopardy: An Exploration of Restrictiveness in Special Education, in* Racial Inequity, *supra* note 4, at 39–70.

20. *See* Linda M. Raffaele Mendez , *Predictors of Suspension and Negative School Outcomes: A Longitudinal Investigation, in* Deconstructing the School-to-Prison Pipeline 30 (Johanna Wald and Daniel J. Losen eds., 2003).

21. *Id.* at 26–27.

22. In 2005, nationally, Blacks constituted approximately 15 percent of the population ages six through twenty-one. Data Accountability Center, *Resident Population and Enrollment* (2004), Table C-8, http://www.ideadata.org/tables28th/ar_C-8.htm. Therefore, if Blacks were identified and disciplined in proportionate numbers, one would expect to find that they would constitute approximately 15 percent of each disciplinary category. In 2005, 32,315 Black students with disabilities were suspended. This number represented nearly half (48 percent) of the 67,966 reported suspensions (for all students with disabilities) of more than ten days. *Compare* Data Accountability Center, *IDEA Part B Discipline* (2003–2004), Table 5-1, http://www.ideadata.org/tables28th\ar_5-1.xls, *with* Data Accountability Center, *IDEA Part B Discipline* (2003–2004), Table 5-3c, http://www.ideadata.org/tables28th\ar_5-3.xls.

23. *See* Osher et al., *supra* note 4, at 93–116. And, once Blacks who have been identified leave public schools, they are far less likely to be employed two years after high school (employed at 25 percent, compared to 53 percent for whites) and are far more likely to be arrested (40 percent, compared to 27 percent for whites). *See* Donald P. Oswald et al., *Community and School Predictors of Overrepresentation of Minority Children in Special Education, in* Racial Inequity, *supra* note 4, at 1.

24. In the IDEA, Congress found that "[g]reater efforts are needed to prevent the intensification of problems connected with mislabeling and high dropout rates among minority children with disabilities." 20 U.S.C. § 1400(c)(12)(A).

25. Howard N. Snyder & Melissa Sickmund, National Center for Juvenile Justice, Juvenile Offenders and Victims: 2006 National Report 83, http://www.ojjdp.ncjrs.org/ojstatbb/nr2006/downloads/NR2006.pdf (citing a study of youth living in high-crime neighborhoods in Seattle).

26. *See* National Council on Disability, Back to School on Civil Rights: Advancing the Federal Commitment to Leave No Child Behind 7 (2000), http://www.ncd.gov/newsroom/publications/2000/backtoschool_1.htm.

27. One study of principals in two districts in Delaware found that about half did not know the procedural requirements for long-term suspension of students with disabilities. *See* Elizabeth Palley, *Balancing Student Mental Health and Discipline: A Case Study of the Implementation of the Individuals with Disabilities Education Act,* 78 Social Service Review 243–66 (2004). Given the numerous and detailed procedural requirements and safeguards found in 20 U.S.C. § 1414, it is nearly certain that if school administrators are unaware of the requirements and have suspended students with disabilities, then they are not in compliance with the IDEA. The IDEA requires states to examine data "to determine if significant discrepancies are occurring in the rate of long-term suspensions and expulsions of children with disabilities." 20 U.S.C. § 1412(a)(22)(A).

28. In many ways the IDEA requires parental involvement and has clear notice requirements and a host of procedural protections to ensure such participation. *See, e.g.,* 20 U.S.C. § 1415.

29. A Washington, D.C., charter school was recently found to have violated the IDEA when it failed to evaluate a high school student for an emotional disturbance within 120 days of a parent's referral. *Integrated Design and Electronics Academy Pub. Charter Sch. v. McKinley ex rel. K.M.,* 570 F. Supp. 2d 28 (D.D.C. 2008). The U.S. Department of Education has conducted investigations to ensure that the rights of students are enforced in

charter schools and, in at least one case, found that the charter school violated students' IDEA rights. Boston (MA) Renaissance Charter School, 3 ECLPR 95 (OCR 1997). The Office for Civil Rights' description of the case is available online at http://ideanet.doe. state.in.us/legal/docs/quarterly_reports/1998_octdec.pdf.

30. Lehr et al., *supra* note 7, at 19.

31. *See generally* Joseph B. Tulman, *Disability and Delinquency: How Failures to Identify, Accommodate, and Serve Youth with Education-Related Disabilities Leads to Their Disproportionate Representation in the Delinquency System,* 3 Whittier J. Child & Fam. Advoc. 3 (2003), http://www.law.udc.edu/resource/resmgr/facultydocs/tulman_disability_delinquenc.pdf.

32. Although this chapter does not review the state-law distinctions, advocates should always thoroughly review the relevant state codes and regulations.

33. 20 U.S.C. §§ 1400–87.

34. 29 U.S.C. § 794. Implementing regulations can be found at 34 C.F.R. § 104 *et seq.*

35. 42 U.S.C. § 12131; implementing regulations can be found at 28 C.F.R. § 35 *et seq.* For the purpose of the legal challenges contemplated in this chapter, Section 504 and Title II of the ADA are identical, and hereinafter only Section 504 will be mentioned. Advocates are advised to review the ADA Amendments Act of 2008, Pub. L. 110-325, 122 Stat. 3553 (to be codified at 42 U.S.C. § 12101 *et seq.*), which affect interpretations of requirements pursuant to the ADA. *See, e.g.,* Equal Employment Opportunity Commission, *Notice Concerning the Americans with Disabilities Act (ADA) Amendments Act of 2008,* http://www.eeoc.gov/ada/amendments_notice.html.

36. 20 U.S.C. § 1401(3).

37. The definition of FAPE is set out at 20 U.S.C. § 1402(9).The state's obligation to provide FAPE is found at 20 U.S.C. § 1412(a)(1).

38. 29 U.S.C. § 794; 34 C.F.R. § 104.33. The Section 504 regulations in the relevant part state,

(b) Appropriate education.

(1) For the purpose of this subpart, the provision of an appropriate education is the provision of regular or special education and related aids and services that (i) are designed to meet individual educational needs of handicapped persons as adequately as the needs of nonhandicapped persons are met and (ii) are based upon adherence to procedures that satisfy the requirements of §§ 104.34, 104.35, and 104.36.

(2) Implementation of an Individualized Education Program developed in accordance with the Education of the Handicapped Act is one means of meeting the standard established in paragraph (b)(1)(i) of this section.

Id.

39. 34 C.F.R. § 104.33(b).

40. *See, e.g.,* Molly L. v. Lower Merion Sch. Dist., 194 F. Supp. 2d 422, 426 (E.D. Pa. 2002) (stating that "[t]he substantive requirements of the Rehabilitation Act in the education context are equivalent to the requirements set forth in the [IDEA]."); *see also Ridgewood Bd. of Educ. v. N.E.,* 172 F. 3d 238, 253 (3d Cir. 1999) ("[T]here are few differences, if any, between IDEA's affirmative duty and § 504's negative prohibition.").

41. For a detailed review of eligibility requirements and related issues, see Mark C. Weber, *The IDEA Eligibility Mess*, 57 Buff L. Rev. 83 (2009).

42. *See* McPherson v. Mich. High Sch. Athletic Ass'n, 119 F. 3d 453, 459–60 (6th Cir. 1997); *see also* Helen L. v. DiDario, 46 F. 3d 325, 330 n.7 (3d Cir. 1995) (holding that law developed under Rehabilitation Act Section 504 mandating nondiscrimination under federal grants and programs is applicable to Title II); Rhodes v. Ohio High Sch. Athletics Ass'n, 939 F. Supp. 584, 588 (N.D. Ohio 1996) (noting that either statute may be invoked by aggrieved individuals alleging discrimination to which each applies).

43. Similar to the IDEA's Child Find requirement, courts recognize that Section 504 imposes a duty on school districts to identify children with disabilities within a reasonable time after school officials are on notice of behavior indicating that the child has a disability. Ridgewood Bd. of Educ. v. N.E., 172 F. 3d 238, 253 (3d Cir. 1999).

44. *See also* chapter 2 (discussing challenges on behalf of homeless children pursuant to the McKinney Vento Act).

45. 20 U.S.C. § 1412(a)(3).

46. 20 U.S.C. § 1414(b)(2).

47. 20 U.S.C. § 1414(a)(1)(B).

48. 20 U.S.C. § 1414(a)(1)(D).

49. 20 U.S.C. § 1414(a)(1)(D). After the evaluation has been administered, the eligibility decision is made by a team of qualified professionals and the child's parent(s). § 1414(b)(4). Once the IEP is developed, the parent also participates in the meetings to review progress and consider changes to the plan, known as the "IEP team," even though this team may differ from the team that determined eligibility. § 1414(c).

50. 20 U.S.C. § 1415(k)(5).

51. *Id.*

52. *See, e.g.,* 20 U.S.C. § 1414(d)(1)(B). The extensive requirements regarding the development and implementation of the IEP are beyond the scope of this chapter but are found at 20 U.S.C. § 1414.

53. 20 U.S.C. § 1414(d)(1)(A)(i)(II)(aa).

54. *See, e.g.,* Bd. of Educ. v. Rowley, 458 U.S. 176, 192 (1982). Students only eligible for protections under Section 504 must be provided with a "504 Plan."

55. *See, e.g.,* K.R. v. Sch. Dist. of Philadelphia, No. 06-2388, 2008 WL 2609810, at *6 (E.D. Pa., June 26, 2008) (citing S.H. v. State-Operated Sch. Dist. of the City of Newark, 336 F. 3d 260, 265 (3d Cir. 2003); M.C. ex rel. J.C. v. Cent. Reg'l Sch. Dist., 81 F. 3d 389, 394 (3d Cir. 1996)).

56. 20 U.S.C. § 1414(d)(1)(A)(i)(IV).

57. 20 U.S.C. § 1415(j).

58. 20 U.S.C. § 1415 (k)(1)(B)

59. 20 U.S.C. § 1415(k)(1)(E). In just four months in 2006, the Office for Civil Rights for the U.S. Department of Education (OCR) issued a combination of six letters of finding or resolution agreements that state that the respondent district had suspended a student with disabilities for over ten days without holding a manifestation determination hearing. In many of these cases there were several violations or potential violations of Section 504 discussed. *See, e.g.,* Letter from Office for Civil Rights, Southern Division, Atlanta (Florida), to Dr. Roger Dearing, Superintendent, Manatee County School District Florida, 107 LRP 4315 (May 31, 2006) (in a negotiated settlement, district that allegedly failed to implement

IEP and had suspended student for forty days over the course of two academic years, without conducting a manifestation determination, agreed to provide the student with compensatory and other services including tutoring, complete the student's functional behavior assessment and behavioral improvement plan, hold monthly monitoring meetings, and retrain staff regarding implementation of Section 504 and IEP plans and discipline of students with disabilities, specifically conducting manifestation determinations); Letter from Office for Civil Rights, Southern Division, D.C. (SC), to Marlboro County (SC) School District, 107 LRP 6250 (Apr. 19, 2006); 107 LRP 4321 (Jonesboro, GA) (June 1, 2006); Letter from Office for Civil Rights, Southern Division, Atlanta (Tennessee), to Dr. Pedro E. Garcia, Director, Metropolitan Nashville Public Schools, 107 LRP 3802 (June 14, 2006); Letter from Office for Civil Rights, Midwestern Division, Kansas City (Kansas), to Marty Kobza, Superintendent, Eudora Unified School District #491, 106 LRP 57035 (Jul. 7, 2006); Letter from Office for Civil Rights, Midwestern Division, Kansas City (Missouri), to Michelle P. Wimes, Spencer Fane Britt & Browne LLP, 106 LRP 60797 (Aug. 15, 2006).

60. 20 U.S.C. § 1415(k)(1)(E)(i).

61. *Id.*

62. 20 U.S.C. § 1415(k)(1)(F)(iii).

63. 34 C.F.R. § 300.536.

64. 20 U.S.C. § 1415 (k)(1)(E), (G) (describing the exceptions of weapons, drugs, and infliction of serious bodily injury under "Special Circumstances—School personnel may remove a student to an interim alternative educational setting for not more than 45 school days without regard to whether the behavior is determined to be a manifestation of the child's disability.").

65. Children may be removed from their placement for up to forty-five days, regardless of whether the misconduct was a manifestation of their disability, when the child committed a weapons or drug offense or committed serious bodily injury. 20 U.S.C. § 1415(k)(1)(G).

66. 20 U.S.C. § 1415(k)(6)(A).

67. *Id. See also* Morgan v. Chris L, 106 F. 3rd 401 (6th Cir. 1997) (affirming 927 F. Supp. 267 (E.D. Tenn. 1994)), *cert. denied,* 520 U.S. 1271 (1999) (holding that a Tennessee school district violated the IDEA by filing juvenile court petition against student with ADHD without following appropriate procedures for "change of placement.")

68. 20 U.S.C. § 1414(k)(1(C).

69. *See* 34 C.F.R. § 300.530(d)(5), § 300.536.

70. 20 U.S.C. § 1415 (k)(1)(D) (describing that children removed will continue receiving services). Some state laws or interpretations may extend FAPE to students with disabilities not eligible under the IDEA and therefore not covered by this protection.

71. *Id.*

72. OCR has stated that students identified as having a disability under Section 504 have not been found to share the IDEA's entitlement to continued supports and services. In one administrative ruling, OCR stated, "If it is determined that the misconduct is not caused by the child's handicap, the child may be excluded from school in the same manner as similarly situated non-handicapped children are excluded. In such a situation, all educational services to the child may cease. The suspension of a handicapped student from transportation can constitute a significant change of placement if a district: has been transporting the student (either under an Individual Education Program or under the

district's regular transportation policies); suspends the student from the transportation as a disciplinary measure; and provides no other form of transportation. If such a suspension goes on long enough, it constitutes a significant change of placement." Letter from Office for Civil Rights, Southern Division, Atlanta (SC), to Dr. T. Paul Vivian, Superintendent, Florence County (SC) Sch. Dist. #2, 16 LRP 924 (Dec. 8, 1989) (finding district not in compliance with Section 504 for suspending a student for seventeen days and expelling her from the bus prior to conducting a manifestation determination hearing but finding district did not violate Section 504 for cessation of services once it was determined that the behavior in question was not a manifestation of her disability).

73. 419 U.S. 565 (1975); *see* chapter 4 for a detailed description of the procedural due process protections afforded to general education students subject to discipline.

74. Telephone interview with Kathleen Boundy, Director of the Center for Law and Education, Nov. 23, 2009.

75. As a general matter, Section 504 has been interpreted by OCR to provide the same "manifestation determination" review as afforded by the IDEA, but as a matter of policy, OCR, pursuant to Section 504 regulations at 34 C.F.R. § 104.35(a), similarly limits the review of suspensions for noncompliance to suspensions of more than ten days, including a cumulative total of suspensions that exceeds ten days. See Letter from OCR, Midwestern Division, Cleveland (OH) to Delaware (OH) City School District, 108 LRP 63653 (Sept. 19, 2008).

76. 20 U.S.C. § 1415(k)(1)(F).

77. 20 U.S.C. § 1415(k)(1)(D).

78. The congressional findings supporting the reauthorization of the IDEA in 2004 cite the use of "scientifically based early reading programs, positive behavioral interventions and supports, and early intervening services . . . in order to address the learning and behavioral needs of such children." 20 U.S.C. §1400(c)(5)(F). Some states, such as New York, have also adopted regulations and guidance specifically outlining the FBA requirements. Many local districts have policies describing how school districts are to develop these assessments.

79. 34 C.F.R. §300.304(b)(3).

80. For example, the state of New York reported that fifteen of eighteen districts had not complied with the legal requirement that they provide behavior intervention plans, monitor them, and evaluate progress; that ten failed to conduct a functional behavioral assessment or intervention plan after the student's conduct was held to be a manifestation of the student's disability; that ten failed to review short-term suspensions to see if there was a pattern of removals; and that eleven had failed to conduct a functional behavioral assessment for students whose initial evaluations showed behaviors that impeded their learning or that of others. *See* New York State Education Department, *Annual Performance Report for 2005–2006* 30–36 (Feb. 2007), http://www.vesid.nysed.gov/specialed/spp/apr2007/june07.pdf.

81. 20 U.S.C. § 1412(b)(5)(A). The IDEA prioritizes required federal and state monitoring of the "[p]rovision of a free appropriate public education in the least restrictive environment." 20 U.S.C. § 1416(a)(3)(A). In the IDEA, Congress finds that "the education of children with disabilities can be made more effective by . . . supporting high-quality, intensive preservice preparation and professional development for all personnel who work with children with disabilities" and that "the education of children with disabilities can be made more effective" by "ensuring their access to the general education curriculum in the regular classroom to the maximum extent possible." 20 U.S.C. § 1400(c)(5).

82. 34 C.F.R. § 104.34.

83. *See* 34 C.F.R. § 104.4(b)(1)(ii).

84. The IDEA defines special education as "specially designed instruction, at no cost to parents, to meet the unique needs of a child with a disability." 20 U.S.C. § 1401(a)(29) (2005).

85. The IDEA requires states to develop plans that ensure, "to the maximum extent appropriate, children with disabilities . . . are educated with children who are not disabled. . . ." 20 U.S.C. § 1412(b)(5)(A).

86. Corey H. v. Bd. of Educ., 27 Individuals with Disabilities Educ. L. Rptr. 713 (N.D. Ill. 1998); For a detailed summary, see Sharon Weitzman Soltman & Donald R. Moore, *Ending Segregation of Chicago's Students with Disabilities: Implications of the Corey H. Lawsuit, in* Racial Inequity, *supra* note 4, at 239–71.

87. *See* 20 U.S.C. § 1416(a)(3)(A).

88. This section on transition services was primarily authored by Elisa Hyman.

89. The IDEA was amended and this age requirement was changed so that this provision of federal law does not apply to incarcerated youths over the age of eighteen who were not previously identified or evaluated. See 20 U.S.C. § 1412(a)(1)(B)(ii); 34 C.F.R. 300.324(d).

90. 20 U.S.C. § 1414(d)(l)(A)(i)(VIII). However, there is a limit on transition plan requirements for students with disabilities incarcerated in adult facilities. See 20 U.S.C. § 1414(d)(7).

91. *Id.*

92. 34 C.F.R. § 300.43(a)(1).

93. 34 C.F.R. § 300.43(a)(1)–(2). For a discussion of these requirements in the context of a lawsuit, *see* Renollett v. Independent Sch. Dist. No. 11, 2005 U.S. Dist. LEXIS 743, at *32–38 (D. Minn. 2005).

94. Pursuant to the IDEA, at 20 U.S.C. § 1416, where the law sets forth priorities for monitoring and enforcement, the U.S. Department of Education's Office for Special Education and Rehabilitative Services (OSERS) created a set of indicators on which districts and states must report to measure IDEA implementation. Each state's performance on the indicators, with the indicator definitions, can be found online. See the Department of Education's response to each state's performance plan and annual performance report online at http://www.ed.gov/fund/data/report/idea/partbspap/index.html. For each state there is a response letter and table posted. For each state, the table document contains the indicator and a description of the state's performance pursuant to that indicator. Indicator 13 is about transitions.

95. For a discussion of a lawsuit brought by Advocates for Children to secure transition services for children released from detention facilities seeking to reenter mainstream public schools, see chapter 7, discussing *J.G. v. Mills.*

96. *See generally* 20 U.S.C. § 1415.

97. *See* 20 U.S.C. § 1415(i); Honig v. Doe, 484 U.S. 305, 326–27 (1988).

98. *See* Freed v. Consol. Rail Corp., 201 F. 3d 188, 192–94 (3d Cir. 2000) (holding that the Rehabilitation Act does not impose an exhaustion requirement); AP v. Anoka-Hennepin Indep. Sch. Dist. No. 11, 538 F. Supp. 2d 1125, 1152 (D. Minn. 2008) (noting that neither Section 504 nor Title II of the ADA includes an exhaustion requirement); Schonfeld v. City of Carlsbad, 978 F. Supp. 1329, 1334 (S.D. Cal. 1997) (finding no exhaustion required under ADA).

99. Cave v. East Meadow Union Free Sch. Dist., 514 F. 3d 240, 246–49 (2d Cir. 2008) (holding that IDEA exhaustion requirements apply equally to relief available under other statutes such as ADA and Rehabilitation Act, if relief sought under those statutes would also be available under the IDEA); Diaz-Fonseca v. Puerto Rico, 451 F. 3d 13, 33–34 (1st Cir. 2006) (holding that where underlying claim is one of violation of the IDEA, plaintiffs may not use Title II of the ADA or Section 504 of the Rehabilitation Act to evade limited remedial structure of IDEA); Blunt v. Lower Merion Sch. Dist., 559 F. Supp. 2d 548 (E.D. Pa. 2008) (finding that because claims raised under the ADA and Rehabilitation Act were based on the same allegations as IDEA claim and sought the same relief, party would be required to exhaust IDEA administrative remedies); cf. James S. v. Sch. Dist. of Philadelphia, 559 F. Supp. 2d 600 (E.D. Pa. 2008) (excusing parent and student from exhausting IDEA procedures in a case brought under the Rehabilitation Act and the ADA, when the damages sought were not available through the IDEA's administrative processes).

100. It may still be prudent to bring a claim under Section 504, even for relief that is also available under the IDEA and even though 504 claims must meet similar exceptions to the exhaustion requirements. If the IDEA claim fails for jurisdictional reasons, the plaintiff may still be able to bring the Section 504 claim to court. See, e.g., M.P. v. Indep. Sch. Dist. No. 721, 439 F. 3d 865, 868 (8th Cir. 2006).

101. See Robinson v. Kansas, 117 F. Supp. 2d 1124, 1143 (D. Kan. 2000) (finding that a student with a disability did not have to exhaust under the IDEA because the claim was a challenge to state legislation and not just an individualized decision); Ronald and Diane D. v. Titusville Area Sch. Dist., 159 F. Supp. 2d 857, 862 (W.D. Pa. 2001) (permitting exception to exhaustion requirement when parents sought retrospective damages, which are unavailable under an IDEA administrative proceeding); see also Meghan Rene v. Reed, 726 N.E. 2d 808, 819–21 (Ind. Ct. App. 2000) (excusing failure to exhaust when plaintiffs challenged state statute).

102. See Honig, 484 U.S. at 326–27.

103. O.F. v. Chester Upland Sch. Dist., 2000 U.S. Dist. LEXIS 6421 (E.D. Pa. 2000).

104. A.A. v. Bd. of Educ., 196 F. Supp. 2d 259 (E.D. N.Y. 2002).

105. See Disability Rights Wisc. v. Wisc. Dep't Pub. Instruction, 463 F. 3d 719, 730 (7th Cir. 2006) (holding that the state P&A agency had the right to certain student records at an alternative school under the federal P&A statutes when there are allegations of abuse and neglect, notwithstanding FERPA); Conn. Office for Protection and Advocacy v. Hartford Bd. of Ed., 464 F. 3d 229, 240–42 (2nd Cir. 2006) (same).

106. 20 U.S.C. § 1415(i)(2)(C)(iii). For frequent updates and commentary on the contours of rights and remedies pursuant to disability law, see http://www.wrightslaw.com.

107. See, e.g., settlements posted online at http://advocatesforchildren.org.

108. See, e.g., Anderson v. Thompson, 658 F. 2d 1205 (7th Cir. 1981); Sellers v. Sch. Bd., 141 F. 3d 524, (4th Cir. 1998), cert. denied, 1998 U.S. LEXIS 5628 (1998).

109. See K.M. v. Sch. Bd., 150 Fed. Appx. 953 (11th Cir. 2005) (unpublished) (reversing award of monetary damages to parents of student whose district denied him a due process hearing, holding that claims for money damages against municipality must show that it had a policy that violated individuals' rights and that parents could not show denial of due process resulted from an official school board policy or custom).

110. See Draper v. Atlanta Pub. Sch. Dist., Civ. Action No. 1:07-CV-0224-MHS (N.D. Ga., Mar. 31, 2008), http://www.wrightslaw.com/law/caselaw/08/GA.draper.aps.504.

damages.pdf (denying district's motion to dismiss in case asserting discrimination and retaliation and requesting damages pursuant to Section 504); *see also* Draper v. Atlanta Indep. Sch. Sys., 480 F. Supp. 2d 1331 (N.D. Ga. 2007) (awarding compensatory education on behalf of dyslexic boy whom district misdiagnosed as mentally retarded, placed in self-contained separate class where he did not learn to read, and failed to provide required three-year reevaluation), *aff'd*, 518 F. 3d 1275 (11th Cir. 2008). For frequent updates on the status of damages awards in cases involving special education violations, *see* http://www.wrightslaw.com.

111. *See generally* Franklin v. Gwinnet County Pub. Sch., 503 U.S. 60 (1992); D.G. v. Somerset Hills Sch. Dist., 559 F. Supp. 2d 484, 496 n.5 (D. N.J. 2008).

112. *See, e.g.,* Nieves-Marquez v. Puerto Rico, 353 F. 3d 108 (1st Cir. 2003).

113. *See* Saucon Valley Sch. Dist. v. Robert and Darlene O., 785 A. 2d 1069, 1076–77 (Pa. Commw. Ct. 2001).

114. *See* Power v. Sch. Bd., 276 F. Supp. 2d 515, 521–22 (E.D. Va. 2003) (holding that Section 504 regulations provided no private right of action to challenge disciplinary procedures when discrimination is not asserted by plaintiff, and therefore court did not have jurisdiction under Section 504 to review challenge to procedures for disciplining students with disabilities).

115. *See* 20 U.S.C. § 1415(i)(3)(B). Any party aggrieved by the findings/decision may bring a civil action with respect to the complaint presented in "any State court of competent jurisdiction or in a district court of the United States, without regard to the amount in controversy." 20 U.S.C. § 1415 (i)(2)(A); 34 C.F.R. § 300.517. *But see* Buckhannon Board and Care Home, Incorporated v. West Virginia Department of Health Resources, 532 U.S. 598 (2001) (limiting the scope and definition of the "prevailing party"). For a more detailed discussion of attorneys' fees in special education cases, see Lynn M. Daggett, *Special Education Attorney's Fees: Of Buckhannon, the IDEA Reauthorization Bills, and the IDEA as Civil Rights Statute,* 8 UC Davis Journal of Juvenile Law and Policy 1–54 (2004), http://jjlp.law.ucdavis.edu/archives/vol-8-no-1/2.%20Article%20IDEA.pdf.

116. 20 U.S.C. § 1415(i)(3)(B)(i)(II).

117. 20 U.S.C. § 1415(i)(3).

118. Arlington Cent. Sch. Dist. Bd. of Educ. v. Murphy, 548 U.S. 291, 300–03 (2006).

119. 34 C.F.R. § 104.3(j)(1). "Is regarded as having an impairment means (A) has a physical or mental impairment that does not substantially limit major life activities but that is treated by a recipient as constituting such a limitation; (B) has a physical or mental impairment that substantially limits major life activities only as a result of the attitudes of others toward such impairment; or (C) has none of the impairments . . . but is treated by a recipient as having such an impairment." 34 C.F.R. § 104.3(j)(2)(IV).

120. M.P. v. Indep. Sch. Dist. No. 721, 439 F. 3d 865, 867 (8th Cir. 2006) (citing Timothy H. v. Cedar Rapids Cmty. Sch. Dist., 178 F. 3d 968, 971 (8th Cir. 1999)).

121. Weixel v. Bd. of Educ., 287 F. 3d 138, 148 (2d Cir. 2002).

122. 34 C.F.R. §104.4(b)(4).

123. *See, e.g.,* Bravin v. Mount Sinai Med. Ctr., 58 F. Supp. 2d 269, 273 (S.D. N.Y. 1999).

124. *See, e.g.,* W.C. v. Cobb County Sch. Dist., 407 F. Supp. 2d 1351, 1363–64 (N.D. Ga. 2005).

125. *See, e.g.,* Alexander v. Choate, 469 U.S. 287, 296–97, 301 (1995) (acknowledging that "much of the conduct that Congress sought to alter in passing the Rehabilitation Act

would be difficult if not impossible to reach were the Act construed to proscribe only conduct fueled by a discriminatory intent" and requiring meaningful access to reasonable accommodations as a way to limit the reach of disparate impact claims); Taylor v. Sec'y of the Navy, 852 F. Supp. 343, 356 (E.D. Pa. 1994); Pushkin v. Regents of Univ. of Colorado, 658 F. 2d 1372, 1384–85 (10th Cir. 1981) ("It would be a rare case indeed in which a hostile discriminatory purpose or subjective intent to discriminate solely on the basis of handicap could be shown").

126. *See, e.g.,* Robinson v. Kansas, 117 F. Supp. 2d 1124, 1145 (D. Kan. 2000); *but see* Timms v. Metro. Sch. Dist., 722 F. 2d 1310, 1318 n.4 (7th Cir. 1983). The court in *Timms* stated that the Eighth Circuit requirement of bad faith or gross misjudgment is undermined by the fact that Section 504 language mirrors Title VI language, because Title VI has been held to apply to unintentional discrimination for compensatory relief. The Supreme Court has since held that private actions under Title VI must demonstrate intentional discrimination.

127. 295 F. 3d 1183, 1187 (10th Cir. 2002) (distinguishing Sandoval, 532 U.S. 275 (2001)), *cert. denied,* 539 U.S. 926 (2003). The case was denied certiorari on appeal. Therefore, it may be possible to pursue disparate impact litigation pursuant to Section 504 (and Section 1983) alleging discrimination on the basis of disability in federal court, even when plaintiffs are now barred to pursue similar claims pursuant to the regulations promulgated under Title VI. The U.S. Supreme Court in *Choate,* for example, distinguished Section 504 (and ADA) from Title VI and Title IX regarding the intent standard. Alexander v. Choate, 469 U.S. 287 (1985). In three cases, *Ability Ctr. v. City of Sandusky,* 385 F. 3d 901, 909 (6th Cir. 2004), *Chaffin v. Kan. State Fair Bd.,* 348 F. 3d 850, 859 (10th Cir. 2003), and *Frederick L. v. Dep't of Pub. Welfare,* 157 F. Supp. 2d 509, 537 (E.D. Pa. 2001), court comments refer to comments in *Choate* that "[d]iscrimination against the handicapped was perceived by Congress to be most often the product, not of invidious animus, but rather of thoughtlessness and indifference—of benign neglect." Moreover, despite the ruling denying a private right of action to allege discrimination pursuant to disparate impact regulations, the *Sandoval* Court did not invalidate these regulations. Therefore advocates should cautiously consider this potential avenue pursuant to both Section 504 and Title VI regulations.

128. *See also* Daniel J. Losen, *Challenging Racial Disparities: The Promise and Pitfalls of the No Child Left Behind Act's Race-Conscious Accountability,* 47 Howard L.J. 243, 287–88 (2004).

129. Alfredo Artiles et al., *English-Language Learner Representation in Special Education in California Urban School Districts, in* Racial Inequity, *supra* note 4.

130. A series of cases referred to as the Jose P. litigation began with the case *Jose P. v. Ambach,* No. 79 Civ. 270 (E.D. N.Y., Dec. 14, 1979), and concerned both the failure to identify students with disabilities and delays in evaluation and inadequacy of placement and quality of special education provided. The case is available at http://advocatesforchildren.org/litigation/litdocs/josepdocs/JosePJudgment_Dec79.pdf. Although the resulting consent decree was not limited to English language learner (ELL) students with disabilities, the remedy focused on ensuring that Hispanic students, many of whom were ELLs or whose parents were not English speakers, were properly identified, evaluated, and subsequently provided with appropriate IEPs and educational placements. Since the original judgment, Advocates for Children and others continue to monitor the implementation of Jose P., with the most recent stipulation having been settled in 2003. *See* Jose P.

v. Ambach, 669 F. 2d 865, 869 (2d Cir. 1982) (not requiring exhaustion because individual cases would not resolve systemic issues affecting the class). Subsequent orders and stipulations in the Jose P. litigation are available at http://advocatesforchildren.org/litigation/Josep.htm [hereinafter Jose P. Orders].

131. In issuing final guidance to states for reporting on a set of IDEA indicators in October 2008, in the comments section, the Department of Education interpreted its regulation at 34 C.F.R. 300.600(d) to require states to look at underrepresentation and stated, "The Department's intent in requiring States to consider underrepresentation in their examination of data concerning disproportionate representation is to ensure that all children who are suspected of being a child with a disability under 34 CFR §300.8 and in need of special education and related services, are identified." See Att_L12-1820-0624 Part B SPP-APR Comments and Discussion 10-02-08(3).doc (on file with the authors).

132. For a full discussion of this phenomenon and possible legal challenges, *see* Daniel J. Losen & Kevin G. Welner, *Disabling Discrimination in Our Public Schools: Comprehensive Legal Challenges to Inappropriate and Inadequate Special Education Services for Minority Children,* 36 Harv. C.R.-C.L. L. Rev. 407, 434–60 (2001).

133. *See* Edward Fierros & James Conroy, *Double Jeopardy: An Exploration of Restrictiveness and Race in Special Education, in* Racial Inequity, *supra* note 4, at 49.

134. 20 U.S.C. § 1416(a)(3)(C).

135. 20 U.S.C. § 1416(b)(2)(C)(ii).

136. 20 U.S.C. § 1418.

137. *See* 20 U.S.C. § 1418(d) and 20 U.S.C. § 1413(f) (requiring reservation of Part B funds granted under the IDEA).

138. 20 U.S.C. §§ 1412(a)(22). Similarly, 20 U.S.C. § 1412(a)(24) calls for states to take preventive measures to address racial disproportionality.

139. One relevant example that predates these provisions is a class action suit against Connecticut's State Board of Education, asserting LRE violations for students with mental retardation. The petitioners included testimony by researchers showing that both Black and Latino students with mental retardation were placed in restrictive educational settings far more often than were white students with the same disabilities. The 2001 settlement, *P.J. v. Connecticut State Board of Education,* included specific provisions intended to reduce the racial disparities in placement and required that the state monitor and provide regular progress reports on the racial subgroups *See* Fierros & Conroy, *supra* note 133, at 62–64. Although the consent decree has ended, it is noteworthy that for Black and Hispanic students in 2006, when restrictiveness of all students with disabilities is broken down by race and measured by the percentage of students inside regular class less than 40 percent of the day, Connecticut ranked seventh best for inclusion for Hispanics and third best for Blacks. Data Accountability Center, Part B Environments Table 5.6, https://www.ideadata.org/docs\RankOrderedTables\artbl5_6s.xls.

140. For public reporting requirements, *see* 20 U.S.C. §§ 1416 and 1418.

141. 519 F. Supp. 2d 870 (E.D. Wis. 2007).

142. *Id.* at 881.

143. *Id.* The court confirmed its certification of the class as "[t]hose students eligible for special education services from the Milwaukee Public School System who are, have been or will be either denied or delayed entry or participation in the processes which

result in a properly constituted meeting between the IEP team and the parents or guardians of the student." *Id.* at 903.

144. *Id.* at 891.

145. *Id.* at 892.

146. *Id.* at 896.

147. *Id.* at 886.

148. *Id.* at 898.

149. *Id.* at 903.

150. *Id.* at 887–88.

151. Negotiated settlement at 3, Jamie S. v. Milwaukee Bd. of Sch. Dirs., No. 01-C-0928 (E.D. Wis., Feb. 27, 2008), http://dpi.wi.gov/eis/pdf/drwdpisettlement.pdf. While the settlement with Wisconsin's Department of Public Instruction was finalized, the court's holding against the Milwaukee Public Schools was appealed by MPS to the 7th Circuit; that appeal remains pending.

152. *See* Jamie S., F. Supp. 2d at 894–95 ("The IDEA, of course, does not contain a 'stigma exception.'").

153. This places Wisconsin among the worst four states in the United States when ranked on this measure in 2005. Racial disparities in long-term suspensions/expulsions (lasting more than ten days) are extraordinarily high in some states, but they also differ dramatically by racial group. Data at the Data Accountability Center shows the state-by-state percentages of children with disabilities that were suspended or expelled for more than ten days, disaggregated by race. *See* http://www.ideadata.org/tables30th/ar_5-4.htm.

154. CV-02-5118 (E.D. N.Y 2002). For a copy of the complaint, the ruling certifying the class, and various pleadings in the case, *see* http://www.advocatesforchildren.org/eb.php.

155. *See* NT v. N.Y. State Educ. Dep't, CV-02-5118 (E.D. N.Y., Jan. 29, 2004) (memorandum and order denying defendant's motion to dismiss), http://www.advocatesforchildren.org/eb.php.

156. 34 C.F.R. §§ 300.151–300.153.

157. 34 C.F.R. §§ 300.506–300.513.

158. 34 C.F.R. § 300.153.

159. For a full review of this work, *see* the Southern Poverty Law Center's website at http://www.splcenter.org.

160. A copy of the complaint and settlement agreement reached for each school district is available at http://www.splcenter.org/legal/docket/docket.jsp.

161. Complaint at 1, P.R. v. Palm Beach Pub. Sch. (Fla. Dep't of Educ., filed Oct. 1, 2008), http://www.splcenter.org/pdf/dynamic/legal/Palm_Beach_Complaint.pdf. "Cool-off removals" include when principals unofficially suspend children by telling them to stay home for several days, without documenting the action as a suspension. *Id.* at 16.

162. *Id.* at 3.

163. *Id.*

164. Developed by a team of researchers, most notably George Sugai and Jeffrey Sprague, PBIS, also known as School-Wide Positive Behavioral Supports, is a well-established systemic intervention that aims to change school environments with an emphasis on changing underlying attitudes and policies around how behavior is addressed. *See* G. Sugai & R. Horner, *The Evolution of Discipline Practices: School-Wide Positive Behavior Supports,* 24 Child and Family Behavior Therapy 23–50, 28 (2002).

165. Studies have found positive results for students with disabilities. Stephen R. Lassen et al., *The Relationship of School-Wide Positive Behavior Support to Academic Achievement in an Urban Middle School*, 43 Psychology in the Schools 701–12 (2006); Carol W. Metzler et al., *Evaluation of a Comprehensive Behavior Management Program to Improve School-Wide Positive Behavior Support*, 24 Education and Treatment of Children 448–79 (2001).

166. *See generally* Sugai & Horner, *supra* note 164.

167. Negotiated settlement at 1, P.R. v. Palm Beach Pub. Sch. (Fla. Dep't of Educ., settled 2009), http://www.splcenter.org/pdf/dynamic/legal/palmbeach_settlement.pdf.

168. *Id.* at 3.

169. *Id.* at 4.

170. *Id.* at 6.

NOTES TO CHAPTER 4

1. Thomas D. Snyder et al., National Center for Education Statistics, Digest of Education Statistics 2007 230–31 (2008), http://nces.ed.gov/pubsearch/pubsinfo.asp?pubid=2008022.

2. Daniel J. Losen & Christopher Edley, Jr., *The Role of Law in Policing Abusive Discipline Policies: Why School Discipline Is a Civil Rights Issue*, in Zero Tolerance: Resisting the Drive for Punishment in Our Schools 230, 231 (William Ayers et al. eds., 2001).

3. The 1973 data were obtained from Children's Defense Fund of the Washington Research Project, School Suspensions: Are they Helping Children? (1975). The 2006 data were obtained from the U.S. Department of Education, Office for Civil Rights. A full analysis of these data will be published this year. Daniel J. Losen & Russell J. Skiba, Southern Poverty Law Center, Suspended Education: Urban Middle Schools in Crisis (forthcoming 2010; on file with the authors).

4. Parents and advocates have expressed suspicion that the rise in disciplinary suspensions is attributable, at least in part, to pressures exerted by high-stakes testing accountability such as those required under the No Child Left Behind Act of 2001, Pub. L. 107-110 (codified as amended in scattered sections of 20 U.S.C.). Empirical evidence provides some support for this suspicion. David N. Figlio, Testing, Crime and Punishment (National Bureau of Economic Research & University of Florida 2003), http://bear.cba.ufl.edu/figlio/crime.pdf (documenting evidence that schools respond to high-stakes testing by selectively disciplining their students because they have an incentive to keep high-performing students in school and low-performing students out of school during the testing window in order to maximize aggregate test scores).

5. Johanna Wald & Daniel Losen, *Out of Sight: The Journey through the School-to-Prison Pipeline*, in Invisible Children in the Society and Its Schools 23, 33 (Sue Brooks ed., 3d ed. 2007); The Advancement Project and the Civil Rights Project at Harvard University, Opportunities Suspended: The Devastating Consequences of Zero Tolerance and School Discipline Policies 13 (2000), http://www.advancementproject.org/publications/opportunity-to-learn.php; American Bar Association & the National Bar Association, Justice by Gender: The Lack of Appropriate Prevention, Diversion and Treatment Alternatives for Girls in the Justice System (2001), http://www.abanet.org/crimjust/juvjus/justiceby-

genderweb.pdf; Daniel J. Losen, *The Color of Inadequate School Resources: Challenging Racial Inequities That Contribute to Low Graduation Rates and High Risk for Incarceration,* 38 Clearinghouse Rev. J. of Poverty Law & Policy 616, 625 (2005) (citing Russell Skiba et al., *Children Left Behind: Series Summary and Recommendations,* Educ. Policy Briefs (Ind. Youth Serv. & Ctr. for Evaluation & Educ. Policy) (Summer 2004), http://www.ceep. indiana.edu/projects/PDF/PB_V2N4_Summary.pdf).

6. *See* N.Y. Education Law § 3214.

7. The Advancement Project reports that, in fact, this perception of school violence is not borne out by the facts:

> By 1999, 62 percent of the public still believed that youth crime was on the rise. The truth was very different, though: while statistics showed an increase in lesser offenses—with simple assaults up 37 percent, disorderly conduct up 33 percent and "other offenses" up 35 percent, youth crime was down almost 30 percent overall between 1991 and 2000 with violent and property crimes decreasing significantly.

Judith A. Browne, The Advancement Project, Derailed! The Schoolhouse to Jailhouse Track 10 (2003), http://www.advancementproject.org/reports/Derailerepcor.pdf.

8. National Center for Education Statistics & Bureau of Justice Statistics, Indicators of School Crime and Safety 2002 135 (2002), http://www.ojp.usdoj.gov/bjs/pub/pdf/iscs02. pdf.

9. *See* Avarita L. Hanson, *Have Zero Tolerance School Discipline Policies Turned into a Nightmare? The American Dream's Promise of Equal Educational Opportunity Grounded in Brown v. Board of Education,* 9 U.C. Davis J. Juv. L. & Pol'y 289, 302 (2005).

10. 20 U.S.C. § 8921 (1994) (repealed 2002 and reenacted under the No Child Left Behind Act, 20 U.S.C. § 7151(b)(1) & (f) (2002)).

11. 20 U.S.C. § 7151(b)(1).

12. ABA Juvenile Justice Commission, Zero Tolerance Policies: A Report (2001), http://www.abanet.org/crimjust/juvjus/zerotolreport.html.

13. 419 U.S. 565 (1975).

14. *Id.* at 574.

15. *Id.* at 574–75.

16. *Id.*

17. Zinermon v. Burch, 494 U.S. 113, 127 (1990).

18. 424 U.S. 319, 335 (1976).

19. 20 U.S.C. § 1400 *et seq.*

20. 29 U.S.C. § 794.

21. Goss, 419 U.S. at 581. But "when a student admits to the conduct giving rise to the suspension, the need for a due process hearing is obviated, since the purpose of a hearing is to safeguard against punishment of students who are innocent of the accusations against them." Cole v. Newton Special Mun. Separate Sch. Dist., 676 F. Supp. 749, 752 (S.D. Miss. 1987), *aff'd,* 853 F. 2d 924 (5th Cir. 1988); *see also* Black Coal. v. Portland Sch. Dist. No. 1, 484 F. 2d 1040, 1045 (9th Cir. 1973); Montoya v. Sanger Unified Sch. Dist., 502 F. Supp. 209, 213 (E.D. Cal. 1980).

22. Goss, 419 U.S. at 584.

23. *Id.* at 583; *see also* Jenkins v. La. State Bd. of Educ., 506 F. 2d 992, 1000 (5th Cir. 1975) (stating that in a student discipline case, the notice of charges "need not be drawn with [the] precision of a criminal indictment").

24. Goss, 419 U.S. at 572–75.

25. *Id.* at 584.

26. *See, e.g.,* Tasby v. Estes, 643 F. 2d 1103 (5th Cir. 1981) (holding that due process does not require opportunity to cross-examine witnesses); Black Coal. v. Portland Sch. Dist. No. 1, 484 F. 2d 1040 (9th Cir. 1973) (holding that due process requires right to be represented by counsel, present witnesses on own behalf, and cross-examine adverse witnesses).

Many courts cite to the Fifth Circuit decision of *Dixon v. Alabama State Board of Education,* 294 F. 2d 150, 159 (5th Cir. 1961), which held that although a "full-dress judicial hearing" was not required to expel a college student for misconduct, "the student should be given the names of the witnesses against him and an oral or written report on the facts to which each witness testifies. He should also be given the opportunity to present . . . his own defense against the charges and to produce either oral testimony or written affidavits of witnesses in his behalf."

27. Thomas Hutton & Kirk Bailey, The Hamilton Fish Institute on School and Community Violence & Northwest Regional Educational Laboratory, School Policies and Legal Issues Supporting Safe Schools 7–8 (2007), http://gwired.gwu.edu/hamfish/merlin-cgi/p/downloadFile/d/20708/n/off/other/1/nae/legalpdf/. *See also* Lawrence F. Rossow & Jerry R. Parkinson, The Law of Student Expulsions and Suspensions 4–7 (2d ed. 1999).

28. Goss, 419 U.S. at 582.

29. *Id.*

30. *Id.* at 582–83.

31. Wash. Admin. Code §§ 148-120-400 to -415 (2008).

32. Procedural due process requires the opportunity to be heard at a "meaningful time and in a meaningful manner." Armstrong v. Manzo, 380 U.S. 545, 552 (1965).

33. *See, e.g.,* Sieck v. Oak Park-River Forest High Sch. Dist., 807 F. Supp. 73 (N.D. Ill. 1992) (holding that a policy of mandatory suspension for theft called into question the "meaningfulness" of student's hearing).

34. 490 F. 2d 458, 460 (5th Cir. 1974). The objectionable behavior included fighting at school, directing abusive language at teachers, missing school at least once without permission, disobeying teachers' directions, and resisting corporal and other forms of punishment. *Id.* at 459.

35. *Id.*

36. 114 F. Supp. 2d 504, 512 (N.D. Miss. 1999); *see also, e.g.,* Lyons v. Penn Hills Sch. Dist., 723 A. 2d 1073 (Pa. Commw. Ct. 1999) (holding that the school board exceeded its statutory grant of authority by adopting a zero-tolerance policy that prevented an exercise of discretion by school officials).

37. 625 F. 2d 660 (5th Cir. 1980).

38. *Id.* at 662.

39. 430 U.S. 651 (1971); for a discussion of substantive due process claims to challenge corporal punishment, *see* Deanna Pollard-Sacks, *State Actors Beating Children: A Call for Judicial Relief* (on file with the authors).

40. San Antonio Indep. Sch. Dist. v. Rodriguez, 411 U.S. 1, 35, 37, 40, 51 (1973); *see also* Butler v. Rio Rancho Pub. Sch. Bd. of Ed., 341 F. 3d 1197, 1200–01 (10th Cir. 2003) (sustaining school suspension because punishment was not "arbitrary" and did not "shock the conscience," given the offense); Brewer v. Austin Indep. Sch. Dist., 779 F. 2d 260, 264 (5th Cir. 1985) (applying rational basis test to substantive due process challenge to school suspension).

41. 420 U.S. 308, 326 (1975).

42. In one of the more egregious cases of federal court deference to school discipline decisions, *Ratner v. Loudoun County Pub. Sch.,* 16 Fed. Appx. 140, 141 (4th Cir. 2001) (unpublished), a classmate told thirteen-year-old Ratner that she was contemplating suicide and that she had brought a knife to school in her binder. Ratner, knowing of the girl's previous suicide attempts and worried for her safety, took the binder away from her and placed it in his locker, intending to tell his parents and her parents of the incident after school. The principal learned of the knife, and Ratner immediately turned it over to her. Importantly, the principal stated that she believed Ratner was trying to act in the girl's best interest and that he posed no threat to anyone with the knife. Notwithstanding, Ratner was expelled for the remainder of the school year. *Id.* at 141–42. On appeal, the Fourth Circuit rejected Ratner's substantive due process claim in summary fashion, stating, "However harsh the result in this case, the federal courts are not properly called upon to judge the wisdom of a zero tolerance policy of the sort alleged to be in place at Blue Ridge Middle School or of its application to Ratner." *Id.* at 142.

43. 229 F. 3d 567 (6th Cir. 2000).

44. *Id.*

45. *Id.* at 581.

46. *Id.* at 575. Addressing the school board's argument that the zero-tolerance policy negated the need to establish knowledge of possession, the court went out of its way to state that it found it "impossible to take this suggestion seriously." *Id.* at 576.

47. No. 1:05CV40, 2006 WL 2850349 (N.D. Miss., Oct. 2, 2006).

48. *Id.* at 3–4.

49. *In re* R.M., 102 P. 3d 868 (Wyo. 2004) (holding that strict scrutiny is the appropriate test to apply to determine whether education must be provided to expelled students).

50. Doe v. Superintendent of Sch. of Worcester, 653 N.E. 2d 1088 (Mass. 1995) (holding that although state constitution provides for right to education, strict scrutiny does not apply to review school officials' decision to expel student); Keith D. v. Ball, 350 S.E. 2d 720 (W. Va. 1986) (finding that expulsion of students did not abridge fundamental state right to education because disruptive conduct by student forfeits that right); *but see* Cathe A. v. Doddridge County Bd. of Educ., 490 S.E. 2d 340 (W. Va. 1997) (applying strict scrutiny to expulsion policy but concluding that it survived).

51. "Research conducted over the past five years has detailed the growing use of suspensions for trivial conduct, much of which is subjectively labeled disrespect, disobedience, and disruption." The Advancement Project, Education on Lockdown: The Schoolhouse to Jailhouse Track 15 (Mar. 2005), http://www.advancementproject.org/reports/FINALEOLrep.pdf.

52. In Seattle high schools during the 1999–2000 school year, for example, 278 African Americans were disciplined for "disobedience," as compared with only 99 Caucasian students, even though African American students make up only 23 percent of the high

school population. Memorandum from June Rimmer, Chief Academic Officer of Seattle Public Schools, et al., to the Principals, Assistant Principals, and other staff at Seattle Public Schools, Disproportionality in Discipline—Rethinking Disobedience (Sept. 24, 2001) (on file with the authors).

53. *See* Sherpell v. Humnoke Sch. Dist. No. 5 of Lonoke County, 619 F. Supp. 670, 677 (E.D. Ark. 1985) (concluding that the subjective elements of a school's discipline code were pretextual, designed to mask racial bias, and resulted in punishment of Black students for conduct for which similarly situated white students were not punished); Hawkins v. Coleman, 376 F. Supp. 1330, 1336 (N.D. Tex. 1974) (noting that cultural differences lead white teachers to perceive conduct by nonwhite students as hostile or disruptive). For a discussion of racial discrimination claims more generally, *see* chapter 2.

54. The concept of notice in the context of a void-for-vagueness analysis—which refers to information of prohibited conduct that must be available to individuals before they have an opportunity to commit the prohibited conduct—should be distinguished from the concept of notice for purposes of procedural due process analyses—which refers to the notice that must be given to an accused, after the alleged misconduct has occurred but usually before punishment is imposed.

55. Grayned v. City of Rockford, 408 U.S. 104, 108 (1972).

56. City of Chicago v. Morales, 527 U.S. 41, 56 (1999).

57. 478 U.S. 675 (1986).

58. *Id.* at 676.

59. U.S. v. Williams, 128 S. Ct. 1830, 1835 (2008) ("Although ordinarily '[a] plaintiff who engages in some conduct that is clearly proscribed cannot complain of the vagueness of the law as applied to the conduct of others,' we have relaxed that requirement in the First Amendment context, permitting plaintiffs to argue that a statute is overbroad because it is unclear whether it regulates a substantial amount of protected speech") (quoting Hoffman Estates v. Flipside, Hoffman Estates, Inc., 455 U.S. 489, 495 (1982)).

60. United States v. Salerno, 481 U.S. 739, 745 (1987).

61. Fraser, 478 U.S. at 678.

62. *Id.*

63. *Id.* at 686.

64. Sypniewski v. Warren Hills Reg'l Bd. of Educ., 307 F. 3d 243, 266–67 (3d Cir. 2002). The Third Circuit set aside a portion of the school rule prohibiting behavior that creates "ill will" on overbreadth grounds. *Id.* at 266.

65. *Id.* (quoting Coates v. City of Cincinnati, 402 U.S. 611, 614 (1971)).

66. Coy v. Bd. of Educ. of N. Canton City Schs., 205 F. Supp. 2d 791, 802–03 (N.D. Ohio 2002); *see also* Spencer v. Unified Sch. Dist. No. 501, 935 P. 2d 242 (Kan. App. 1997) (relying on Fraser, 478 U.S. 675, to reject challenge to school rule prohibiting "unruly conduct that disrupts schools" brought on behalf of student who was expelled after a passenger in his car jokingly pointed a pellet gun at classmates).

67. Coy, 205 F. Supp. 2d at 796, 802. The court reasoned that this prohibition "does not give students any indication of what actions or behaviors would lead to discipline. . . . On its face, the wording of [that section] invites arbitrary, discriminatory and overzealous enforcement." *Id.* at 802 (internal quotations omitted).

68. Smith v. Mount Pleasant Pub. Sch., 285 F. Supp. 2d 987, 996 (E.D. Mich. 2003). *See also* Flaherty v. Keystone Oaks Sch. Dist., 247 F. Supp. 2d 698, 702–04 (W.D. Pa. 2003)

(invalidating on vagueness grounds a school rule that prohibited conduct "that school officials deem to be 'inappropriate, harassing, offensive or abusive' without defining those terms or limiting them in relation to geographic boundaries . . . or to speech that causes a material and substantial disruption to the school day").

69. Miller v. Penn Manor Sch. Dist., 588 F. Supp. 2d 606 (E.D. Pa. 2008).

70. Stephenson v. Davenport Cmty. Sch. Dist., 110 F. 3d 1303, 1305 (8th Cir. 1997) (alteration in original).

71. *Id.* at 1311. Other cases that have invalidated antigang rules as unconstitutionally vague include *Chalifoux v. New Caney Independent School District,* 976 F. Supp. 659, 667–69 (S.D. Tex. 1997) (invaliding school prohibition against "gang-related apparel" on vagueness grounds and noting that it would not be "overly burdensome for the District to provide a definite list of prohibited items and to update that list as needed"), and *Copper v. Denlinger,* 667 S.E. 2d 470 (N.C. App. 2008) (rejecting motion to dismiss vagueness challenge to school district's antigang rule).

72. 251 F. 3d 662, 666 (7th Cir. 2001).

73. *Id.*

74. *Id.* at 667–68.

75. Complaint, A.W. v. DeSoto County Sch. Dist., No. 2:09-cv-00155 (N.D. Miss., filed Sept. 1, 2009).

76. *Id.*

77. Complaint, D.G. v. DeSoto County Sch. Dist., No. 2:09-cv-00187 (N.D. Miss. filed Oct. 19, 2009).

78. 717 A. 2d 117, 122 n.8 (Conn. 1998).

79. *Id.* at 130 (internal quotations omitted).

80. 393 U.S. 503, 506 (1969).

81. *Id.* at 507.

82. *Id.* at 504.

83. *Id.* at 513.

84. *See, e.g.,* Holloman v. Harland, 370 F. 3d 1252, 1272 (11th Cir. 2004) (stating that "student expression must cause (or be likely to cause) a material and substantial disruption, and more than a brief, easily overlooked, *de minimus* impact, before it may be curtailed") (internal quotations and alterations omitted); LaVine v. Blaine Sch. Dist., 257 F. 3d 981 (9th Cir. 2001) (requiring school officials to show "facts which might reasonably have led school authorities to forecast substantial disruption of or material interference with school activities"; quoting Tinker, 393 U.S. 503, but noting that *Tinker* held that officials are "not required to wait until disruption actually occurs before they may act, nor need they have certainty that disruption will occur"); Boucher v. Sch. Bd. of Sch. Dist. of Greenfield, 134 F. 3d 821 (7th Cir. 1998) (holding that test must focus on whether school authorities have "reason to believe" that expression would be disruptive).

85. Alexander v. United States, 509 U.S. 544, 555 (1993); Bd. of Trustees of State Univ. of N.Y. v. Fox, 492 U.S. 469, 483 (1989).

86. Smith, 285 F. Supp. 2d 987 (finding that rule prohibiting "verbal assaults" is impermissibly overbroad but sustaining suspension of a student pursuant to that rule when student had criticized teacher).

87. Fraser, 478 U.S. at 677–78; *see also* Lowery v. Euverard, 497 F. 3d 584 (6th Cir. 2007) (sustaining removal of students from football team who had circulated petition

critical of the coach, stating, "I hate [the school's football coach] and I don't want to play for him," on the ground that school officials were reasonable in concluding that the speech was disruptive to the team by eroding the coach's authority); Smith, 285 F. Supp. 2d 987 (sustaining suspension of student for "verbal assault" when student read commentary in school cafeteria criticizing "turd-licking" tardiness policy purportedly made by a Nazi and supported by "teacher gestapos," speculating as to principal's marital infidelity and assistant principal's confused sexual identity, and including terms such as "skank" and "tramp").

88. Fraser, 478 U.S. at 685. Cf. *Guiles v. Marineau,* 461 F. 3d 320 (2d Cir. 2006) (holding that a school may not prohibit a student from wearing a shirt portraying President Bush that, through an amalgam of images and text, criticizes the president as a chicken-hawk president and accuses him of being a former alcohol and cocaine abuser. To make its point, the shirt displays images of drugs and alcohol. The court held that the student had a First Amendment right to wear the T-shirt and that because it was not obscene or patently offensive, *Fraser* did not apply).

89. 127 S. Ct. 2618 (2007).

90. *Id.* at 2622.

91. 240 F. 3d 200, 215 (3d Cir. 2001).

92. *Id.*

93. 247 F. Supp. 2d 698, 704 (W.D. Pa. 2003).

94. *Id.*

95. *Id.; see also* Miller, 588 F. Supp. 2d 606 (sustaining overbreadth challenge to school rule prohibiting "anything that is a distraction"); Gillman v. Sch. Bd. for Holmes County, 567 F. Supp. 2d 1359 (N.D. Fla. 2008); Killion v. Franklin Reg'l Sch. Dist., 136 F. Supp. 2d 446, 458–59 (W.D. Pa. 2001) (invalidating on overbreadth grounds a rule authorizing suspension or expulsion for any student who "verbally or otherwise abuses a staff member").

96. Virginia v. Black, 538 U.S. 343, 344 (2003).

97. Boim v. Fulton County Sch. Dist., 494 F. 3d 978 (11th Cir. 2007).

98. *Id.* at 983.

99. LaVine v. Blaine Sch. Dist., 257 F. 3d 981 (9th Cir. 2001); *see also* Riehm v. Engelking, 538 F. 3d 952 (8th Cir. 2008) (holding that student essay depicting student's murder of teacher and suicide constituted true threat and was not protected speech); Ponce v. Socorro Indep. Sch. Dist., 508 F. 3d 765 (5th Cir. 2007) (sustaining discipline of student over personal journal entries about "Columbine"-style attacks); A.G. v. Sayreville Bd. of Educ., 333 F. 3d 417 (3rd Cir. 2003) (sustaining suspension of a kindergarten student for saying "I'm going to shoot you" to a friend at recess, concluding that the decision was reasonably related to pedagogical concerns).

100. *See* LeBlanc v. Ascension Parish Sch. Bd., 301 F. Supp. 2d 576 (M.D. La. 2004) (sustaining discipline of student who brought to school a graphic and violent drawing depicting public school being soaked with gasoline, with missile aimed at it, obscene and racial expletives written on the drawing, and students holding guns and throwing a brick at the principal); Demers v. Leominster Sch. Dep't, 263 F. Supp. 2d 195 (D. Mass. 2003) (finding no violation of free-speech rights when school officials suspended student for drawing a picture of school surrounded by explosives and repeatedly writing phrases "I hate life" and "I want to die" on sheet of paper).

101. 526 F. 3d 419 (9th Cir. 2008).

102. 290 Fed. Appx. 273 (11th Cir. 2008); *see also* Lowry v. Watson Chapel Sch. Dist., 508 F. Supp. 2d 713 (E.D. Ark. 2007) (upholding mandatory school-uniform policy against First Amendment challenge given that policy was adopted in accordance with state legislative findings that uniforms further government interest of making students' socioeconomic disparities less obvious).

103. Jacobs v. Clark County Sch. Dist., 373 F. Supp. 2d 1162 (D. Nev. 2005).

104. 538 F. 3d 554 (6th Cir. 2008); *see also* B.W.A. v. Farmington R-7 Sch. Dist., 508 F. Supp. 2d 740 (E.D. Mo. 2007) (finding that school rule banning the display of the Confederate flag did not violate the First Amendment).

105. Gillman v. Sch. Bd. for Holmes County, 567 F. Supp. 2d 1359 (N.D. Fla. 2008) (holding that school ban on wearing or displaying symbols or slogans advocating the fair treatment of homosexuals is viewpoint discriminatory and violates the First Amendment).

106. *See* Pollnow v. Glennon, 594 F. Supp. 220, 221 n.2 (S.D. N.Y. 1984) (permitting school discipline for out-of-school conduct because conduct may adversely affect the educative process or endanger the health, safety, or morals of pupils within the education system for which the school authorities are responsible); *see generally* Daniel E. Feld, Annotation, *Right to Discipline Pupil for Conduct Away from School Grounds or Not Immediately Connected with School Activities,* 53 A.L.R. 3d 1124 (2006) (collecting cases on right of schools to discipline pupils for off-campus conduct).

107. *See* Healy v. James, 408 U.S. 169, 189 (1972) (holding that, in the school context, the government may punish conduct that "materially and substantially disrupt[s] the work and discipline of the school") (internal quotations omitted).

108. 635 F. Supp. 1440 (D. Me. 1986).

109. 136 F. Supp. 2d 446 (W.D. Pa. 2001).

110. 527 F. 3d 41 (2d Cir. 2008). Additional cases sustaining student discipline for off-campus Internet speech include *J.S. ex rel. Snyder v. Blue Mountain School District,* 2008 WL 4279517 (M.D. Pa., Sept. 11, 2008) (finding no First Amendment violation for punishing student who created parodic profile of principal on MySpace), and *Barnett ex rel. Barnett v. Tipton County Board of Education,* No. 07-2055-JPM-dkv (W.D. Tenn., Jan. 26, 2009).

111. *See, e.g.,* Mass. Gen. Laws ch. 71, § 37H 1/2 (1996) (authorizing suspension of students who have been charged with felonies); Ga. Code Ann. § 20-2-751.5(c) (providing that students will be disciplined for off-campus misconduct, including conduct that is prohibited by the Georgia or U.S. criminal codes; conduct that is punishable as a felony if committed by adults; and conduct for which a student has been arrested, indicted, adjudicated to have committed, or convicted).

112. *See supra* note 106 and accompanying text.

113. For a statute that is worded so as to take into account the substantive nature of the off-campus act, see Mass. Gen. Laws ch. 71, § 37H 1/2 (1996) (requiring determination that "student's continued presence in school would have a substantial detrimental effect on the general welfare of the school" before suspending a student for being charged with a felony).

114. In *Woods v. Wright,* 334 F. 2d 369 (5th Cir. 1964), the Fifth Circuit held unlawful the suspensions and expulsions of Black students on the basis of arrests for their participation in a demonstration against segregation. More broadly, the *Wright* court held that

discipline protocols could not be used to deprive students of a constitutionally guaranteed right. *See id.* at 374–75; *cf.* Tinker, 393 U.S. 503 (students' wearing of armbands was "pure speech," and as a constitutional right, school had to show that conduct would materially and substantially interfere with requirements of appropriate discipline in the operation of the school).

NOTES TO CHAPTER 5

1. The Advancement Project & the Civil Rights Project at Harvard University, Opportunities Suspended: The Devastating Consequences of Zero Tolerance and School Discipline 12 (2000), http://www.advancementproject.org/pdfs/opsusp.pdf ("With the burgeoning number of children being suspended and expelled, there is clearly a need for high quality alternative education programs.").

2. *See* Camilla A. Lehr et al., Institute of Community Integration, Alternative Schools: Policy and Legislation across the United States: Research Report 1, 5 (2003) http://ici. umn.edu/alternativeschools/publications/Legislative_Report.pdf [hereinafter Lehr et al., Alternative Schools Report 1] (finding that by 2003, forty-seven states and the District of Columbia had legislation regarding alternative schools or programs); Education Commission of the States, Alternative Education: What States Are Doing, http://ecs.org/ecs-main.asp?page=/html/issuesK12.asp (providing periodically updated summaries of state legislation).

3. *See* Lehr et al., Alternative Schools Report 1, *supra* note 2, at 8 (discussing the diversity of definitions across states and between scholars).

4. *See, e.g.,* Laura Green, *Education Company Banking on Heat Star to Fill Charter Schools,* Palm Beach Post, Aug. 15, 2008, at 1A (describing contract between public school district and for-profit corporation to provide alternative school); Editor, *Leaving School Early: SRC Head Nevels Resigns, and a New Chapter of Uncertainty Begins,* Philadelphia Daily News, Aug. 13, 2007, at 17 (discussing for-profit corporation operating alternative schools).

5. *See* Lehr et al., Alternative Schools Report 1, *supra* note 2, at 7 (stating that thirty-four states have legislation indicating that enrollment in alternative programs occurs as a consequence of suspension or expulsion).

6. Brian Kleiner et al., National Center for Education Statistics, Public Alternative Schools and Programs for Students at Risk of Education Failure: 2000–01 1 (2002), http://nces.ed.gov/pubs2002/2002004.pdf (listing factors for placement in an alternative school or program, including poor grades, truancy, pregnancy, disruptive behavior, or referral by a juvenile court).

7. Camilla A. Lehr et al., Institute of Community Integration, Alternative Schools: Findings from a National Survey of the States, Research Report 2, 12 (2004), http://ici. umn.edu/alternativeschools/publications/alt_schools_report2.pdf [hereinafter Lehr et al., Alternative Schools Report 2] (estimating that, within the twenty states that responded to surveys to state departments of education, 1,023,260 students enrolled in such programs in 2001–02).

8. Kleiner, *supra* note 6, at 6. This study, based on a survey of sample school districts, estimates that in the 2000–01 school year there were 10,900 alternative schools/programs, defined to include public alternative schools or programs administered by districts for

at-risk students where the majority of students attended for at least half of their instructional time, including charter schools, programs within juvenile detention centers, community-based schools or programs, and those that operated during weekday evenings and weekends. *Id.* at 2–3, 10.

9. *Id.* at 6.

10. *See, e.g.,* Lauren Roth, *New Alternative School Puts Future on Display,* Virginia Pilot and Ledger Star, Dec. 6, 2008, at 3 (noting a brand-new separate facility); Kevin C. Dilworth, *E. Orange to Discuss Fate of an Old School: State to Help Chart Plan for Shut Carver,* Newark Star-Ledger, Oct. 3, 2008, at 25 (noting trailers near the mainstream school).

11. Lehr et al., Alternative Schools Report 2, *supra* note 7, at 14.

12. *Compare* Kleiner, *supra* note 6, at 10 (estimating 612,900 students enrolled in alternative schools and programs in 2000–01, based on survey of national sample of districts), *with* Lehr et al., Alternative Schools Report 2, *supra* note 7, at 11 (estimating that, within the twenty states that responded to surveys to state departments of education, 1,023,260 students enrolled in such programs in 2001–02).

13. Lehr et al., Alternative Schools Report 2, *supra* note 7, at 11. In California, between 10 and 15 percent of high school students enroll in an alternative education program for at-risk students each year. Elizabeth Hill, Legislative Analyst's Office, Improving Alternative Education in California 3 (2007), http://www.lao.ca.gov/2007/alternative_educ/ alt_ed_020707.pdf.

14. Kleiner, *supra* note 6, at 8.

15. *See id.* at 10 (finding that more than a third of districts surveyed maintained alternative schools where more than a fifth of the student body had IEPs); American Civil Liberties Union, Missing the Mark: Alternative Schools in the State of Mississippi (Feb. 2009).

16. *See* Texas Appleseed, Texas' School-to-Prison Pipeline: Dropout to Incarceration: The Impact of School Discipline and Zero Tolerance 50 (2007).

17. *See also* Camilla A. Lehr, National Center on Secondary Education and Transition, Alternative Schools and Students with Disabilities: Identifying and Understanding the Issues 1 (Oct. 2004), http://www.ncset.org/publications/info/NCSETInfoBrief_3.6.pdf; Camilla A. Lehr & Cheryl M. Lange, Institute on Community Integration, Alternative Schools and the Students They Serve: Perceptions of State Directors of Special Education (2003), http://ici.umn.edu/products/prb/141/141.pdf.

18. *See, e.g.,* Texas Appleseed, *supra* note 16, at 36–47 (documenting racial disparities in referrals to disciplinary alternative education programs in Texas public school districts).

19. Hill, *supra* note 13.

20. *See generally* Augustina H. Reyes, *Disciplinary Alternative Education Programs, in* Discipline, Achievement, and Race: Is Zero Tolerance the Answer? 47 (Augustina H. Reyes ed., 2006); Margaret Hadderman, Clearinghouse on Educational Policy and Management, *Alternative Schools, in* Trends and Issues: School Choice (2002), http://eric. uoregon.edu/trends_issues/choice/alternative_schools.html.

21. For a discussion of the incentives created by the No Child Left Behind Act to deny alternative education to expelled students, *see* Maureen Carroll, *Comment, Educating Expelled Students after No Child Left Behind: Mending an Incentives Structure That Discourages Alternative Education and Reinstatement,* 55 UCLA L. Rev. 1909 (2008). But some progressive education advocates reason that this exemption may be warranted because

the progress of these students may be better measured through a manner other than high-stakes testing.

It is also worth noting that in some jurisdictions, students are placed in disciplinary alternative schools for longer than a full academic year. In theory, then the state should be held accountable for these students' performance.

22. 411 U.S. 1, 35 (1973).

23. *Id.*

24. Turley v. Sauquoit Valley Sch. Dist., 307 F. Supp. 2d 403, 407 (N.D. N.Y. 2003); Hill v. Rankin County, Mississippi Sch. Dist., 843 F. Supp. 1112, 1116 (S.D. Miss. 1993).

25. *Cf.* Kleiner, *supra* note 6, at 13–14 (documenting capacity constraints on alternative schools and indicating that a third of surveyed school districts were not able to place students in alternative schools because of overenrollment).

26. *See* 20 U.S.C. §§ 1400(d)(1)(A), (B), 1401(8), and 1412 (2006).

27. For a discussion of the state right to alternative education for expelled students, *see* Carroll, *supra* note 21, at 1915–24.

28. Cal. Educ. Code § 48916.1 (West 2006) (requiring districts to ensure an education program is provided upon the expulsion of a student and requiring separate programs for grades 1 through 6 and grades 7 through 12).

29. Colo. Rev. Stat. Ann. § 22-33-203 (West 1998) (requiring districts to provide services to expelled students upon request).

30. Del. Code Ann. tit. 14, § 1604 (1997) (requiring provision of alternative education services for expelled students).

31. Ky. Rev. Stat. Ann. § 158.150 (West 2008) (requiring local school boards to provide educational services to expelled students in appropriate settings).

32. La. Rev. Stat. Ann. § 17:416.2 (2001) (requiring suspended and expelled students to participate in alternative education program approved by the state).

33. Minn. Stat. § 121A.55 (2008) (requiring school boards to promulgate policies "recogniz[ing] the continuing responsibility of the school for the education of the pupil during the dismissal period).

34. Miss. Code. Ann. § 37-13-92, -93 (West 2008) (mandating that districts provide educational programs for expelled students).

35. Neb. Rev. Stat. § 79-266 (2008) (requiring districts to have alternative education programs or an expulsion procedure that provides for an education plan and monthly progress review).

36. N.J. Stat. Ann. § 18A:37-8 (1999) (stating that students expelled for firearms must be placed in an alternative education program or receive home instruction or other suitable facilities or programs until placement becomes available).

37. N.Y. Educ. Law § 3214 (McKinney 2001) (requiring instruction, supervision, or detention for suspended students).

38. R.I. Stat. § 16-21-27 (2008) (requiring districts to adopt a plan to assure continued supervision of students suspended more than ten days or chronically truant).

39. Tenn. Code Ann. § 49-2-203, § 49-6-3402 (2008) (requiring districts to provide access to alternative program for students in grades 7 through 12 who have been suspended or expelled).

40. 490 S.E. 2d 340, 344 (W. Va. 1997).

41. *Id.* at 345.

42. *Id.* at 351; *see also* Phillip Leon M. v. Greenbrier County Bd. of Educ., 484 S.E. 2d 909, 911 (W. Va. 1996) (holding that state constitution guaranteed "fundamental" right to education and that denial of all educational services to child who had been adjudicated delinquent and expelled for one year for bringing firearm to school failed strict scrutiny required for denial of fundamental right).

43. 749 A. 2d 902, 903 (N.J. Super. Ct. Ch. Div. 2000).

44. *Id.* at 908.

45. 615 N.E. 2d 516 (Mass. 1993).

46. 653 N.E. 2d 1088, 1095 (Mass. 1995).

47. *Id.*; *see also id.*, at n.4 (listing cases from other states); *id.* at 1096 ("a student's interest in a public education can be forfeited by violating school rules.").

48. D.B. v. Clarke County Bd. of Educ., 469 S.E. 2d 438, 440 (Ga. Ct. App. 1996) (finding that state constitutional right to education is not fundamental and upholding permanent expulsion of twelve-year-old student).

49. *In re* Jackson, 352 S.E. 2d 449, 455 (N.C. Ct. App. 1987) (reversing lower court conclusion that districts must provide alternative educational services to suspended students, notwithstanding state constitutional right to education).

50. R.M. v. Washakie County Sch. Dist. No. 1, 102 P. 3d 868, 876 (Wyo. 2004) (finding that state constitution guarantees "fundamental" right to education but upholding denial of alternative education to expelled students as narrowly tailored to further a compelling state interest).

51. Op. Att'y Gen. of Mich., 6271, at 13 (1985) (interpreting state constitutional provision creating free public schools as not requiring a board of education to provide alternative education to suspended or expelled students, except those students eligible for services under the Handicapped Children Act).

52. 419 U.S. 565, 572–75 (1975).

53. Everett v. Marcase, 426 F. Supp. 397, 400 (E.D. Pa. 1977).

54. Buchanan v. City of Bolivar, Tenn., 99 F. 3d 1352, 1359 (6th Cir. 1996) (suggesting that "absent some showing that the education received at the alternative school is significantly different from or inferior to that received at [Plaintiff's] regular public school," a disciplinary transfer to an alternative school implicates no protected interest and procedural due process protections are not required); Breeding v. Driscoll, 82 F. 3d 383, 389 n.5 (11th Cir. 1996) (stating, in dicta, that "we doubt [Plaintiff] has a property interest under Georgia law in attending [Plaintiff's mainstream public school] instead of the alternative school to which he was assigned," where the alternative program gave Plaintiff work assigned by his regular teachers but prohibited him from attending regular classes).

55. 111 F. 3d 25, 26 (5th Cir. 1997).

56. Nevares v. San Marcos Consol. Sch. Dist., 954 F. Supp. 1162, 1167 (W.D. Tex. 1996), *rev'd*, 111 F. 3d 25 (5th Cir. 1997).

57. *Id.* at 1166.

58. *Id.*

59. *Id.*

60. *Id.* at 1167.

61. 111 F. 3d at 26; *see also* Zamora v. Pomeroy, 639 F. 2d 662, 670 (10th Cir. 1981) (denying standing to student raising procedural due process challenge against transfer to alternative program absent evidence that the placement was "substantially prejudicial,"

e.g., showing that alternative school was so inferior as to amount to expulsion); Marner v. Eufala City Sch. Bd., 204 F. Supp. 2d 1318, 1324 (M.D. Ala. 2002) (concluding that a lack of "classical classroom instruction" was insufficient to meet this high standard and holding that minimal *Goss* requirement of notice and an opportunity to be heard were sufficient to impose forty-five-day transfer to an alternative school); *but see* Riggan v. Midland Indep. Sch., 86 F. Supp. 2d 647, 655 (W.D. Tex. 2000) (holding that five-day transfer to alternative school during study period for final exams could trigger procedural due process protections because it would deny the student the opportunity to "participat[e] in or benefit[] from the comments of his teachers and peers during in-class reviews." The court noted that, "The primary thrust of the educational process is classroom instruction; therefore minimum due process procedures may be required if an exclusion from the classroom would effectively deprive the student of instruction or the opportunity to learn").

62. 419 U.S. at 574–75 (footnote omitted; citations omitted; internal quotation marks omitted).

63. 879 A. 2d 408, 420 (Pa. Commw. Ct. 2005).

64. 424 U.S. 693 (1976).

65. 424 U.S. at 701–12.

66. 879 A. 2d at 416.

67. *Id.* at 417–18.

68. *Id.* at 418–19.

69. Lehr et al., Alternative Schools Report 2, *supra* note 7, at 4; Mary Magee Quinn & Jeffrey Poirier, American Institutes for Research, Study of Effective Alternative Education Programs: Final Grant Report 16 (2006), http://www.lehigh.edu/centennial/assets/pdf/AIR_report_effective_alt_education.pdf; *see generally* National Alternative Education Association, Exemplary Practices in Alternative Education: Indicators of Quality Programming (2009), http://www.tennessee.gov/education/learningsupport/alted/doc/ExemplaryPracticesinAE.pdf.

70. Lehr et al., Alternative Schools Report 2, *supra* note 7, at 15–16.

71. *See* Kleiner, *supra* note 6, at 27.

72. *See id.*

73. *See supra* notes 19–21, and accompanying text.

74. Lehr et al., Alternative Schools Report 1, *supra* note 2, at 11.

75. Ga. Code Ann. § 20-2-154.1 (2008).

76. Ark. Code Ann. § 6-18-508 (2008).

77. Ohio Rev. Code Ann. § 3313.533 (West 2008).

78. Lehr et al., Alternative Schools Report 1, *supra* note 2, at 11.

79. *See* Tenn. Code Ann. § 49-1-207; *see generally* Tennessee State Board of Education, Alternative Education Programs, Models, and Standards (2008), http://www.taea.net/images/ProgramStandards.pdf.

80. Fla. Stat. § 1008.34 (2008).

81. N.C. Gen. Stat. § 115C-12(24) (2008).

82. *See* Md. Code Regs. § 13A.08.01.12-1 (2008).

83. Complaint, M.H. v. Atlanta Indep. Sch. Dist., No. 2008-CV-147828 (Super. Ct. Fulton County, Mar. 11, 2008), http://www.aclu.org/images/asset_upload_file173_34423.pdf. For more information about this lawsuit, *see* http://www.aclu.org/crimjustice/juv/34422prs20080311.html.

84. Order Denying Motion to Dismiss, M.H. v. Atlanta Indep. Sch. Sys., No. 08-cv-1435 (N.D. Ga., filed Mar. 27, 2009).

85. Opposition to Motion to Dismiss Comm. Educ. Partners as a Def., M.H. v. Atlanta Indep. Sch. Sys., No. 08-cv-1435 (N.D. Ga., filed Aug. 17, 2009).

86. No. 06-087, 2006 WL 3731304, at 6 (Tenn. Ct. App., Dec. 19, 2006).

87. *Id.* at 1.

88. *Id.* at 7–8, 12. Yet, the same court awarded statutory attorneys' fees to counsel for the plaintiffs for establishing the right to some form of alternative education. No. 06-01155, 2007 WL 1519543 (Tenn. Ct. App., May 25, 2007).

89. 478 F. Supp. 418, 430 (D. Minn. 1979) (addressing Minn. Stat. § 127.29).

90. *Id.* at 423.

91. Lehr et al., Alternative Schools 2, *supra* note 7, at 19.

92. Kleiner, *supra* note 6, at 21.

93. *Id.*

94. Ga. Comp. R. & Regs. 160-4-8-12 (2008).

95. Md. Code Regs. § 13A.08.01.12-1 (2008).

96. *See, e.g.,* Tenn. Code Ann. § 49-6-3402(i)(1) (2008).

97. Integrated Design and Electronics Academy Pub. Charter Sch. v. McKinley *ex rel.* K.M., 570 F. Supp. 2d 28 (D.D.C. 2008) (finding that a charter school violated the IDEA).

NOTES TO CHAPTER 6

1. Rachel Dinkes et al., National Center for Education Statistics, Indicators of School Crime and Safety: 2007 113, 116 (2007).

2. One such collaboration that has been severely criticized by advocates is the development of "roundtables" in Massachusetts, under which school officials, juvenile justice personnel, and law enforcement officers meet periodically to discuss particular students. Advocates have argued that these roundtables serve to target at-risk youth for more frequent negative interactions with both school officials and school resource officers. For a discussion of the Massachusetts roundtables, see Lisa Thurau-Gray, *The Trend towards Turning Public Education into a Gated Community,* 11 Cornell J.L. & Pub. Pol'y 665, 670–75 (2002).

3. *See, e.g.,* Paul J. Hirschfield, *Preparing for Prison? The Criminalization of School Discipline in the USA,* 12 Theoretical Criminology 79, 80 (2008) (describing that "problems that once invoked the idea and apparatus of student discipline have increasingly become criminalized"); Daveen Rae Kurutz, *School Arrests, Citations Jump by 46 Percent,* Pittsburgh Tribune-Review, Aug. 23, 2008 (documenting 46 percent increase in number of school-based arrests and citations in Allegheny County in a single year); Children's Defense Fund, America's Cradle to Prison Pipeline 125 (2007) (noting tripling in number of school-based arrests in Miami-Dade County from 1999 to 2001); The Advancement Project, Education on Lockdown: The Schoolhouse to Jailhouse Track 15 (Mar. 2005) (documenting growth in the number of school-based arrests in select jurisdictions).

4. South Carolina Department of Juvenile Justice, Annual Statistical Report 2007–2008 13 (2009).

5. Mark A. Greenwald, Florida Department of Juvenile Justice, Delinquency in Florida's Schools: A Four Year Study 7, 12 (2009).

6. *See, e.g.,* Sharif Durhams, *Tosa East Student Arrested, Fined after Repeated Texting,* Milwaukee Journal Sentinel, Feb. 18, 2009, at B8 (describing arrest of a fourteen-year-old girl for text-messaging); *Student Arrested for Passing Gas and Turning Off Classmates' Computers,* South Florida Sun-Sentinel, Nov. 22, 2008 (reporting the arrest of a thirteen-year-old boy for repeatedly passing gas in class); Martin Cassidy, *Requests for Taser Recording Rejected,* Greenwich Time, May 31, 2008, at A1 (documenting the use of a Taser to shock a student after he knocked over a chair); Ann N. Simmons, *Scuffle Exposes a Racial Rift,* L.A. Times, Oct. 11, 2007, at B1 (reporting the arrest of a sixteen-year-old girl for battery after dropping a piece of birthday cake in the school lunch area and failing to clean it up to the satisfaction of the school resource officer); Bob Herbert, *6-Year-Olds under Arrest,* N.Y. Times, Apr. 9, 2007, at A17 (describing arrest of a six-year-old girl for felony battery on a school official and two misdemeanor counts of disruption of school and resisting arrest after throwing a temper tantrum at school); American Civil Liberties Union, Criminalizing the Classroom: The Over-Policing of New York City Schools 6, 14 (2007) (documenting arrests of students for bringing cell phone to school and walking into class late).

7. David E. Grossmann & Maurice Portley, National Council of Juvenile & Family Court Judges, Juvenile Delinquency Guidelines: Improving Court Practice in Delinquency Cases 151 (2005); *see also* Marie Leech & Carol Robinson, *City Schools Rely on Arrests to Keep Order,* Birmingham News, Mar. 22, 2009, at 1A (documenting concerns regarding the criminalization of students resulting in the "flooding of Family Court with cases that once would have been handled in a principal's office" and quoting Presiding Family Court Judge Brian Huff as stating, "But we're arresting children for offenses no one should be arrested for"); American Civil Liberties Union, Race and Ethnicity in America: Turning a Blind Eye to Injustice 149 (2007) (documenting statement by a juvenile-court judge in Massachusetts that he handles more school discipline in his courtroom today than he did in his former position, as a public school principal); Sara Rimer, *Unruly Students Facing Arrest, Not Detention,* N.Y. Times, Jan. 4, 2004 (reporting that juvenile-court judges in Ohio, Virginia, Kentucky, and Florida have complained about the volume of school misconduct cases overwhelming their courtrooms).

8. For example, social-work researcher Matthew T. Theriot has found a correlation between the presence of a school resource officer and the number of school-based arrests for disorderly conduct. Matthew T. Theriot, *School Resource Officers and the Criminalization of Student Behavior,* 37 J. of Crim. Just. 280, 280 (2009); *see also* Clayton County Public Schools, Blue Ribbon Commission on School Discipline: A Written Report Presented to the Superintendent and Board of Education 47 (2007) (documenting strong correlation between deployment of school resource officers and the more than tenfold increase in school-based arrests); American Civil Liberties Union, Hard Lessons: School Resource Officer Programs and School-Based Arrests in Three Connecticut Towns 35–43 (2008); American Civil Liberties Union, Criminalizing the Classroom: The Over-Policing of New York City Schools (2007); National Economic and Social Rights Initiative, Deprived of Dignity: Degrading Treatment and Abusive Discipline in New York City and Los Angeles Public Schools (2007).

9. Catherine Y. Kim & India Geronimo, American Civil Liberties Union, Policing in Schools: Developing a Model Governance Document for School Resource Officers in K–12 Schools (Aug. 2009); Cathy Girouard, Office of Juvenile Justice and Delinquency Prevention, U.S. Department of Justice, OJJDP Fact Sheet: School Resource Officer Training Program (2001).

10. Paul Hirschfield, *The Uneven Spread of School Criminalisation in the United States*, 74 Crim. Just. Matters 28, 28 (2008); Dinkes et al., *supra* note 1, at 60.

11. *See* Judith A. Browne, Advancement Project, Derailed: The Schoolhouse to Jailhouse Track 18–20, 23 (2003) (documenting disparities by race and special education status in school-based arrests in select jurisdictions).

12. Greenwald, *supra* note 5, at 5.

13. ACLU, Hard Lessons, *supra* note 8, at 35–43.

14. *See* Gary Sweeten, *Who Will Graduate? Disruption of High School Education by Arrest and Court Involvement*, 23 Just. Q. 462, 473, 478–79 (2006); Advancement Project, *supra* note 3, at 12; Terence P. Thornberry et al., *The Causes and Correlates Studies: Findings and Policy Implications*, 9 Juvenile Just. 3, 12 (Sept. 2004); Jeff Grogger, *Arrests, Persistent Youth Joblessness, and Black/White Employment Differentials*, 74 Rev. Econ. & Stat. 100, 105–06 (1992).

15. For an excellent discussion of challenges to such practices in a defensive context, that is, representing individuals accused in delinquency and criminal cases, see Marsha L. Levick & Robert G. Schwartz, *Changing the Narrative: Convincing Courts to Distinguish between Misbehavior and Criminal Conduct in School Referral Cases*, 9 D.C. L. Rev. 53 (2007); Elizabeth Calvin et al., National Juvenile Defender Center, Juvenile Defender Delinquency Notebook (2d ed. 2006), http://www.njdc.info/delinquency_notebook/interface.swf.

16. *See* York v. Wahkiakum Sch. Dist. No. 200, 178 P. 3d 995, 1001–02 (Wash. 2008) (concluding that the Washington constitution provides greater protection than its federal counterpart and thus prohibits suspicionless random drug testing of students); R.D.S. v. State, 245 S.W. 3d 356, 362 (Tenn. 2008) (noting in student questioning case that state constitutional right against self-incrimination more protective than federal right); Commonwealth v. Berry, 570 N.E. 2d 1004, 1007 n.2 (Mass. 1991) (providing more protective juvenile right against self-incrimination under state law than afforded under federal law); Theodore v. Delaware Valley Sch., 761 A. 2d 652, 660 (Pa. Commw. Ct. 2000) (noting in student search case that state constitution is more protective than federal Constitution and that it prohibits drug testing as a condition for participation in extracurricular activities and obtaining driving and parking privileges), *aff'd*, 836 A. 2d 76 (Pa. 2003).

17. For a discussion of these issues, see Erwin Chemerinsky, Federal Jurisdiction §§ 2.3, 7.5, 8.5–8.7 (5th ed. 2007).

18. Heck v. Humphrey, 512 U.S. 477, 486–87 (1994) (holding that in order to recover damages in a Section 1983 case for unlawful conviction, the plaintiffs must prove that the conviction or sentence has been overturned).

19. Vernonia Sch. Dist. 47J v. Acton, 515 U.S. 646, 654 (1995) (describing historical doctrine of *in loco parentis* and quoting 1 William Blackstone, Commentaries on the Laws of England 441 (1769)).

20. *See, e.g.,* Bd. of Educ. of Indep. Sch. Dist. No. 92 of Pottawatomie County v. Earls, 536 U.S. 822, 840 (2002) ("Today's public expects its schools not simply to teach the fundamentals, but 'to shoulder the burden of feeding students breakfast and lunch, offering before and after school child care services, and providing medical and psychological services,' all in a school environment that is safe and encourages learning."); Acton, 515 U.S. at 655–56 (recognizing the duty of school officials to "inculcate the habits and manners of civility"); Bethel Sch. Dist. No. 403 v. Fraser, 478 U.S. 675, 683 (1986) ("The process of educating our youth for citizenship in public schools is not confined to books,

the curriculum, and the civics class; schools must teach by example the shared values of a civilized social order.").

21. Indeed, a large number of legal scholars have published articles discussing this issue in recent years. *See* Bryan C. Hathorn, *Case Note, Constitutional Law—Searches, Seizures, & Confessions—Constitutional Protections for Students in Public Schools,* 76 Tenn. L. Rev. 211 (2008); Eleftharia Keans, *Note, Student Interrogation by School Officials: Out with Agency Law and In with Constitutional Warnings,* 27 B.C. Third World L.J. 375 (2007); Paul Holland, *Schooling Miranda: Policing Interrogation in the Twenty-First Century Schoolhouse,* 52 Loy. L. Rev. 39 (2006); Jennie Rabinowitz, *Note, Leaving Homeroom in Handcuffs: Why an Over-Reliance on Law Enforcement to Ensure School Safety Is Detrimental to Children,* 4 Cardozo Pub. L. Pol'y & Ethics J. 153 (2006); Gregory R. Mueller, *Detectives Dressed like Teachers: Circumventing the Constitutional Rights of New Jersey Students,* 236 N.J. Lawyer 25 (2005); Christina L. Anderson, *Double Jeopardy: The Modern Dilemma for Juvenile Justice,* 152 U. Pa. L. Rev. 1181, 1194–1200 (2004); Josh Kagan, *Reappraising T.L.O.'s "Special Needs" Doctrine in an Era of School–Law Enforcement Entanglement,* 33 J.L. Educ. 291 (2004); Michael Pinard, *From the Classroom to the Courtroom: Reassessing Fourth Amendment Standards in Public School Searches Involving Law Enforcement Authorities,* 45 Ariz. L. Rev. 1067 (2003); Jacqueline A. Stefkovich & Judith A. Miller, *Law Enforcement Officers in Public Schools: Student Citizens in Safe Havens?* 1999 B.Y.U. Educ. & L.J. 25 (1999); Betsy Levin, *Educating Youth for Citizenship: The Conflict between Authority and Individual Rights in the Public School,* 95 Yale L.J. 1647 (1986).

22. 469 U.S. 325, 341–42 (1985).

23. *Id.* at 341.

24. *Id.* at 342; *see also* Acton, 515 U.S. at 654–66 (citing to *T.L.O.* and concluding a school search policy is reasonable based on "the decreased expectation of privacy, the relative unobtrusiveness of the search, and the severity of the need met by the search"); Beard v. Whitmore Lake Sch. Dist., 402 F. 3d 598, 605 (6th Cir. 2005) ("[A] search undertaken to find money serves a less weighty governmental interest than a search undertaken for items that pose a threat to the health or safety of students, such as drugs or weapons."); Cornfield *ex rel.* Lewis v. Consol. High Sch. Dist. No. 230, 991 F. 2d 1316, 1320 (7th Cir. 1993) ("[W]hether a search is 'reasonable' in the constitutional sense will vary according to the context of the search. . . . A nude search of a student by an administrator or teacher of the opposite sex would obviously violate this standard. Moreover, a highly intrusive search in response to a minor infraction would similarly not comport with the sliding scale advocated by the Supreme Court."). *See generally* Michael J. Dale et al., 2 Representing the Child Client § 10.07[2][b] (2008) (discussing cases applying *T.L.O.*).

25. 469 U.S. at 345–47.

26. *Id.* at 342 n.8 (expressly declining to determine "whether individualized suspicion is an essential element of the reasonableness standard we adopt for searches by school authorities").

27. *See, e.g.,* Doe *ex rel.* Doe v. Little Rock Sch. Dist., 380 F. 3d 349, 356 (8th Cir. 2004) (invaliding a search requiring all students to empty their pockets and subject their backpacks and bags to search, where the purported state interest was a "generalized concern[] about the existence of weapons and drugs in its schools"); In re William G., 709 P. 2d 1287, 1297 (Cal. 1985) (invalidating a search of student's calculator case when there was no prior information connecting the student to any contraband); In re Pima, 733 P. 2d 316, 317–18

(Ariz. Ct. App. 1987) (invalidating a search of student's pockets in the absence of any information regarding this particular student's use or possession of drugs, notwithstanding general reports of drug use in the school); *cf.* DesRoches *ex rel.* DesRoches v. Caprio, 156 F. 3d 571, 577–78, 578 n.3 (4th Cir. 1998) (holding that a search of a student's backpack for stolen sneakers was reasonable because it was supported by individualized suspicion but declining to hold that individualized suspicion is always required).

28. 87 F. 3d 979, 980, 982–83 (8th Cir. 1996).

29. 469 U.S. at 337 n.5.

30. *See, e.g.,* Zamora v. Pomeroy, 639 F. 2d 662, 670–71 (10th Cir. 1981); Singleton v. Bd. of Educ. USD 500, 894 F. Supp. 386, 391 (D. Kan. 1995).

31. *See In re* Patrick Y., 746 A. 2d 405, 413–14 (Md. 2000); *In re* Isiah B., 500 N.W. 2d 639, 649 (Wis. 1993); Shoemaker v. State, 971 S.W. 2d 178, 182 (Tex. App. 1998).

32. *See, e.g.,* State v. Jones, 666 N.W. 2d 142, 148 (Iowa 2003) (affirming the legitimate expectation of privacy in school lockers notwithstanding state law and school rules contemplating and regulating locker searches); *In re* Dumas, 515 A. 2d 984, 985–56 (Pa. Super. Ct. 1986) (recognizing the legitimate privacy expectation in a student's locker and invalidating a locker search of a student who was caught with cigarettes in her hand).

33. *In re* Adam, 697 N.E. 2d 1100, 1107 (Ohio Ct. App. 1997); *accord In re* Dumas, 515 A. 2d at 985.

34. *See* Doe, 380 F. 3d at 355 (characterizing the use of metal detectors in schools as minimally intrusive administrative searches that do not require individualized suspicion); United States v. McDonald, 100 F. 3d 1320, 1325 (7th Cir. 1996) (noting the acceptance of using metal detectors at airports, courthouses, hospitals, and schools).

35. People v. Dukes, 580 N.Y.S. 2d 850, 852–53 (N.Y. Crim. Ct. 1992) (holding that the intrusion involved in a school metal-detector search was not greater than necessary to satisfy governmental interest underlying the need for search); *accord* Doe v. Little Rock Sch. Dist., No. LR-C-99-386, 1999 WL 33945744, at *3 (E.D. Ark., Aug. 26, 1999) (unreported); *In re* S.S., 680 A. 2d 1172, 1176 (Pa. Super. Ct. 1996).

36. *Cf.* United States v. Hartwell, 436 F. 3d 174, 178 (3d Cir. 2006) (affirming metal detector search at airport by relying, in part, on the fact that every passenger is searched).

37. *See* B.C. v. Plumas Unified Sch. Dist., 192 F. 3d 1260, 1267–68 (9th Cir. 1999) (holding that a search by a drug-sniffing dog infringes on a person's reasonable expectation of privacy and rejecting a random, suspicionless dog-sniff of student as unreasonable absent individualized suspicion); Horton v. Goose Creek Indep. Sch. Dist., 690 F. 2d 470, 481–82 (5th Cir. 1982) ("The intrusion on dignity and personal security that goes with the type of canine inspection of the student's person involved in this case cannot be justified by the need to prevent abuse of drugs and alcohol when there is no individualized suspicion, and we hold it unconstitutional.").

38. *See, e.g.,* Doe v. Renfrow, 475 F. Supp. 1012, 1021–22 (N.D. Ind. 1979) (holding that the use of drug-sniffing dogs to detect narcotics does not constitute a search triggering Fourth Amendment concerns when the dogs walked up and down the aisles of classrooms but did not closely approach individual students), *aff'd,* 631 F. 2d 91 (7th Cir. 1980); Commonwealth v. Cass, 709 A. 2d 350, 357 (Pa. 1998) (approving of the use of dogs to sniff two thousand lockers and search those lockers flagged by the dogs because, "[g]iven the limited expectation of privacy in that unique setting, we conclude that a search of the lockers was a minimally intrusive invasion of the students [*sic*] privacy interest").

By contrast, the ACLU of Washington successfully persuaded a school district to abandon its plans to implement drug-sniffing dogs at schools, absent individualized suspicions, by threatening to file a lawsuit under the state constitution's privacy clause, which requires individualized suspicion for all searches. For more information, see ACLU of Washington, press release, *Nine Mile Fall School District Abandons Dog Searches* (Mar. 30, 2006), http://www.aclu-wa.org/detail.cfm?id=430.

39. 129 S. Ct. 2633 (2009).

40. *Id.* at 2641.

41. *Id.* at 2642.

42. Phaneuf v. Fraikin, 448 F. 3d 591, 598 (2d Cir. 2006) (invalidating a strip search of an eighteen-year-old student suspected of possessing marijuana based on student tip because school officials failed to investigate, corroborate, or substantiate the tip further prior to the search).

43. Cornfield *ex rel.* Lewis v. Sch. Dist. No. 230, 991 F. 2d 1316, 1323 (7th Cir. 1993) (upholding a strip search of student suspected of placing drugs in his crotch, in part because search was performed in the privacy of boys' locker room, where no one else was present; officials stood at least ten feet away from the student while he removed his clothes; the student was never physically touched; and the officials permitted the student to put on a gym uniform while they searched his clothes).

44. *See* Cal. Educ. Code § 49050 (West 2006); Iowa Code Ann. § 808A.2(4)(a) (West 2003); N.J. Stat. Ann. § 18A:37-6.1 (West 1999); Okla. Stat. tit. 70, § 24-102 (West 2005); S.C. Code Ann. § 59-63-1140 (2008); Wash. Rev. Code § 28A.600.230(3) (West 2009); Wis. Stat. Ann. § 948.50(3) (West 2005).

45. 515 U.S. at 664–65.

46. *Id.* at 658.

47. 536 U.S. 822.

48. *Id.* at 833–34.

49. *See, e.g.,* Willis *ex rel.* Willis v. Anderson Cmty. Sch. Corp., 158 F. 3d 415, 418–19 (7th Cir. 1998) (invalidating a policy requiring drug tests for all students suspended for fighting absent any demonstrable link between drug use and fighting); Tannahill *ex rel.* Tannahill v. Lockney Indep. Sch. Dist., 133 F. Supp. 2d 919, 930 (N.D. Tex. 2001) (invalidating a mandatory drug-testing policy for all junior and senior high school students).

50. *See* Joye v. Hunterdon Cent. Reg'l High Sch. Bd. of Educ., 826 A. 2d 624, 654 (N.J. 2003).

51. The Fifth Amendment, applicable to states through the Fourteenth Amendment, provides that no person shall "be compelled in any criminal case to be a witness against himself." U.S. Const. amend. V.

52. *See* Complaint at 18–20, Antoine v. Winner Sch. Dist., No. Civ. 06-3007 (D.S.D., filed Mar. 24, 2006).

53. *Id.*

54. *See* Consent Decree at 2–3, Antoine, No. Civ. 06-3007 (D.S.D. filed Dec. 10, 2007).

55. *See* Pollnow v. Glennon, 594 F. Supp. 220, 224 (S.D. N.Y. 1984), *aff'd,* 757 F. 2d 496 (2d Cir. 1985); Boynton v. Casey, 543 F. Supp. 995, 997 (D. Me. 1982). Additionally, a school official's intent to turn over incriminating student statements to the police does not transform the interview into a custodial interrogation. *See* Commonwealth v. Snyder, 597 N.E. 2d 1363, 1369 (Mass. 1992); *see also* State v. Tinkham, 719 A. 2d 580, 583 (N.H.

1998) (affirming that a school principal does not need to administer *Miranda* warnings before questioning a student when there is "no affirmative act by any police officer inducing [the principal] to question the [student]"); *In re* Navajo County Juvenile Action No. JV91000058, 901 P. 2d 1247, 1249 (Ariz. Ct. App. 1995) (holding there was no custodial interrogation because a school principal is not an agent or instrumentality of the police).

56. The privilege against self-incrimination may be asserted in any forum, so long as the testimony might subject the witness to criminal prosecution. *See* Malloy v. Hogan, 378 U.S. 1, 11–12 (1964).

57. Butler v. Oak Creek-Franklin Sch. Dist., 172 F. Supp. 2d 1102, 1125–26 (E.D. Wis. 2001) (holding that a student had the right to assert the Fifth Amendment and to remain silent before school officials because the student's conduct could have resulted in criminal prosecution); Gonzales v. McEuen, 435 F. Supp. 460, 471 (C.D. Cal. 1977) (holding that comment by counsel on two students' refusal to testify at an expulsion hearing, and arguments that guilt could be inferred from such refusal, violated the students' Fifth Amendment rights).

58. A student who has been required to make self-incriminating statements by school officials may not civilly challenge the questioning eliciting those statements; the only remedy available is the exclusion of those incriminating statements from criminal proceedings. Chavez v. Martinez, 538 U.S. 760, 767-69 (2003).

59. Minnesota v. Murphy, 465 U.S. 420, 434–35 (1984).

60. Additionally, any waiver of the right must be knowingly, intelligently, and voluntarily made. *See* Fare v. Michael C., 442 U.S. 707, 724 (1979) (citing North Carolina v. Butler, 441 U.S. 369, 373 (1979)).

61. *See* State v. Benoit, 490 A. 2d 295, 301 (N.H. 1985).

62. *Id.* at 725.

63. *See, e.g.,* United States v. D.F., 115 F. 3d 413, 421 (7th Cir. 1997) (concluding that a juvenile's confession to staff at a mental-health facility was not voluntary because the staff members "encouraged" her to confess, developed her trust, and granted her privileges based on her admissions).

64. Benoit, 490 A. 2d at 302; *see* Commonwealth v. McCra, 694 N.E. 2d 849, 852 (Mass. 1998) (noting that juveniles under the age of fourteen must actually consult with an interested adult for a waiver of the right against self-incrimination to be valid); *In re* E.T.C., 449 A. 2d 937, 940 (Vt. 1982).

65. *See, e.g.,* Smith v. State, 918 A. 2d 1144, 1149–50 (Del. 2007) (rejecting the "interested adult rule" but noting that the opportunity to consult with an interested adult is a factor in the "totality of the circumstances"); *In re* Jerrell C.J., 699 N.W. 2d 110, 120 (Wis. 2005) (following the "totality of the circumstances" approach but noting that depriving the juvenile of the opportunity to consult with an interested adult is "strong evidence that coercive tactics were used to illicit the incriminating statements"; citing Theriault v. State, 223 N.W. 2d 850, 857 (Wis. 1974)).

66. *See supra* note 7 and accompanying text.

67. *See* Kagan, *supra* note 21, at 316–25; Pinard, *supra* note 21, at 1119–25.

68. Complaint, Benitez v. Montoya, No. 03-0392 (N.D. Cal., Jan. 30, 2003). The district settled the case and agreed to permit searches of students and lockers only when there is individualized, reasonable suspicion; school officials agreed to summon law enforcement to campus only when necessary to protect the safety of people on campus, when required

by law, or when school officials have individualized, reasonable suspicion that a student is breaking the law; and police officers who question or search students on campus agreed to follow the same rules that apply when questioning or searching students off campus. For more information, *see* ACLU of Northern California, *Cases: Benitez v. Montoya,* http://www.aclunc.org/cases/landmark_cases/benitez_v._montoya.shtml?ht.

69. Pursuant to a negotiated agreement, the defendants agreed to destroy the photographs and other information collected during the search and lineup and to adopt policies for when the police may photograph, search, and question students on school campuses or at school functions. For more information, *see* ACLU of Northern California, press release, *Fairfield Families Win New Policies for Police in Schools* (June 7, 2007), http://www.aclunc.org/news/press_releases/fairfield_families_win_new_policies_for_police_in_schools.shtml?ht.

70. The district agreed to remove school resource officers at all the district's schools as a condition of settling the case. For more information, *see* ACLU of Northern California, *ACLU Protects Native American Children in Landmark School Settlement,* http://www.aclunc.org/issues/racial_justice/aclu_protects_native_american_children_in_landmark_school_settlement.shtml.

71. T.L.O., 469 U.S. at 341 n.7 (declining to determine the standards that govern school searches and seizures conducted in conjunction with or at the behest of law enforcement agencies).

72. *In re* C.H., 763 N.W. 2d 708 (Neb. 2009) (finding custodial interrogation, which requires *Miranda* warnings, when law enforcement questions student in principal's office); *In re* R.H., 791 A. 2d 331, 333–34 (Pa. 2002) (finding custodial interrogation when school resource officer assigned to school questioned student); *In re* D.A.R., 73 S.W. 3d 505, 512–13 (Tex. App. 2002) (same); State v. Doe, 948 P. 2d 166, 169 (Idaho Ct. App. 1997) (same),

73. *Compare In re* W.R., 634 S.E. 2d 923, 926 (N.C. Ct. App. 2006) (finding custodial interrogation in questioning by a uniformed police officer and school officials acting together), *allowing review,* 653 S.E. 2d 877 (N.C. 2007); *In re* G.S.P., 610 N.W. 2d 651, 658 (Minn. Ct. App. 2000) (finding custodial interrogation in questioning by school liaison officer and school principal), *with* Cason v. Cook, 810 F. 2d 188, 193 (8th Cir. 1987) (finding no custodial interrogation when school principal questioned student in the presence of officer), *In re* W.R., 675 S.E. 2d 342, 344 (N.C. 2009) (finding no custodial interrogation when school official and officer questioned student); State v. D.J., 132 Wash. App. 1055 (Wash. Ct. App. 2006) (unreported) (finding no custodial interrogation when principal and officer questioned student); State v. J.T.D., 851 So. 2d 793, 796 (Fla. Dist. Ct. App. 2003) (same). For further discussion of this issue, *see* Holland, *supra* note 21.

74. Cason v. Cook, 810 F. 2d 188, 192 (8th Cir. 1987) (holding that a search conducted by school officials in conjunction with police was subject to relaxed reasonableness standard rather than probable cause when school officials initiated the search and police involvement was minimal); Tarter v. Raybuck, 742 F. 2d 977, 983–84 (6th Cir. 1984) (predating *T.L.O.* but applying the same standard to a search initiated by school officials but in the presence of law enforcement); Vassallo v. Lando, 591 F. Supp. 2d 172, 194 (E.D. N.Y. 2008) (applying *T.L.O.* and finding reasonable suspicion for a search initiated by school officials but conducted in conjunction with police); Johnson v. City of Lincoln Park, 434 F. Supp. 2d 467, 475 (E.D. Mich. 2006) (applying *T.L.O.* standard to search conducted by

school resource officer in the presence of school principal); Rudolph *ex rel.* Williams v. Lowndes County Bd. of Educ., 242 F. Supp. 2d 1107, 1114 (M.D. Ala. 2003) (applying *T.L.O.* standard to search conducted by police officers at the request of, but not in the presence of, school officials); *In re* Angelia D.B., 564 N.W. 2d 682, 690–91 (Wis. 1997) (applying *T.L.O.* standard to search by school liaison officer at the request of and in conjunction with school officials); *In re* J.F.M., 607 S.E. 2d 304, 307 (N.C. Ct. App.), *appeal dismissed,* 612 S.E. 2d 320 (N.C. 2005) (applying *T.L.O.* standard to search by school resource officer in conjunction with school officials); *In re* Josue T., 989 P. 2d 431, 436 (N.M. Ct. App. 1999) (applying *T.L.O.* to search by school resource officer made at the request of school official); Coronado v. State, 835 S.W. 2d 636, 639 (Tex. Crim. App. 1992) (applying *T.L.O.* to search by school resource officer at the request of and in conjunction with assistant principal); *but see* State v. K.L.M., 628 S.E. 2d 651, 653 (Ga. Ct. App. 2006) (requiring probable cause anytime a law enforcement officer participates in a search, even if the search is directed by a school official). *See generally* Alexander C. Black, *Annotation, Search Conducted by School Official or Teacher as Violation of Fourth Amendment or Equivalent State Constitutional Provision,* 31 A.L.R. 5th 229 §§ 21, 38 (1995) (discussing cases).

75. 309 F. 3d 1054, 1062 (8th Cir. 2002).

76. *Id.* at 1060.

77. State v. Heirtzler, 789 A. 2d 634, 638 (2001) (applying "agency rule" to prevent the police from ordering third parties, in this case school officials, to conduct search or seizure that would be unlawful if conducted by the police themselves); F.P. v. State, 528 So. 2d 1253, 1255 (Fla. Dist. Ct. App. 1988) (applying probable cause standard when an outside police officer investigating an auto theft initiated the search of a student at school); *cf.* Vassallo, 591 F. Supp. 2d at 196 (emphasizing that there was "absolutely no evidence that the school officials' actions were used as a pretext by the police officer to circumvent the warrant and probable cause requirements" and concluding that *T.L.O.* standard applied to a search conducted by school officials in conjunction with police); *but see* Milligen v. City of Slidell, 226 F. 3d 652, 656 (5th Cir. 2000) (applying relaxed *T.L.O.* standard to a seizure that was initiated and requested by two police officers, on the ground that the vice principal was the one to summon the students into her office and remained present during the questioning by police).

78. Cases treating school resource officers as school officials, subject to relaxed *T.L.O.* standards even when they initiate or conduct searches acting alone, include People v. Dilworth, 661 N.E. 2d 310, 317 (Ill. 1996) (applying reasonable suspicion standard to search by school resource officer acting alone); *In re* William V., 4 Cal. Rptr. 3d 695, 698 (Cal. Ct. App. 2003) (applying the reasonable suspicion standard to a search by uniformed police officer on a two-year contract with the school); People v. Williams, 791 N.E. 2d 608, 610 (Ill. App. Ct. 2003) (subjecting a weapons search by a school resource officer to the reasonable suspicion standard even though it was related to burglary investigation that arose outside school); Russell v. State, 74 S.W. 3d 887, 892–93 (Tex. App. 2002) (quoting *Dilworth* and concluding that school resource officers acting on their own initiative are subject to the relaxed *T.L.O.* standard); Commonwealth v. J.B., 719 A. 2d 1058, 1066 (Pa. Super. Ct. 1998) (treating school resource officers as school officials, subject to relaxed *T.L.O.* standard); State v. D.S., 685 So. 2d 41, 43 (Fla. Dist. Ct. App. 1996) (same); Wilcher v. State, 876 S.W. 2d 466, 467 (Tex. Ct. App. 1994) (applying the reasonable suspicion standard when the searcher was "a police officer for the Houston

Independent School District"); *In re S.F.*, 607 A. 2d 793, 794 (Pa. Super. Ct. 1992) (applying the reasonable suspicion standard to a search by a "plainclothes police officer for the School District of Philadelphia").

Cases reaching the opposite conclusion include Shade v. City of Farmington, 309 F. 3d 1054, 1060 (8th Cir. 2002) (treating school resource officers identically to ordinary police officers); State v. Scott, 630 S.E. 2d 563, 566 (Ga. Ct. App. 2006) (holding that school resource officers, unlike school officials, must have probable cause rather than mere reasonable suspicion to search or seize a student); Patman v. State, 537 S.E. 2d 118 (Ga. Ct. App. 2000) (holding police officers working on special detail in a school to the probable cause standard for searches of students); A.J.M. v. State, 617 So. 2d 1137, 1138 (Fl. Dist. Ct. App. 1993) (holding that a school resource officer employed by a sheriff's office must have probable cause to search).

79. 532 U.S. 67, 83–84 (2001).

80. *Id.* at 71–73.

81. *Id.* at 73.

82. *Id.* at 83.

83. *Id.* at 84.

84. *See, e.g.,* Gray *ex rel.* Alexander v. Bostic, 458 F. 3d 1295, 1305–06 & n.7 (11th Cir. 2006) (holding that a school resource officer's handcuffing of nine-year-old girl for disciplinary purposes violated Fourth Amendment), *cert. denied,* 127 S. Ct. 2428 (2007); *see also* A.W. v. State, 928 So. 2d 1243 (Fla. Dist. Ct. App. 2006) (concluding that a school resource officer was not "engaged in the lawful execution of a legal duty" and thus the student could not be adjudicated delinquent for resisting arrest when the officer demanded that the student, who was skipping school and hanging out in a car in the school parking lot against school rules but not against criminal law, hand over his car keys).

85. Some districts employ their own police departments and promulgate regulations or board policies defining the roles and responsibilities of these officers. Other districts employ the services of ordinary municipal police departments by entering into a memorandum of understanding (MOU) with the police department, explicitly defining the respective roles and duties of SROs. See Kim & Geronimo, *supra* note 9; Girouard, *supra* note 9; Browne, *supra* note 11, at 16–17.

86. In response to advocacy by the ACLU of Washington, the Clarkston School District maintains a policy in which school disciplinary issues, including minor violations of law, are handled exclusively by school officials; law enforcement intervene only for serious crimes in which "there is a substantial threat to the health and safety of students." See Clarkston Sch. Dist., Policy No. 4310 (Sept. 10, 2001), http://www.csdk12.org/BoardPolicies/Content/NEW_4000_SECTION.pdf. Similarly, the efforts of a local juvenile-court judge from Clayton County, Georgia, resulted in an agreement between the police and the school district limiting referrals of students to the juvenile justice system for minor school-discipline issues including affray, disrupting public school, disorderly conduct, and criminal trespass. See Cooperative Agreement, http://www.gpdsc.com/resources-juvenile-cooperative_agreement_070804.pdf.

87. The suit raises an unlawful-arrest claim on behalf of two teachers who were arrested for interfering with a police officer's attempt to arrest a student at school. For more information, see N.Y. Civil Liberties Union, *Kronen v. NYC,* http://www.nyclu.org/node/1099.

88. Baker v. Couchman, 721 N.W. 2d 251, 256 (Mich. Ct. App. 2006), *rev'd on other grounds,* 729 N.W. 2d 520 (Mich. 2007) (finding that the superintendent had no authority to interfere with a school resource officer's investigations because "[w]hile investigation of misconduct on school grounds is foremost within the province of the school administration, once the administration opens the schoolhouse doors to assistance from law enforcement personnel, it concedes some of its authority to that autonomous agency").

89. *See supra* notes 3–7 and accompanying text.

90. *See generally* Julius Menacker & Richard Mertz, *State Legislative Responses to School Crime,* 85 Educ. L. Rep. 1 (1993) (reviewing state statutes in thirty-six states relating to school crime specifically).

91. In keeping with the rest of this book, the goal here is to identify strategies for systemic reform, rather than tips for defenders representing individual cases. For excellent resources for juvenile defenders representing individual cases, *see* Calvin et al., *supra* note 15, and Levick & Schwartz, *supra* note 15. For a discussion on affirmatively challenging school-based arrests generally, outside the context of school-specific crimes, *see* chapter 7.

92. The use of these two doctrines to challenge school discipline codes, as opposed to criminal statutes, is discussed in chapter 4.

93. City of Chicago v. Morales, 527 U.S. 41, 56 (1999).

94. Parker v. Levy, 417 U.S. 733, 756 (1974).

95. United States v. Salerno, 481 U.S. 739, 745 (1987) (holding that, outside the First Amendment context, a facial challenge requires a litigant "to establish that no set of circumstances exists under which the Act would be valid").

96. Alexander v. United States, 509 U.S. 544, 555 (1993).

97. Bd. of Trustees of State Univ. of N.Y. v. Fox, 492 U.S. 469, 483 (1989).

98. 408 U.S. at 108.

99. *Id.* at 112.

100. *Id.* at 114.

101. *Id.* at 119.

102. *See, e.g., In re* Amir X.S., 639 S.E. 2d 144, 145 (S.C. 2006) (sustaining a statute that makes it unlawful "to interfere with or to disturb in any way or in any place the students or teachers of any school or college in this State" or "to act in an obnoxious manner thereon"); Commonwealth v. Bohmer, 372 N.E. 2d 1381, 1384 & n.2 (Mass. 1978) (sustaining a statute criminalizing anyone who "wilfully interrupts or disturbs a school"); M.C. v. State, 695 So. 2d 477, 478–79 (Fla. Dist. Ct. App. 1997) (rejecting overbreadth and vagueness challenges to a statute making it a crime to "[k]nowingly disrupt or interfere with the lawful administration or function of an educational institution"); *cf.* State v. McCooey, 802 A. 2d 1216, 1217–18 (N.H. 2002) (avoiding a constitutional challenge to a conviction for disorderly conduct that occurred during a class because it was not established that the appellant's conduct actually disrupted school activities).

103. No. 1999CA00128, 2000 WL 222033, at *2 (Ohio Ct. App., Feb. 22, 2000).

104. *Id.*

105. 92 P. 3d 521 (Idaho 2004).

106. *Id.* at 522 (citing Idaho Code Ann. § 33-512(11)).

107. *Id.* at 525.

108. Idaho Code Ann. § 18-916 (2008); *see also* Ark. Code Ann. § 6-17-106(a)(1) (West 2008) (making it a crime to address a public school employee using language "that in its common acceptation is calculated to . . . arouse the person to whom it is addressed to anger to the extent likely to cause imminent retaliation").

109. 354 So. 2d 869, 870 (Fla. 1978).

110. *Id.* at 872.

111. *See, e.g.,* Shoemaker v. State, 38 S.W. 3d 350 (Ark. 2001) (discussing and relying on similar cases and invalidating a statute punishing anyone who "abuses or insults a public school teacher while that teacher is performing normal and regular assigned school responsibilities").

112. *See, e.g.,* Ariz. Rev. Stat. Ann. § 15-507 (2008); Ark. Code Ann. § 6-17-106(a) (West 2008); Idaho Code Ann. § 18-916 (2008); Mont. Code Ann. § 20-4-303 (2007); N.D. Cent. Code § 15.1-06-16 (2007).

113. S.C. Code Ann. § 16-17-420(2)(b) (2008).

114. *See* J.L.S. v. State, 947 So. 2d 641, 646–47 (Fla. Dist. Ct. App. 2007), *denying review,* 958 So. 2d 919 (Fla. 2007) (rejecting constitutional challenges to a statute prohibiting trespass on school grounds by persons without "legitimate purpose" at the school; citing Fla. Stat. § 810.0975(2)(b) (2008)).

115. *See* State v. Debnam, 542 P. 2d 939, 941 (Ore. Ct. App. 1975) (invaliding a statute prohibiting "loiter[ing]" at schools on void-for-vagueness grounds because "the term 'loiter' standing alone is 'so elastic that men of common intelligence must necessarily guess (its) meaning'").

116. 873 So. 2d 485, 487 (Fla. Dist. Ct. App. 2004).

117. "Following the murders of thirteen students and one teacher at Columbine High School in Colorado in 1999, schools and law enforcement cracked down on students' verbal expressions that directly or indirectly threatened violence toward other students, teachers, or the school community in general. Whether in the form of oral threats, written hit lists, drawings, web-based messages, or other forms of expression, suspension, expulsion, and arrest rapidly became the predictable response." Levick & Schwartz, *supra* note 15, at 66–67 (footnote omitted).

118. 18 Pa. Cons. Stat. Ann. § 2706(a) (West 2008); *see also* Ga. Code Ann. § 16-11-37 (2008); Haw. Rev. Stat. § 707-715 (2008); Minn. Stat. Ann. § 609.713 subdiv. 1 (2008); Neb. Rev. Stat. § 28-311.01(1) (2008); N.J. Stat. Ann. § 2C:12-3 (2009); Wyo. Stat. Ann. § 6-2-505(a) (2008).

119. *See, e.g., In re* Ernesto H., 24 Cal. Rptr. 3d 561, 561 (Cal. Ct. App. 2004) (rejecting a free-speech challenge to a statute prohibiting threats against public employees brought by a student who said to his teacher, "Yell at me and see what happens"); *accord* State v. Milner, 571 N.W. 2d 7, 14–15 (Iowa 1997); State *ex rel.* R.T., 748 So. 2d 1256, 1261 (La. Ct. App. 1999), *rev'd on other grounds,* 781 So. 2d 1239 (La. 2001).

120. *See, e.g.,* State v. Nelson, 739 N.W. 2d 199, 206 (Neb. 2007); People v. VanPatten, 850 N.Y.S. 2d 213, 216 (N.Y. App. Div. 2007), *appeal denied,* 889 N.E. 2d 91 (N.Y. 2008); Saidi v. State, 845 So. 2d 1022, 1026 (Fla. Dist. Ct. App. 2003); Commonwealth v. Green, 429 A. 2d 1180, 1182 (Pa. Super. Ct. 1981).

1. As with each chapter in this book, this chapter focuses on systemic litigation to challenge the pipeline, rather than practice tips for direct legal services providers. For an excellent resource for juvenile defenders providing direct legal services, *see* Marsha L. Levick & Robert G. Schwartz, *Changing the Narrative: Convincing Courts to Distinguish between Misbehavior and Criminal Conduct in School Referral Cases*, 9 U.D.C.L. Rev. 53 (2007); Elizabeth Calvin et al., National Juvenile Defender Center, Juvenile Defender Delinquency Notebook (2006), http://www.njdc.info/delinquency_notebook/interface.swf.

2. The Annie E. Casey Foundation, 2008 Kids Count Data Book 7 (2008), http://www.aecf.org/KnowledgeCenter/PublicationsSeries/KCDatabookProds.aspx [hereinafter 2008 Kids Count Data Book].

3. Melissa Sickmund et al., U.S. Department of Justice, Census of Juveniles in Residential Placement Databook (2008), http://www.ojjdp.ncjrs.gov/ojstatbb/cjrp/.

4. South Carolina Department of Juvenile Justice, Annual Statistical Report 2007–2008 13 (2009).

5. Mark A. Greenwald, Florida Department of Juvenile Justice, Delinquency in Florida's Schools: A Four Year Study 7, 12 (2009).

6. *See* Gary Sweeten, *Who Will Graduate? Disruption of High School Education by Arrest and Court Involvement*, 23 Just. Q. 462, 473, 478–79 (2006); Terence P. Thornberry et al., *The Causes and Correlates Studies: Findings and Policy Implications*, 9 Juvenile Just. 3, 12 (Sept. 2004); Jeff Grogger, *Arrests, Persistent Youth Joblessness, and Black/White Employment Differentials*, 74 Rev. Econ. & Stat. 100, 105–06 (1992).

7. He Len Chung et al., MacArthur Foundation, Juvenile Justice and the Transition to Adulthood (Feb. 2005), http://www.transad.pop.upenn.edu/downloads/chung-juvenile%20just%20-formatted.pdf.

8. Barry Holman & Jason Zeidenberg, Justice Policy institute, The Dangers of Detention: The Impact of Incarcerating Youth in Detention and Other Secure Facilities (Nov. 2006), http://www.cfjj.org/Pdf/116-JPI008-DOD_Report.pdf.

9. 2008 Kids Count Data Book, *supra* note 2, at 10.

10. *See In re* Gault, 387 U.S. 1, 14–18 (1967) (describing the Juvenile Court movement); *see also* Howard N. Snyder & Melissa Sickmund, National Center for Juvenile Justice, Juvenile Offenders and Victims: 2006 National Report 94–96, http://www.ojjdp.ncjrs.org/ojstatbb/nr2006/downloads/NR2006.pdf. Recent brain-imaging research and behavioral studies confirm that adolescents are "far less able to gauge risks and consequences, control impulses, handle stress, and resist peer pressure" than are adults. 2008 Kids Count Data Book, *supra* note 2, at 9 (citing Brief of the American Medical Association et al., as Amici Curiae in Support of Respondent, Roper v. Simmons, 543 U.S. 551 (2005) (No. 03-633)). Most important, "most youthful offenders will cease lawbreaking as a part of the normal maturation process." *Id.* (citing D.S. Elliot, *Youth Violence: An Overview,* paper presented at the Aspen Institute's Children's Policy Forum: Children and Violence Conference, in Queenstown, MD (Feb. 1994)).

11. *In re* Gault, 387 U.S. at 15.

12. *Id.* at 14. In more recent years, however, a growing number of juveniles are being processed through the adult criminal system rather than the juvenile justice system. Each

year, up to two hundred thousand youth are tried in adult criminal courts, an alarming statistic given that the U.S. Centers for Disease Control and Prevention has found that "[t]ransfer of youth to the adult criminal justice system typically results in greater subsequent crime, including violent crime, among transferred youth; therefore, transferring juveniles to the adult system is counterproductive as a strategy for preventing or reducing violence," and that such transfers have no discernable deterrent effect. 2008 Kids Count Data Book, *supra* note 2, at 9. The transfer may occur either pursuant to state statutes or through the exercise of the judge's or prosecutor's discretion. *See* National Juvenile Defender Center, Policy Summary: Juvenile Transfer Reform (2005), http://www.njdc.info/pdf/CPATransfer.pdf; Christopher Hartney, National Council on Crime and Delinquency, Fact Sheet: Youth under Age 18 in the Adult Criminal Justice System (June 2006), http://www.nccd-crc.org/nccd/pubs/2006may_factsheet_youthadult.pdf. For an unsuccessful challenge to the constitutionality of prosecutorial discretion in transfers of juveniles to adult criminal court, *see* Manduley v. Superior Court, 41 P. 3d 3 (Cal. 2002).

13. *In re* Gault, 387 U.S. at 15.

14. Kent v. U.S., 383 U.S. 541, 556 (1966).

15. 387 U.S. at 33, 41, 47, 56, 58.

16. Approximately 18 percent of all juvenile arrests are for status offenses, and in 2004, over four hundred thousand children were arrested or held in police custody for status offenses. U.S. Department of Justice, Office of Justice Programs, Office of Juvenile Justice and Delinquency Prevention, OJJDP Statistical Briefing Book, Washington, D.C. (2006).

17. Although the Supreme Court requires a probable-cause hearing within forty-eight hours of arrest for adults, County of Riverside v. McLaughlin, 500 U.S. 44, 56 (1991), states vary greatly in the length of time they permit juveniles to be detained before a probable-cause hearing can be held. Elizabeth Calvin, National Juvenile Defender Center, Legal Strategies to Reduce the Unnecessary Detention of Children 8–10 (2004), http://www.njdc.info/pdf/detention_guide.pdf. For example, state statutes in Alabama, Arkansas, Georgia, Nevada, New York, North Dakota, Ohio, Pennsylvania, Virginia, and Wyoming permit children to be held for up to seventy-two hours prior to the initial court appearance. *Id.* The California Supreme Court has held the rule inapplicable to juvenile proceedings, permitting children to be detained upon arrest for up to seventy-eight hours before the first court appearance. Alfredo A. v. Superior Court, 865 P. 2d 56 (Cal. 1994). The U.S. Supreme Court has not addressed this issue.

18. *In re Gault* makes clear that juveniles retain the right to counsel for juvenile proceedings. 387 U.S. at 15. A disturbing number of juveniles, however, purportedly waive this right. In April 2008, the Juvenile Law Center filed a successful petition in the Pennsylvania Supreme Court to expunge thousands of delinquency adjudications on grounds that the juveniles' waiver of counsel was not knowing and voluntary. Petition, *In re* J.V.R., No. 81 MM 2008 (Penn. S. Ct., filed Apr. 28, 2008); Order regarding expungement of records at 4, *In re* J.V.R., No. 81 MM 2008 (Pa. 2008) (per curiam). A copy of the complaint and related briefs are available at http://www.jlc.org/news/4/luzernecounty/. In other jurisdictions, protection of juvenile rights with respect to waivers of counsel has been accomplished by legislative means. *See* National Juvenile Defender Center, Policy Summary: Juvenile Waiver of Counsel (2005), http://www.njdc.info/pdf/CPAWaiver.pdf.

19. In *Schall v. Martin*, 467 U.S. 253 (1984), the Supreme Court upheld the constitutionality of preventive preadjudication detention for juveniles. States vary significantly in the

extent to which they authorize this practice. Florida requires a showing of "substantial risk of bodily harm as evidenced by recent behavior," and Kansas demands that a youth have a "history of violent behavior toward others" or exhibit a "seriously assaultive or destructive behavior at the time of being taken into custody." Colorado, by contrast, prohibits the pretrial release of a child without bond, unless the prosecutor consents, when the child has been adjudicated for a felony or Class 1 misdemeanor within the past year. Calvin, *supra* note 17, at 10. For a thorough analysis of pretrial juvenile detention in Massachusetts, *see* Robin Dahlberg, ACLU, Locking Up Our Children: The Secure Detention of Massachusetts Youth after Arraignment and before Adjudication (May 2008). For an example of a successful post-*Schall* settlement agreement obtained by the Juvenile Law Center to limit the use of pretrial juvenile detention, *see* Settlement Agreement, Coleman v. Stanziani, No. 81-2215 (E.D. Pa., filed Dec. 15, 1986), http://clearinghouse.wustl.edu/detail.php?id=374.

20. Sue Burrell & Loren Warboys, Office for Juvenile Justice and Delinquency Prevention, Special Education and the Juvenile Justice System (July 2000), http://www.ncjrs.gov/html/ojjdp/2000_6_5/contents.html.

21. Calvin, *supra* note 17, at 56–80.

22. Snyder & Sickmund, *supra* note 10, at 104–08.

23. *In re* Gault, 387 U.S. at 15.

24. McKeiver v. Pennsylvania, 403 U.S. 528 (1971). Absent a federal constitutional right to a jury trial for juveniles, advocates have engaged in litigation to secure the right under state law. Advocates in Kansas have been successful; in *In re L.M.,* the Kansas Supreme Court, acknowledging that delinquency proceedings have lost their benevolent *parent patriae* character, concluded that juveniles retain a right to jury trial in delinquency proceedings. *In re* L.M., 186 P. 3d 164, 170 (Kan. 2008). Advocates in other jurisdictions have been less successful, however. State v. Chavez, 163 Wash. 2d 262 (2008); State *ex rel.* D.J. (La. S. Ct.); *In re* J.F. (Pa. Super. Ct.).

25. 467 U.S. at 263.

26. *Id.* at 265.

27. 42 U.S.C. § 5633(a)(11).

28. 42 U.S.C. § 5633(a)(11)(A)(ii).

29. Melissa Sickmund et al., Department of Justice, Office of Juvenile Justice and Delinquency Prevention, Census of Juveniles in Residential Placement Databook (2008), http://www.ojjdp.ncjrs.gov/ojstatbb/cjrp/. That same year, 3 percent of the youth detained prior to adjudication, or 836 children, were detained for status offenses. *Id.* According to the OJJDP, in 2003, more than 4,800 children were detained for status offenses. Snyder & Sickmund, *supra* note 10, at 198. The proposal for reauthorization of the JJDPA, pending at the time of this writing, would narrow the valid court-order exception, requiring the juvenile court to issue findings of fact to determine that there is no less restrictive alternative available and that the secure detention would be capped at seven days. S. 3155, 110th Cong. (2008).

30. N.Y. Family Court Act § 305.2 (McKinney 2005).

31. Letter from Arthur Eisenberg, NYCLU, and Catherine Kim, ACLU, to Commissioner Raymond Kelley, New York Police Department (Oct. 7, 2008), http://www.aclu.org/crimjustice/juv/37086prs20081008.html (describing findings from analysis of the public records).

32. Cooperative Agreement between the Juvenile Court of Clayton County, the Clayton County Public School System, the Clayton County Police Department et al., http://www.gpdsc.com/resources-juvenile-cooperative_agreement_070804.pdf (setting forth agreement to limit the use of school-based arrests for "misdemeanor type delinquent acts involving offenses against public order including affray, disrupting public school, disorderly conduct, obstruction of police (limited to acts of truancy where a student fails to obey an officer's command to stop or not leave campus), and criminal trespass (not involving damage to property)").

33. For a discussion of memoranda of understanding between police departments and public school districts, *see* Catherine Y. Kim & India Geronimo, American Civil Liberties Union, Policing in Schools: Developing a Model Governance Document for School Resource Officers in K–12 Schools (Aug. 2009).

34. Mary Magee Quinn et al., *Youth with Disabilities in Juvenile Corrections: A National Survey*, 71 Exceptional Child 339 (2005); Gail A. Wasserman et al., *Assessing the Mental Health Status of Youth in Juvenile Justice Settings*, OJJDP Juvenile Justice Bulletin 1 (Aug. 2004), http://www.ncjrs.gov/pdffiles1/ojjdp/202713.pdf; Lex Frieden, National Council on Disability, Addressing the Needs of Youth with Disabilities in the Juvenile Justice System (May 2003), http://www.ncd.gov/newsroom/publications/2003/juvenile.htm.

35. Morgan v. Chris L., No. 94-6561, 1997 WL 22714 (6th Cir., Jan. 21, 1997).

36. Flint Bd. of Educ. v. Williams, 276 N.W. 2d 499 (Mich. Ct. App. 1979) (involving violation of school rules and regulations); *In re* McCann, 17 Educ. for the Handicapped L. Rep. [now IDELR] 551 (Tenn. Ct. App. 1990) (involving truancy and unruly behavior).

37. 20 U.S.C. § 1415(k)(6)(A).

38. Valentino C. v. Sch. Dist. of Phila., No. CV-01-2097, 2003 WL 177210 (E.D. Pa., Jan. 23, 2003); *In re* Trent, 569 N.W. 2d 719 (Wisc. Ct. App. 1997).

39. For further discussion of these and other strategies for children with disabilities in the juvenile and criminal justice systems, *see* Joseph B. Tulman, *Applying Disability Rights to Equalize Treatment for People with Disabilities in the Delinquency and Criminal Systems,* 8(2) Children's Rights Litig. Comm. of the Am. Bar Ass'n (Spring 2006); Joseph B. Tulman, *Disability and Delinquency: How Failures to Identify, Accommodate and Serve Youth with Education-Related Disabilities Leads to Their Disproportionate Representation in the Delinquency System,* 3 Whittier J. Child & Fam. Advoc. 3 (2003).

40. Bart Lubow & Dennis Barron, Office of Juvenile Justice and Delinquency Prevention, Fact Sheet: Resources for Juvenile Detention Reform (Nov. 2000), http://www.ncjrs.gov/pdffiles1/ojjdp/fs200018.pdf. For an excellent discussion on the history and current status of disproportionate minority contact with the juvenile justice system, *see* James Bell & Laura John Ridolfi, W. Haywood Burns Institute, Adoration of the Question: Reflections on the Failure to Reduce Racial & Ethnic Disparities in the Juvenile Justice System (Dec. 2008), http://burnsinstitute.org/article.php?list=type&type=16.

41. National Council on Crime and Delinquency, And Justice for Some: Differential Treatment of Youth of Color in the Justice System (Jan. 2007), http://www.nccd-crc.org/nccd/pubs/2007jan_justice_for_some.pdf [hereinafter And Justice for Some].

42. 2008 Kids Count Data Book, *supra* note 2, at 9.

43. And Justice for Some, *supra* note 41, at 2.

44. *Id.*

45. 42 U.S.C. § 5633(a)(22).

46. 2008 Kids Count Data Book, *supra* note 2, at 10. Litigation involving conditions of confinement for children—whether it involves pretrial detention conditions, juvenile commitment facilities, or placement in adult correctional facilities—is much like litigation involving conditions of confinement for adults, and impact litigators have achieved significant victories in this area. For example, the Youth Law Center obtained a comprehensive settlement agreement against the Ohio Department of Youth Services in *S.H. v. Strickrath,* Stipulation for Injunctive Relief, S.H. v. Strickrath, No. 2-04-cv-1206 (S.D. Ohio, filed Apr. 4, 2008), securing the hiring of additional staff; an increase in training; revision of its policies on the use of force, seclusion, and discipline; and improvement of mental health, educational, medical, and dental services. For more information on this litigation, *see* http://www.ylc.org/viewDetails.php?id=63. Similarly, the Juvenile Justice Project of Louisiana entered into a comprehensive settlement agreement with the U.S. Department of Justice and the state of Louisiana regarding conditions at various secured detention facilities for juveniles, addressing issues related to juvenile justice, medical, dental, and mental health. Settlement Agreement, A.A. v. Wackenhut Corrections, Corp., Civ. No. 00-246-C-M1 (M.D. La., filed Aug. 17, 2000), http://www.jjpl.org/PDF/settlement_agreement.pdf. More recent cases relating to conditions of confinement for detained youth that remain pending include *Morgan v. Nagin,* No. 2:07-cv-09755 (E.D. La., filed Dec. 21, 2007), filed by the Juvenile Justice Project of Louisiana, and *ACLU v. New Mexico Children, Youth and Families Department (CYFD),* No. D-101-cv-200702921 (N.M. 1st Jud. Dist. Ct., filed Nov. 20, 2007), filed by the ACLU of New Mexico and the Youth Law Center.

47. *See* Katherine Twomey, *The Right to Education in Juvenile Detention under State Constitutions,* 94 Va. L. Rev. 765 (2008); P.E. Leone, T. Price & R.K. Vitolo, *Appropriate Education for All Incarcerated Youth: Meeting the Spirit of P.L. 94-142 in Youth Detention Facilities,* 7 Remedial and Special Education 4, 9–14 (1988). For an excellent discussion of this subject in the context of human rights law, *see* Marsha Weissman et al., Dignity in Schools Campaign, The Right to Education in the Juvenile and Criminal Justice Systems in the United States, Submission to Vernor Munoz, Special Rapporteur on the Right to Education 6 (Dec. 2008), http://www.dignityinschools.org/files/US_Prisoner_Education. pdf (citing R.M. Foley, *Academic Characteristics of Incarcerated Youth and Correctional Educational Programs,* 9 J. of Emotional and Behavioral Disorders 248–59 (2001)).

48. P.E. Leone & S.M. Meisel, *Improving Education Services for Students in Detention and Confinement Facilities,* 17(1) Child. Legal Rts. J. 2–12 (1997).

49. Sarah Livsey, Melissa Sickmund & Anthony Sladky, U.S. Department of Justice, Juvenile Residential Facility Census, 2004: Selected Findings 10 (Jan. 2009), http://www. ncjrs.gov/pdffiles1/ojjdp/222721.pdf.

50. *Id.*

51. *Id.*

52. *Id.* at 9.

53. Tommy P. v. Bd. of County Comm'rs of Spokane County, 645 P. 2d 697 (Wash. 1982).

54. D.B. v. Clark County Bd. of Educ., 469 S.E. 2d 438 (Ga. Ct. App. 1996).

55. *See, e.g.,* Cal. Educ. Code § 48645–48646; Fla. Stat. § 1003.52

56. *See supra* note 46 for a sample of such cases.

57. Leone & Meisel, *supra* note 48, at 2 (noting that estimates of the percentage of incarcerated children who have disabilities range from 30 to 60 percent and concluding

that "the percentage of young people in juvenile correctional facilities who were previously identified and served in special education before their incarceration is at least three to five times the percentage of the public school population identified as disabled").

58. 20 U.S.C. §§ 1400–87; 29 U.S.C. §794.

59. 20 U.S.C. § 1414; 30 C.F.R. § 300.2.

60. Leone & Meisel, *supra* note 48, at 2.

61. *Id.* at 5–6 (providing chart of each case and its status).

62. Snyder & Sickmund, *supra* note 10, at 236–37.

63. *See, e.g.,* Cal. Educ. Code § 48645 *et seq.* (providing minimum education standards for "public schools in juvenile halls, juvenile homes, day centers, juvenile ranches, juvenile camps, regional youth educational facilities, or Orange County youth correctional centers"); Fla. Stat. § 1003.52 (providing minimum education standards for youth in the custody of Department of Juvenile Justice programs).

64. 20 U.S.C. § 1412(a)(1)(B)(ii); *see* 34 C.F.R. §§ 300.122(a)(2), 300.311(a).

65. 34 C.F.R. § 300.311(b)(1).

66. 34 C.F.R. § 300.311(b)(2).

67. 34 C.F.R. § 300.311(c)

68. 829 F. Supp. 1016 (N.D. Ill. 1993).

69. *Id.* at 1018.

70. *Id.* at 1019.

71. 230 F. 3d 582 (3d Cir. 2000).

72. 5 P. 3d 691 (Wash. 2000).

73. *Id.* at 697.

74. Cora Roy-Stevens, OJJDP Fact Sheet, Overcoming Barriers to School Reentry (Oct. 2004), http://www.ncjrs.gov/pdffiled/ojjdp/fs200403.pdf.

75. Ronald D. Stephens & June Lane Arnette, Office for Juvenile Justice and Delinquency Prevention, From the Courthouse to the Schoolhouse: Making Successful Transitions 8 (Feb. 2000), http://www.ncjrs.gov/pdffiles1/ojjdp/178900.pdf.

76. Roy-Stevens, *supra* note 74, at 1.

77. 484 S.E. 2d 909, 911 (W. Va. 1996).

78. 749 A. 2d 902 (N.J. Super. Ct. Ch. Div. 2000),

79. 352 S.E. 2d 449, 454 (N.C. Ct. App. 1987).

80. 102 P. 3d 868, 876 (Wyo. 2004).

81. 879 A. 2d 408, 409–10 (Pa. Commw. Ct. 2005).

82. *Id.* at 419.

83. *Id.* at 415.

84. *Id.* at 417–18.

85. *Id.* at 418.

86. *Id.*

87. *Id.* As to the precise procedural requirements of such a hearing to challenge the placement in an alternative school, the court held that the procedures should be identical to those provided for other students challenging disciplinary decisions, including written notice of the reasons for the proposed action, an offer to hold an informal hearing within five days, notice of the time and place of the hearing, and the right to question witnesses present at the hearing and to speak and produce witnesses in support of the child's position. *Id.* at 420.

88. Second Amended Complaint, J.G. v. Mills, No. 1:04-cv-5415 (E.D. N.Y., filed Feb. 8, 2005).

89. *Id.*

90. Magistrate's Report and Recommendation, J.G. v. Mills, No. 1:04-cv-5415 (E.D. N.Y., filed July 6, 2006). The district court's decision on the motion for preliminary relief was stayed pending settlement negotiations between the parties.

91. *Id.*

92. *Id.* at 34–45.

93. *Id.* at 50.

94. *Id.* at 54.

95. *Id.* at 57 (emphasis in original).

96. Stipulation and Order of Settlement with State Defendant, J.G. v. Mills, No. 1:04-cv-5415 (E.D. N.Y., filed Oct. 7, 2008).

97. 20 U.S.C. §§ 6421, 6422, 6438, 6455.

98. For a description of state legislation, *see* Angeline Spain, The National Evaluation and Technical Assistance Center for the Education of Children and Youth Who Are Neglected, Delinquent, or At-Risk, State Legislation Strengthening Transition, http://www.neglected-delinquent.org/nd/resources/trans_strength.asp.

Index

Alternative schools/programs (*continued*), race and, 14n10, 99, 190n18; right to education and, 6, 100–102, 191n25n, 191nn28–39, 192n42, 192nn47–51; special education in, 56, 61, 109–10, 173n70; under state laws, 101, 191nn28–39, 192n42, 192nn47–51; suspensions/expulsions and, 98, 101–2, 157nn117–20, 157n122, 189n5; teachers at, 99–100. *See also* Due process

American Bar Association, 42; recommendation from, 32; on zero-tolerance discipline policies, 80

American Civil Liberties Union (ACLU), 23–24, 116–18, 120, 200n68, 201nn69–70, 203n86; discriminatory discipline and, 37–38; drug-sniffing dogs and, 198n38; gang-related activity and, 90; international human rights law and, 31; *M.H. v. Atlanta Independent School District*, 107–8; school police conduct v., 120, 200n68, 201nn69–70

Americans with Disabilities Act of 1990, 57, 171n35

Annie E. Casey Foundation, 128, 134

Antidiscrimination protections: children of color and, 34–44; for ELL, 44–47, 165n88, 165n96; for foster care students, 48; for homeless students, 47–48, 49–50, 166n105, 167n107, 167n109; race and, 34–43; for undocumented students, 47

AP v. Anoka-Hennepin Independent School District No. 11, 175n98

Arizona, 165n96

Arkansas: alternative education in, 107; *Doe ex rel. Doe v. Little Rock School District*, 197n27; *Doe v. Little Rock School District*, 198n35; *Sherpell v. Humnoke School District No. 5*, 36

Arrests: children of color v., 35; impact of, 113; out-of-school, 95–96, 188n111, 188nn113–14; questionable, 112, 195n6; race and, 2, 113, 133–34, 196n11; school misconduct criminalization and, 112, 194n3; special education and, 113, 132–33, 196n11. *See also* Challenging initial referral/arrest; School-based arrests

As-applied, facial challenges v., 87, 123, 185n59, 204n95

Attorney's fees, litigating disabilities rights and, 66, 177n115

Automatic/mandatory penalties: *Colvin v. Lowndes County*, 84, 183n34; *Lee v. Macon County Board of Education*, 84, 183n36; meaningful hearing for, 84; *Mitchell v. Board of Trustees*, 84–85; procedural due process and, 84–85, 183nn33–34, 183n36

A.W. v. State, 203n84

Baker v. Couchman, 204n88

Baltimore City Public Schools, 22

Bar-Navon v. Brevard County School Board, 94, 188n102

Barnett ex rel. Barnett v. Tipton County Board of Education, 188n110

B.C. v. Plumas Unified School District, 198n37

Beard v. Whitmore Lake School District, 197n24

Behavioral intervention plan (BIP), 62–63, 174n78, 174n80

Bethel School District No. 403 v. Fraser, 87, 88, 92, 196n20

BIP. *See* Behavioral intervention plan

Black Coal v. Portland School District No. 1, 183n26

Blasi, Gary, 33

Blunt v. Lower Merion School District, 176n99

Board of Education of Independent School District No. 92 of Pottawatomie County v. Earls, 117, 196n20

Board of Education of the City of Los Angeles, 23

Boim v. Fulton County School District, 94

Boisseau v. Picard, 50

Boucher v. School Board of School District of Greenfield, 186n84

Boynton v. Casey, 199n55

Bradford v. Maryland State Board of Education, 22

Breeding v. Driscoll, 192n54

Coronado v. State, 201n74
Coy v. Board of Education of North Canton City Schools, 88–89, 185nn66–67
CRC. See Convention on the Rights of the Child
Crime rates, graduation v., 9–10. See also School-specific crimes
Crispim v. Athanson, 161n37
Crowley v. Pinellas County School Board, 23, 153n55
C.S.C. v. Knox County Board of Education, 108–10

Darensburg v. Metropolitan Transportation Commission, 163n56
Dartmouth Review v. Dartmouth Coll., 160n20
Data Accountability Center, 180n153
Davis v. Monroe County Board of Education, 39, 161n37
D.B. v. Clarke County Board of Education, 192n48
D.C. v. School District of Philadelphia, 105, 141
Delaware: alternative education in, 101, 191n30; disabilities/suspension and, 170n27; foster care students in, 48
Demers v. Leominster School Department, 187n100
Department of Education, U.S., 23
DesRoches ex. rel. DesRoches v. Caprio, 197n27
Detention, for status offenses, 208n29
Detention rates: of African Americans, 35, 133–34; of Hispanics, 35, 133–34
Diaz-Fonseca v. Puerto Rico, 176n99
Different treatment: discriminatory discipline v., 36–39; disparate impact v., 35–36; federal claims of, 36–39; intentional discrimination as, 36–39
Dignity Denied: The Effect of "Zero Tolerance" Policies on Students' Human Rights, 31
Disabilities: accountability v., 52, 168n8; adequacy lawsuits and, 20; alternative schools/programs and, 52, 99, 101, 168n7, 190n15; in charter schools, 170n29; discrimination against, 52–53, 168n9, 169n12; due process and, 105; ELL v., 68,

178n130; employment v., 170n23; Equal Protection Clause and, 27; evaluation of, 58, 172n49; expulsion v., 54; federal rights/protections and, 51–64, 68, 171n32, 171n35, 172n49, 176n110; graduation rates v., 52, 168n5; identification of, 58–59, 68–70, 172n43, 176n110, 179n143; instruction quality v., 53–54, 169n17; juvenile corrections v., 51–77; juvenile facilities education and, 136, 210n57; juvenile justice system v., 2, 5, 132–33, 210n57; legal protections and, 56–70; manifestation determination and, 60–61, 75, 172n59, 173nn64–65, 174n75; Mills v. Board of Education, 27; Pennsylvania Association for Retarded Children (PARC) v. Commonwealth, 27; population with, 51, 167n1, 168n4; procedural due process and, 82; school discipline v., 54, 170n22; school misconduct criminalization and, 113; suspensions and, 52, 54, 170n27; Title II and, 75. See also Individuals with Disabilities Education Act; Special education
Disability discrimination claims, 176n101; administrative complaints in, 67–68; disparate impact in, 68, 177n125, 178nn126–27; federal/administrative complaints in, 67–68; individual discrimination in, 67; in pipeline litigation, 67–68, 177n119, 177n125, 178nn126–27. See also Litigating disabilities rights
Disability law, implementation failure and, 55–56, 170nn27–29
Disability Rights Wisconsin v. Wisconsin Department Public Instruction, 176n101
Disciplinary alternative schools and programs. See Alternative schools/programs
Disciplinary exclusion, 60; long-term, 61–62, 173n72
Disciplinary/nondisciplinary removals, 72–73, 180n155
Discrimination: different treatment and, 35–39; against disabilities, 52–53, 168n9, 169n12; disparate impact and, 35–36, 160n16. See also Antidiscrimination protections; Disability discrimination claims

Discriminatory discipline: intentional discrimination and, 36–39; race and, 36–39, 160n20

Disenrollment, accountability v., 9–10

Disparate impact: in California, 41–42, 162n53, 162nn55–58; in Connecticut, 43–44; different treatment v., 35–36; in disability discrimination claims, 68, 177n125, 178nn126–27; discrimination and, 35–36, 160n16; federal law and, 39–40, 161nn42–43; in Illinois, 42; intention and, 35–36, 160nn16–17; language access and, 40, 162n48; in Minnesota, 42–43, 164n67, 164n72; state law and, 40–44; Title VI and, 160n17, 161nn42–43; U.S. Justice Department and, 40; writ of mandamus and, 40, 162nn46–47

Disparate treatment. *See* Different treatment

Dixon v. Alabama State Board of Education, 183n26

Doe ex rel. Doe v. Little Rock School District, 197n27

Doe v. Little Rock School District, 198n35

Doe v. Renfrow, 198n38

Doe v. Superintendent of Schools, 29

Doe v. Superintendent of Schools of Worchester, 102, 184n50

Doninger v. Niehoff, 95, 188n110

Donnell C. v. Illinois State Board of Education, 137–38

Draper v. Atlanta Public School District, 176n110

Dropouts: ELL and, 44; testing and, 1

Drugs: school misconduct criminalization and, 112; testing for, 3, 117, 149n18, 199n49

Due process, 30; admittance of guilt v., 182n21; alternative schools/programs and, 102–5, 192n54, 192n61; *D.C. v. School District of Philadelphia*, 105; disabilities and, 105; education quality and, 103–4, 192n54, 192n61; *Goss v. Lopez* and, 80–81, 83–84, 103, 104, 192n61; involuntary transfer and, 103–4, 105,

192n54, 192n61; liberty interest and, 80–81, 104–5; *Nevares v. San Marcos Consolidated Independent School District*, 103–4, 192n61; in New York, 79; out-of-school arrests v., 95–96; stigma and, 104–5; timing and, 83–84. *See also* Procedural due process rights; Substantive due process

Durant v. State, 21, 155n84

E.B. v. Board of Education, 72–73, 180n155

Education: equality in, 11–12; funding in, 1, 4, 9–13; in juvenile facilities, 135–36, 210n57, 211n63

Educational reentry: alternative school and, 141; expulsion and, 140; *J.G. v. Mills*, 142–43, 212n90; in juvenile justice system, 139–44, 211n87; in Kentucky, 139; in New York City, 139; public schools transition failure and, 142–44; *In re Jackson*, 140; *In re R.M.*, 140; *State ex rel. G.S.*, 140; state laws for, 143–44; stigma and, 142–43; timing v., 142–43

Education for All Handicapped Act, 27. *See also* Individuals with Disabilities Education Act

Education funding, incarceration funding v., 9–10

Education quality: in alternative schools/programs, 3, 106–10, 194n88; due process and, 103–4, 192n54, 192n61; federal laws and, 106; state laws and, 106–7

EEOA. *See* Equal Educational Opportunity Act

Eighth Circuit: *Shady v. City of Farmington*, 120–21; *Thompson v. Carthage School District*, 115

Elementary and Secondary Education Act of 1965 (ESEA), 12; Title I, 151nn21–22. *See also* No Child Left Behind

Eleventh Circuit: *Boim v. Fulton County School District*, 94; school dress codes and, 94

ELL. *See* English Language Learner

Employment, race/disability v., 170n23

Foster care students, 48
Fourteenth Amendment, 30
Fourth Amendment: alternative education and, 108; drug-sniffing dogs and, 198n38; *Ferguson v. City of Charleston*, 121–22; school police conduct and, 121–22, 203nn84–86; school searches and, 115, 116; *Shady v. City of Farmington*, 120–21
Franklin J. Lane High School, 30–31
Franklin v. Sandoval, 39, 161n37, 161n40, 161n42, 178n127
Frederick L. v. Department of Public Welfare, 178n127
Free appropriate public education (FAPE): in juvenile facilities, 136; noncessation, 61–62, 173n70, 173n72; right to, 57–58, 136, 171n38, 171n40, 172n42; Section 504 and, 57, 136, 171n35, 171n38, 171n40, 172n42
Freedom of Information Act, 132
Freed v. Consolidated Rail Corporation, 175n98
Free speech: in school-specific crimes, 123–24. *See also* First Amendment
Fuller ex rel. Fuller v. Decator Public School Board, 89–90
Functional behavioral assessments (FBA), 62–63, 174n78
Funding: academic failure and, 9–13; of education, 1, 4, 9–13; of incarceration, 9–10; inequities in, 22–24; lawsuits and, 152n33; problems and, 4, 150n1; states and, 151n21

Gang-related activity: First Amendment v., 89; *Stephenson v. Davenport Community School District*, 89, 90, 186n71; suspensions/expulsions and, 89–90, 186n71; void for vagueness and, 89–90, 186n71
Gant v. Wallingford Board of Education, 161n37
GED program, 30, 31
Gender, suspensions v., 2, 34–35
Georgia: alternative education in, 102, 107, 192n48; *Breeding v. Driscoll*, 192n54;

juvenile facilities education in, 135; mainstream school return in, 110; *M.H. v. Atlanta Independent School District*, 107–8; out-of-school arrests in, 188n111; school misconduct criminalization in, 203n86
Gillman v. School Board for Holmes County, 187n95, 188n104
Goss v. Lopez, 28, 62; due process and, 80–81, 83–84, 103, 104, 192n61
Gould v. Orr, 153n49
Graduation: adequacy v., 18; crime rates v., 9–10; pipeline v., 3; race and, 23; right to education v., 18–19, 154nn66–67
Graduation rates: for accountability, 25; disabilities v., 52, 168n5; NCLB and, 25; systemic issues v., 74
Grassroots Organizing, Social Movement, and the Right to High-Quality Education (Oakes, Rogers, Blasi, and Lipton), 33
Gray ex rel. Alexander v. Bostic, 203n84
Grayned v. City of Rockford, 124
Guiles v. Marineau, 187n88
Gun Free Schools Act (1994), 79

Hancock v. Commissioner of Education, 14–15, 24, 153n42, 154n58
Hawkins v. Coleman, 185n53
Heckman, James, 9–10
Heck v. Humphrey, 196n18
Heller v. Hodgin, 37
Hispanics, 178n130; detention rates of, 35, 133–34; school misconduct criminalization and, 113; suspensions of, 2
Hobson v. Hansen, 53
Holloman v. Harland, 186n84
Homeless students: antidiscrimination protections for, 47–48, 49–50, 166n105, 167n107, 167n109; IDEA and, 167n112
Horton v. Goose Creek Independent School District, 198n37
Huff, Brian, 195n7
Hunt v. Alabama, 20

ICESCR. *See* International Covenant on Economic, Social and Cultural Rights

arraignments in, 130, 207n18; beginning of, 129–30; challenging initial referral/arrest, 131–34, 209n32; cost of, 129; disabilities v., 2, 5, 132–33, 210n57; dispositions in, 131, 208n29; educational reentry right in, 139–44, 211n87; IEPs in, 136, 137; jury trials in, 130–31, 208n24; juvenile facilities education and, 135–36, 210n57; life chances v., 128–29; numbers in, 128, 207n16; overview of, 129–31, 206n10, 207n1, 207nn16–19, 208n24, 208n29; pre-adjudicatory hearing, 130, 207n19; probable cause hearings in, 130, 207n17; *In re Gault*, 130, 207n18; right to education in, 134–39, 210n46, 210n57, 211n63; *Schall v. Martin*, 131, 207n19; status offenses in, 130, 207n16, 208n29; transition services from, 139–44, 211n87
J.W. v. DeSoto County School District, 90

Kansas: *Chaffin v. Kansas State Fair Board*, 178n127; *Montoy v. Kansas*, 28; preventive preadjudication in, 207n19; *In re L.M.*, 208n24; *Robinson v. Kansas*, 68, 176n101, 178n126, 178n127
Keith D. v. Ball, 157n119, 184n50
Kentucky: adjudicated youth in, 150n24; alternative education in, 101, 191n31; educational reentry in, 139
Killion v. Franklin Regional School District, 95, 187n95
King v. Martin, 162n47
Klein v. Smith, 95
K.M. v. School Board, 176n109
Kozol, Jonathan, 22–23

Langley v. Monroe County School District, 86
Language access: disparate impact and, 40, 162n48; for parents, 45, 46, 165n88. *See also* Equal Educational Opportunity Act
LaShonda D. v. Monroe County Board of Education, 157n115
Latinos. *See* Hispanics
Lau v. Nichols, 27, 45, 46
LaVine v. Blaine School District, 94, 186n84, 187n99

Law enforcement: as school discipline, 3, 6, 148n10, 149n17, 149nn19–20, 194n3, 195nn6–8. *See also* School resource officers
LEA. *See* Local educational agency
Least restrictive environment (LRE), 63, 174n81, 175nn84–85
LeBlanc v. Ascension Parish School Board, 187n100
Lee v. Macon County Board of Education, 84, 183n34
Legal Aid Society, 142
Legal Assistance Foundation, 137–38
Legal protections/disabilities, federal rights and, 56–70
LEP. *See* Limited in English proficiency
Levin, Betsy, 149n17
Lewis E. v. Spagnolo, 153n49
Liberty interest, due process and, 80–81, 104–5
Limited in English proficiency (LEP), 27. *See also* English Language Learner
Lipton, Martin, 33
Litigating disabilities rights: attorney's fees and, 66, 177n115; exhaustion of administrative remedies and, 64–65, 175nn98–101; jurisdiction/private right of action and, 66, 177n114; scope of remedies and, 65–66, 176nn109–10
Lobato v. State of Colorado, 16, 20; NCLB and, 24–25
Local educational agency (LEA), 49, 166n105
Locker searches, 116, 149n18, 198n32
Los Angeles County Unified School District, 23
Losen, Daniel, 168n6
Louisiana: alternative education in, 101, 191n32; *Boisseau v. Picard*, 50; class action state administrative complaints in, 74; juvenile detention conditions in, 210n46
Lowery v. Euverard, 186n87
Lowry v. Watson Chapel School District, 188n102
LRE. *See* Least restrictive environment

Manifestation determination, 60–61, 75, 172n59, 173nn64–65, 174n75

Marner v. Eufala City School Board, 192n61
Maryland: alternative education standards in, 107; Bradford v. Maryland State Board of Education, 22; mainstream school return in, 110
Massachusetts: alternative education in, 102, 192n47; Doe v. Superintendent of Schools, 29; foster care students in, 48; Hancock v. Commissioner of Education, 14–15, 24; roundtables in, 194n2
Mathews v. Eldridge, 81, 83
M.C. v. State, 204n102
McCall v. State, 125–26
McDuffy v. Secretary of Executive Office of Education, 14–15, 102
McFadden v. Board of Education for Illinois School District U-46, 42
McKeiver v. Pennsylvania, 208n24
McKinney-Vento Act, 47–50, 152n25, 166n105, 167n107, 167n109
Meghan Rene v. Reed, 176n101
Memorandum of understanding (MOU), 203n85
Metal detectors, 116, 149n18, 198nn34–36
M.H. v. Atlanta Independent School District, 107–8
Michigan, 21, 102, 192n51
Middle school, 2, 35
Miller v. Penn Manor School District, 89
Miller v. Woods, 162n47
Milligen v. City of Slidell, 202n77
Mills v. Board of Education, 27, 53, 169n12
Milwaukee Public Schools (MPS), 70–72, 179n143, 180n151
Minnesota: alternative education in, 101, 191n33; disparate impact in, 42–43, 164n67, 164n72; drugs in, 42–43, 164n67
Miranda, 118, 199n55, 200n56, 201n72
Mississippi, 101, 191n34
Mitchell v. Board of Trustees, 84–85
Monetary damages, 65–66, 176n109
Monteiro v. Tempe Union High School District, 161n37
Montoy v. Kansas, 28
Morgan v. Chris L., 173n67
Morgan v. Nagin, 210n46

Morse v. Frederick, 92
MOU. See Memorandum of understanding
Mrs. A.J. v. Special School District No. 1, 109

NAACP Legal Defense and Educational Fund, Inc., 4; Boisseau v. Picard, 50
National Center for Education Statistics, 149n18; on school misconduct criminalization, 112; on school violence, 79
National Center on Education, Disability and Juvenile Justice, 4
National Council of Juvenile and Family Court Judges, 112, 119
Native Americans, suspensions of, 2, 37
NCLB. See No Child Left Behind
Nebraska, 101, 191n35
Nevares v. San Marcos Consolidated Independent School District, 103–4, 192n61
New Jersey: alternative education in, 101, 191n36; resource litigation in, 13; State ex rel. G.S., 140
New Jersey v. T.L.O., 115, 116, 119–21, 197n24, 201n74, 202n78
New York: alternative education in, 101, 191n37; BIP/FBA in, 174n80; case study in, 72–73, 180n155; E.B. v. Board of Education, 72–73, 180n155; procedural due process context in, 79; Ruiz v. Pedota, 30–31
New York City, 147n1, 150n24; educational reentry in, 139; ELL in, 44; J.G. v. Mills, 142–43, 212n90
New York Civil Liberties Union, 122, 203n87
New York Immigration Coalition, 44–45, 165n88
Title IX, 161n37
Ninth Circuit: on ELL, 45–46, 165n96; LaVine v. Blaine School District, 94, 186n84, 187n99; school dress codes and, 94
No Child Left Behind (NCLB), 12–13, 151n26, 156n96; alternative schools/programs and, 100, 190n21; graduation rates and, 25; Lobato v. State of Colorado and, 24–25; McKinney-Vento Act, 47–50, 152n25, 166n105, 167n107, 167n109; right-to-education lawsuits and, 24–26; states v., 152nn25–26; subgroups and, 25

Seventh Circuit, 46
Shady v. City of Farmington, 120–21, 202n78
Sheff v. O'Neill, 43–44, 164n74, 164n77
Sherpell v. Humnoke School District No. 5,
    36, 185n53
Shoemaker v. State, 205n111
Smith v. Mount Pleasant Public Schools, 89,
    185n68
South Carolina, 128; school misconduct
    criminalization in, 112, 194n3
South Dakota, 118
Southern Poverty Law Center (SPLC), 74
Special education, 52, 175n84; adequacy
    lawsuits and, 21; in alternative schools/
    programs, 56, 109–10; arrests and, 113,
    132–33, 196n11; challenging initial refer-
    ral/arrest and, 132–33; school-based
    arrests v., 113, 196n11
Speech: free speech, 123–24; threats/speech
    involving violence, 93–94, 187nn99–100
Spencer v. Unified School District No. 501,
    185n66
SPLC. *See* Southern Poverty Law Center
Sprague, Jeffrey, 180n164
SROs. *See* School resource officers
States: disparate impact and, 41; EEOA
    and, 27, 157n113; funding and, 151n21;
    NCLB v., 152nn25–26; suspensions/
    expulsions and, 86, 184nn49–50
State ex rel. G.S., 102, 140
State laws: access denial and, 27–28;
    alternative education right under, 101,
    191nn28–39, 192n42, 192nn47–51; *Cathe
    A. v. Doddridge County Board of Educa-
    tion*, 101, 192n42; differences among,
    13–14; disparate impact and, 40–44; for
    educational reentry right, 143–44; edu-
    cation quality and, 106–7; federal law
    v., 13, 27–28, 56, 113–14, 196n16; pipeline
    remedy and, 16–26; "push-outs" and, 28,
    29, 157nn117–20, 157n22; resource litiga-
    tion and, 13–26; right to education v.,
    13–26; state constitutions and, 13
State v. Chavez, 208n24
State v. Doe, 125

State v. Heirtzler, 202n77
State v. Jones, 198n32
State v. J.T.D., 201n73
State v. K.L.M., 201n74
State v. McCooey, 204n102
State v. Russell, 42–43
State v. Scott, 202n78
Statewide adequacy suits, 154n58; imple-
    mentation safeguards and, 19; pipeline
    and, 17–19; pipeline-specific remedies in,
    18–19; resource import in, 17–18
Status offenses: detention for, 208n29; in
    juvenile justice system, 130, 207n16,
    208n29
*Stephenson v. Davenport Community School
    District*, 89, 90, 186n71
Strip searches, 116–17, 199n42–43
Substantive due process: rational basis
    review for, 85–86, 184n46; school
    administrators v., 85; for suspensions/
    expulsions, 85–86, 184n40, 184n42,
    184n46, 184nn49–50; *Wood v. Strickland*,
    85, 184n42
Sugai, George, 180n164
Suspensions: accountability v, 181n4;
    adequacy v., 18; of African Americans,
    2, 34–35, 72, 78, 180n153; disabilities and,
    52, 54, 170n27; federal rights/protec-
    tions and, 61–62, 173n70, 173n72, 174n75,
    174n80; gender v., 2, 34–35; of Hispanics,
    2; IDEA and, 170n27; in middle school,
    2, 35; MPS and, 71; of Native Americans,
    38; race and, 2, 34–35, 38, 72, 78, 180n153;
    race/disability v., 54; results of, 3, 78; as
    school discipline, 1–3, 147n3; Section
    504 and, 62, 174n75; in Wisconsin, 72,
    180n153
Suspensions (long-term), procedural due
    process and, 81–83
Suspensions (short-term), procedural due
    process and, 81–84, 182n21, 183n26
Suspensions/expulsions, 61–62, 173n72;
    alternative schools/programs and, 98,
    101–2, 157n122, 157nn117–20, 157n122,
    189n5; challenging, 78–96; First

Void for vagueness: as-applied v. facial challenges in, 87, 185n59; *Bethel School District Number 403 v. Fraser*, 87, 88, 92; *Coy v. Board of Education of North Canton City Schools*, 88–89, 185n66; definition v., 87–88, 185n54; drugs and, 90; First Amendment and, 87; gang-related activity and, 89–90, 186n71; inappropriate conduct and, 88–89, 185n64; *Miller v. Penn Manor School District*, 89; notice and, 87, 185n54; off-campus conduct and, 90; *Smith v. Mount Pleasant Public Schools*, 89, 185n68; subjective assessments and, 86–87, 184nn51–52, 185n53; suspensions/expulsions and, 86–90, 184nn51–52, 185nn53–54, 185n59, 185n64, 185nn66–68, 186n71; *Sypniewski v. Warren Hills Regional Board of Education*, 88, 185n64

Waddy, Judge, 53
Washington: juvenile facilities education in, 135; Seattle, 184n52; *Tunstall v. Bergeson*, 138–39
Washington, D.C., 53
Wendt v. Wendt, 43–44
West Virginia: alternative education in, 101, 192n42; *Philip Leon M. v. Greenbrier County Board of Education*, 140

Wilcher v. State, 202n78
Williams, 18
Willis ex rel. Willis v. Anderson Community School Corporation, 199n49
Wisconsin: *Disability Rights Wisconsin v. Wisconsin Department Public Instruction*, 176n101; *Jamie S. v. Milwaukee Public Schools*, 70–72, 179n143, 180n151, 180n153; race/suspensions in, 72, 180n153
Woods v. Wright, 188n114
Wood v. Strickland, 85, 184n42
Writ of mandamus, disparate impact and, 40, 162nn46–47
Wyoming: alternative education in, 102, 192n50; *In re R.M.*, 140

York v. Wahkiakum School District No. 200, 196n16

Zamora v. Pomeroy, 192n61
Zero-tolerance discipline policies, 31; American Bar Association on, 80; current application of, 79–80; rise of, 79–80, 182n7; *Seal v. Morgan*, 85, 184n46; suspensions/expulsions and, 79–80, 182n7

About the Authors

CATHERINE Y. KIM spent seven years as an attorney with the American Civil Liberties Union National Legal Department in its Racial Justice Program, specializing in the intersection between education and the juvenile justice system. She currently teaches at the University of North Carolina School of Law at Chapel Hill.

DANIEL J. LOSEN is a senior education law and policy associate at the Civil Rights Project at UCLA.

DAMON T. HEWITT is director of the Education Project at the NAACP Legal Defense and Educational Fund and the founder of its "Dismantling the School to Prison Pipeline" initiative.